MUST A JEW BELIEV

THE LITTMAN LIBRARY OF
JEWISH CIVILIZATION

Dedicated to the memory of
LOUIS THOMAS SIDNEY LITTMAN
who founded the Littman Library for the love of God
and as an act of charity in memory of his father
JOSEPH AARON LITTMAN
יהא זכרם ברוך

'Get wisdom, get understanding:
Forsake her not and she shall preserve thee'
PROV. 4:5

The Littman Library of Jewish Civilization is a registered UK charity
Registered charity no. 1000784

Must a Jew Believe Anything?

◆

MENACHEM KELLNER

◆

Second Edition

Oxford · Portland, Oregon
The Littman Library of Jewish Civilization

The Littman Library of Jewish Civilization

Chief Executive Officer: Ludo Craddock
Managing Editor: Connie Webber

PO Box 645, Oxford OX2 0UJ, UK
www.littman.co.uk

Published in the United States and Canada by
The Littman Library of Jewish Civilization
c/o ISBS, 920 NE 58th Avenue, Suite 300
Portland, Oregon 97213-3786

First published 1999
2nd edition, with corrections and Afterword, 2006
Reprinted 2008

A catalogue record for this book is available from the British Library

Library of Congress Cataloging in publication data applied for

ISBN 978–1–904113–38–6

Publishing co-ordinator: Janet Moth
Copy-editing: Gillian Bromley and Lindsey Taylor-Guthartz
Index: Menachem Kellner
Production: John Saunders
Design: Pete Russell, Faringdon, Oxon.
Printed in Great Britain on acid-free paper by
Biddles Ltd., Kings Lynn, Norfolk

For Jolene
now and forever

Acknowledgements

I WOULD never have written this work were it not for the encouragement and example of Ken Seeskin. Ken is the model of the academically dispassionate scholar of Jewish topics who is also deeply concerned about the state of the Jewish community and convinced that retreating to the ivory towers of academe is irresponsible. In a world in which rabbis are more and more social workers and less and less scholars (and this is no criticism of rabbis), academics have to be active within the Jewish community if our ancient tradition of intellectual engagement with and scholarly approach to the texts and traditions of classical Judaism is to be maintained. Ken's marvellous *Maimonides: A Guide for Today's Perplexed*, written in a lively and engaging style and directly addressed to the reader, deals with complex, serious, and important topics in an accessible fashion, without either condescending to the reader or making unnecessarily difficult demands. It is the model I have sought to emulate here.

It is a pleasant duty to thank the many individuals who have helped me in various ways in the writing of this book. My wife, Jolene, has read every line several times and argued with me about most of them. In a very serious sense this book is as much hers as mine. For this, and for much, much else, I am grateful. Kenneth Seeskin and Jonathan Berg have been generous with their comments, criticisms, and encouragement. Menachem Hirshman read and criticized the first three chapters; I am grateful for his assistance. David R. Blumenthal read an earlier draft of the text and made many discerning suggestions. The book has been vastly improved by his perceptive critique. Marc Shapiro and Shmuel Morell gave me the benefit of detailed criticism of the entire text. Shmuel in particular forced me to rethink many of my arguments and to be more self-conscious about what I was trying to do. I am profoundly grateful to him for his exemplary collegiality. I have (electronically) discussed aspects of the book with Michael Broyde, Eitan Fiorino, and Eli Clark. I thank them for their assistance. I worked out many of the ideas here in lectures given under the warm and hospitable aegis of the Foundation for Jewish Studies in Washington, DC, and in a seminar which I had the privilege of teaching at the École Pratique des Hautes Études in Paris; I am grateful to Rabbi Joshua Haberman and Ms Ruth Frank in Washington and to

Professor Charles Touati in Paris for their intellectual stimulation and wonderful hospitality.

My thanks to Professor David R. Blumenthal and to E. J. Brill, publishers, for permission to reprint Blumenthal's fine translation of Maimonides' Thirteen Principles from his *The Commentary of R. Ḥoter ben Shelomo to the Thirteen Principles of Maimonides.*

I would also like to thank Connie Webber, Janet Moth, and Gillian Bromley of the Littman Library for their many important contributions to this book. Each of these talented individuals contributed unstintingly of her skill and intelligence; whatever the book's faults, many of its strengths can be traced to them. My special thanks go to Ludo Craddock, Littman's chief executive officer, for his efficient and good-humoured shepherding of this book all the way to the hands of its readers.

Contents

Introduction

I HAVE written this book because I have something to say to my fellow Jews about the nature of our religion and how we may best relate to one another. Additionally, the book presents further evidence for a claim that I have been defending in my scholarly writings over the past twenty years, namely that Maimonides' theological formulations and halakhic decisions are conditioned by his philosophical positions. In this study, furthermore, I draw together ideas and insights scattered among some two dozen books and articles of mine, forming them into a consistent and, I hope, useful whole.

There is a sense in which this is two books. In the first six chapters I present, analyse, and defend a particular understanding of what religious faith means in classical Judaism. These chapters will, I hope, be of interest to anyone, Jew or non-Jew, seeking insights into what might bombastically be called the 'nature of Judaism'. The seventh and last chapter is addressed to Orthodox Jews in particular. In that chapter I build upon the conclusions of the first six chapters in order to argue for a new way of looking at and relating to non-Orthodox Jews and institutions. The first six chapters are thus primarily analytical, the last primarily polemical and apologetic (in the sense of defending a particular religious stance).

I wrote this book because of my concern that there is a crisis looming over Jews and Judaism. The crucial question we face, I think, is not whether we will have Jewish grandchildren, but how many different sorts of mutually exclusive and mutually intolerant Judaisms our grandchildren will face. Orthodoxy insists that God revealed the (one, uniquely true, immutable) Torah to Moses at Sinai. This bedrock commitment seems to rule out a pluralist approach (accepting that different valid and legitimate approaches to the Torah may coexist in mutual respect). Orthodoxy in today's world is less and less amenable to respectful dialogue with a non-Orthodoxy—a range of non-Orthodoxies—which it sees as growing ever more radical, ever more willing to jettison traditional values, beliefs, and practices. It sees itself not as pushing away the non-Orthodox, but as reacting and responding to their excesses. More and more, Orthodoxy seems willing to 'cut its losses', give up on the rest of the Jewish people, and concentrate on a 'saving remnant' as the only hope for a Jewish future. This book is an expression of my unwillingness to accept this approach.

Conservative, Reform, and Reconstructionist Jews, on the other hand, feel that every one of their overtures to Orthodoxy has been rebuffed, that 'there is no one to talk to there'. They see Orthodoxy as growing ever more fundamentalist, ever more intransigent, and ever more triumphalist. They see themselves not as pushing away the Orthodox, but as reacting and responding to their excesses.

As an 'Orthodox' Jew, I am more concerned with what Orthodoxy can and should do to lessen these tensions than with pointing the finger of blame at non-Orthodox streams. I put the term 'Orthodox' in quotation marks here because, while I am a believing, Torah-observant Jew and as such would ordinarily be called Orthodox, I prefer not to use the term in this sense. 'Orthodoxy' in the strict sense, not as a way of life but as a way of structuring our thinking about other Jews, makes sense only in the context of the Maimonidean Judaism which is precisely what I am arguing against in this book. My argument in what follows is that Orthodoxy has backed itself into a corner by making a virtue out of what was originally a term of opprobrium, namely 'orthodoxy' in the strict sense of the term. If Judaism is defined in terms of dogmatic orthodoxy, non-Orthodox Jews automatically become heretics, and the halakhic tradition (at least from the time of Maimonides) is very clear on how to treat heretics: working with them, and not against them, to create a Jewish future for all of us simply is not an option.

It is the burden of this book to argue that traditionalist Judaism in the modern world did not have to adopt this approach, and that it still can, and certainly ought to, frame the argument in other terms altogether. These other terms are not pluralist—I do not think that the belief that the Torah was given by God to Moses on Sinai which underlies the Jewish tradition can coexist with the sort of pluralism demanded by non-Orthodoxy today—but they do allow for mutual respect and tolerance and, even more important, allow all Jews to work together towards a less polarized Jewish future.

This book is also my response to two different sorts of challenge. One of its germs was the suggestion of Rabbi A. Mark Levin that I adapt my book *Dogma in Medieval Jewish Thought* to a more general audience (he also urged me to write a book on the most important theological jokes in Judaism, but that is a different story). A second impetus was a review of another book of mine, *Maimonides on Judaism and the Jewish People*, in which I had sought to prove that Maimonides rejected the idea that Jews are defined by some inherent characteristic which makes them essentially unlike non-Jews.[1] This idea has a long history in the Jewish tradition: it is central, for example, to the vision of Judaism held by the Iberian philosopher-poet Judah Halevi (d. 1141) and to that held by the author of the Zohar, the core text of the type of Jewish mysticism known as kabbalah. Maimonides, I argued, maintained that being Jewish has less to do with where one comes from and more to do with where one is going. For Maimonides, a Jew is defined by belief and behaviour, not by some mystical or metaphysical principle, and certainly not just by the brute fact of having been born with a particular set of genes. In contemporary terms, and to adopt a helpful analogy coined by my friend Daniel J. Lasker, Jews are defined by software, not hardware. As I will try to show in this book, Maimonides went so far as to summarize the heart of Judaism as he understood it in a series of dogmatic statements, his well-known Thirteen Principles.[2]

Maimonides on Judaism and the Jewish People was written as a scholarly work and aimed at a scholarly audience. No work of scholarship, however, no matter how dry, boring, and distant from the claims and concerns of 'real life', can be entirely divorced from the life, concerns, hopes, and fears of the scholar who produced it. If this is the case generally, it is all the more true of a person living in Israel and dealing with Judaic scholarship. While writing the book I was aware that I had found in Maimonides traditional authority for a position with which I strongly identified personally. One of the reasons I hold that position so strongly is that I am convinced that the alternative approach is dangerous.

It is a short step from maintaining that Jews are essentially different from non-Jews to affirming that Jews are inherently superior to non-Jews (a belief hardly borne out by any objective consideration of the evi-

[1] On the essentialist vs. the Maimonidean approach to the nature of the Jewish people, see Menachem Kellner, *Maimonides on Judaism and the Jewish People* (Albany: SUNY Press, 1991).

[2] Much of this book is given over to a discussion of Maimonides. For general audiences by far the single best introduction to the master's thought is Kenneth Seeskin, *Maimonides: A Guide for Today's Perplexed* (West Orange, NJ: Behrman House, 1991). For readers interested in a more technical approach, I recommend Marvin Fox, *Interpreting Maimonides* (Chicago: University of Chicago Press, 1990). With verve and insight, Fox stakes out a closely reasoned position on how to interpret Maimonides, a hotly debated topic now and in the past. On how Fox's approach fits into the history of Maimonides interpretation, see Menachem Kellner, 'Reading Rambam: Approaches to the Interpretation of Maimonides', *Jewish History*, 5 (1991), 73–93.

dence). It is also a short step from the conviction that Jews are essentially unlike non-Jews to the position that non-Jews can never be trusted and that they bear within them an ineradicable hatred for Jews (a belief which I reject, but which a rational person could deduce from the sad facts of recent and less recent Jewish history). In the context of an Israel seeking to live at peace with its neighbours, Jews holding this 'essentialist' view of the nature of the Jewish people more than occasionally fall prey to the tendency to demonize our enemies and often incline to believe that any accommodation with these enemies will simply lead the latter to continue seeking our destruction. In other words, instead of seeing Arabs as human beings like us, with similar fears and hopes, frustrations and joys, they see them as the latest incarnation of the quintessential Jew-hating Gentile bent upon nothing but our destruction. When the essentialist vision of the Jewish people is coupled with the profound disdain for non-Jews found in the Zohar and other kabbalistic and hasidic texts, the temptation to reject any movement towards peace or accommodation on the part of Arabs as nothing more than a tactical step towards the ultimate goal of our destruction becomes almost overwhelming.

As a Jew who believes that God created all human beings equally in the divine image, and as one eager to live in peace and equality with my Arab neighbours, I was delighted to find in Maimonides traditional authority for the position that, obvious differences of talent aside, all human beings are born equal. But, in so doing, I may have jumped from the frying pan into the fire. In a perceptive review of *Maimonides on Judaism and the Jewish People*, David Novak pointed out that by turning the Jews from a nation defined by shared descent, or by some shared metaphysical or mystical characteristic, into a communion of true believers, Maimonides opened the door to accusations of heresy and the concomitant theological witch-hunts.[3] Knowing that I had no more sympathy with that outcome than with some sort of religio-ethnic triumphalism, Novak challenged me to write another book, exploring the possibilities for theological tolerance within a Judaism which rejects nationalist essentialism. This book is my answer to Novak's challenge.

Now the full extent of the problem which prompted me to write this book comes clear: can I reject or modify Maimonides' theological definition of what it is to be a Jew without adopting some sort of essentialist definition of the nature of Jewishness, with all its attendant dangers, and without doing what I take Conservative and contemporary Reform Jews

[3] David Novak, Review of Menachem Kellner, *Maimonides on Judaism and the Jewish People*, *Shofar*, 11 (1992), 150–2.

to do—namely, turn Judaism into a kind of religious nationalism, whose main doctrine seems to be a sentimental attachment to half-remembered myths about what 'true' Jewish life used to be like? There is a second problem: can I reject what I will show below to be Maimonides' 'theologification' of Judaism without rejecting the allied claims that Judaism teaches truth and that there is one absolute truth? I certainly do not want to give these up! The book before you is my attempt to meet these challenges.

Rabbi Moses ben Maimon (1138–1204), known in English as Maimonides and in Hebrew by the acronym Rambam, figures on almost every page of this book. The name 'Maimonides' itself suggests the fact that there are as many ways of understanding him as there are individuals seeking to understand him. As I once heard Shalom Rosenberg remark, each of us has a 'Mymonides', as opposed to 'Hermonides' or 'Hismonides'. A number of my recent scholarly publications were written in order to define and defend a particular view of Maimonides. There is no need to go into that issue here. The account of Maimonides presented in this book is one with which my intended audience should have no problems—with the exception, probably, of one aspect, namely my exposition of Maimonides' understanding of the nature of human perfection and the criteria which must be satisfied for inclusion in the world to come. As I (and almost all other scholarly interpreters of his thought with whom I am familiar) understand Maimonides, the only criterion he stipulates for inclusion in the world to come is intellectual perfection. In order to achieve intellectual perfection one must first achieve a very high level of moral perfection. In Maimonides' eyes, the best, most effective, and most efficient tool for achieving and maintaining moral perfection is fulfilment of the commandments of the Torah. Nevertheless, in principle, one could achieve a very high level of intellectual perfection (as did Aristotle, according to Maimonides) without fulfilling the commandments. Furthermore, fulfilling the commandments without achieving intellectual perfection does not get one into the world to come. This interpretation of Maimonides is likely to raise the hackles of those who approach him from a strictly traditionalist perspective, and I have thus written a special appendix (Appendix 1 below) defending it through an examination of Maimonides' introduction to his commentary on the tenth chapter of Mishnah *Sanhedrin* ('Perek ḥelek').

There may be some readers who will be put off by my willingness to engage Maimonides in debate, dismissing it as an act of unparalleled hubris on my part. To that, a number of things must be said. First,

Maimonides is today treated with more veneration than he himself would want. Such veneration often leads to horrible misrepresentation of his thought. The best example I have of this is a lecture I once heard by a well-known scientist and Habad hasid. He maintained that since Maimonides had written the *Mishneh torah* with divine inspiration, everything in it must be literally true, including the pre-Copernican description of the cosmos found in the opening chapters of 'Laws of the Foundations of the Torah'. In fact, Maimonides presented scientific matters in the *Mishneh torah* as an exposition of the most up-to-date science of his day—an exposition which he certainly did not think was infallible.[4]

Second, it is one of the theses of this book that in matters of theology the attitudes of earlier authorities carry less weight than they do in matters of halakhah. It would be inconsistent of me, then, to feel that it was forbidden for me occasionally to take respectful issue with Maimonides on matters of theology. In addition, I have argued in detail in a separate work that Maimonides himself denies the claim that earlier generations (including the *tannaim* and *amoraim*, that is, the authorities cited in the Mishnah and Talmud) have inherently greater authority than later generations to make binding decisions in non-halakhic matters.[5]

Third, and most important for those for whom this question is an issue of significance, there are traditional authorities upon whom I can rely for every one of my reservations about Maimonides' positions; these authorities will be cited below where relevant and appropriate. In general our medieval forebears were quite willing to be sharply critical of Maimonides. The glosses of R. Abraham ben David of Posquières, known in Hebrew as Rabad (*c*.1125–98) on the *Mishneh torah* are a notorious case in point, as we shall see below (p. 58). Similarly, R. Shem Tov ibn Shem Tov (*c*.1380–1441) was unrestrained and downright vituperative in his criticisms of the Jewish Aristotelians, Maimonides prominent among them.[6] R. Isaac ben Sheshet Perfet (1326–1408; also known in Hebrew as Rivash) addressed a halakhic responsum to the question (*inter alia*) whether it was permitted to study the philosophical works of figures like

[4] For proof of this, see Menachem Kellner, 'Maimonides on the Science of the *Mishneh Torah*: Provisional or Permanent?', *AJS Review*, 18 (1993), 169–94.

[5] Menachem Kellner, *Maimonides on the 'Decline of the Generations' and the Nature of Rabbinic Authority* (Albany: SUNY Press, 1996).

[6] These criticisms are found in Shem Tov ibn Shem Tov, *Book of Beliefs* (Heb.) (Ferrara, 1556; photo-edition, Jerusalem, 1969); a good example of what I have in mind may be found on fo. 45*b*, where Maimonides' discussion of angels as 'separate intellects' in the second chapter of the 'Laws of the Foundations of the Torah' is dismissed as 'contradicting the entire Torah'.

Maimonides and Gersonides (R. Levi ben Gershom, 1288–1344, known in Hebrew as Ralbag). In the end, he was loath to forbid their works, even though they wrote things 'which it is forbidden to hear', having been led astray by foreign teachings.[7]

I should add a word here about the 'world to come'. Classical Judaism (i.e. the Judaism of the Mishnah and Talmud) includes the clear assumption that some of us, at least, will survive our deaths in one form or another and that after we die the righteous are in some way rewarded and the wicked in some way punished. Beyond that, there is very little agreement in Jewish tradition about how the world to come is constituted or what happens there. Maimonides is one of the few authoritative Jewish figures to have devoted much systematic attention to the nature of the world to come and to the matter of how one achieves entry into it. It is one of the main aims of this book to show that Maimonides' discussion of these questions was innovative as opposed to traditional, and that its use in today's Jewish world has dangerous consequences.

To put my thesis in the simplest possible terms, I will argue here that Maimonides was right in rejecting the essentialist view of the Jewish people, but wrong in replacing it with a definition of the Jew as a person who adheres to a strictly defined set of dogmas. This is simple to state, but not so simple to explain, and certainly not so simple to defend. What do I mean by 'right' and 'wrong' in this context? The Jewish religious tradition, as it had developed to his day, presented Maimonides with a number of well-entrenched options concerning the nature of the Jewish people. He chose one of those options and rejected others. The same religious tradition presented Maimonides with a series of options concerning the nature of Jewish belief. He chose an option which had only recently been made available, so to speak—having been imported into Judaism by the theologian and polemicist R. Sa'adia Gaon (882–942)—one which still clearly bore the marks of its Graeco-Muslim origin, and one which cohered only poorly with the rest of the Jewish tradition.[8] Thus, the first choice was 'right', the second 'wrong'. Moreover, the first

[7] On this issue, see Menachem Kellner, 'R. Isaac bar Sheshet's Responsum Concerning the Study of Jewish Philosophy', *Tradition*, 15 (1975), 110–18. Further on the resistance to Maimonidean philosophy in medieval Judaism, see idem, 'Gersonides and his Cultured Despisers: Arama and Abravanel', *Journal of Medieval and Renaissance Studies*, 6 (1976), 269–96.

[8] The claim that Maimonides used categories of thought which betray their Graeco-Muslim origin is indirectly defended in the first two chapters of this book. See also the text from Maimonides' commentary on *Pirkei avot* ('Ethics of the Fathers') cited below (p. 63). For detailed discussion, see Menachem Kellner, *Dogma in Medieval Jewish Thought: From Maimonides to Abravanel* (Oxford: Oxford University Press, 1986), 1–9, 34–49.

choice, I believe, helped move Jews and Judaism along the path to messianic fulfilment; the second did not.

The claim that Maimonides was influenced by non-Jewish sources, incidentally, is not a new one. It was made—as an accusation—by many of his medieval opponents, as noted above.[9] The accusation was renewed in the modern era by Rabbi Samson Raphael Hirsch (1808–88):

> [Maimonides] sought to reconcile Judaism with the difficulties which confronted it from without, instead of developing it creatively from within, for all the good and the evil which bless and afflict the heritage of the father. His peculiar mental tendency was Arabic–Greek, and his conception of the purpose of life the same. He entered into Judaism from without, bringing with him opinions of whose truth he had convinced himself from extraneous sources and—he reconciled. For him, too, self-perfecting through the knowledge of truth was the highest aim, the practical he deemed subordinate. For him knowledge of God was the end, not the means; hence he devoted his intellectual powers to speculations upon the Deity, and sought to bind Judaism to the results of his speculative investigations as to postulates of science or faith. The Mizvoth became for him merely ladders, necessary only to conduct to knowledge or to protect against error.[10]

Hirsch's claims here are stronger than anything I will be saying in this book.[11]

In broad strokes, the argument of this book depends upon distinguishing two types of religious faith: one which understands faith as primarily trust in God expressed in concrete behaviour, as against another which understands faith as primarily the acknowledgement of the

[9] For an accessible discussion, see Daniel Jeremy Silver, *Maimonidean Criticism and the Maimonidean Controversy, 1180–1240* (Leiden: Brill, 1965).

[10] See Samson Raphael Hirsch, *The Nineteen Letters of Ben Uziel*, trans. Bernard Drachman (New York: Funk & Wagnalls, 1899), eighteenth letter, 181–2.

[11] I find it hard to believe, incidentally, that Hirsch could get away with a comment like this in the contemporary Orthodox world. For an illuminating study of the background to Hirsch's attack, see Jay Harris, 'The Image of Maimonides in Nineteenth Century Jewish Historiography', *Proceedings of the American Academy for Jewish Research*, 54 (1987), 117–39 at 139. *The Nineteen Letters*, as Marc Shapiro noted to me in a personal communication, is one of Hirsch's earliest works; in his later works he no longer criticizes Maimonides overtly, he simply ignores him. It is interesting to note further that the German halakhic authority and polemicist R. Jacob ben Zvi Emden (1697–1776) in at least some places seriously entertained the possibility that Maimonides was not the author of a book he found so objectionable as the *Guide of the Perplexed*. See Jacob J. Schacter, 'Rabbi Jacob Emden's *'Iggeret Purim'*, in Isadore Twersky (ed.), *Studies in Medieval Jewish History and Literature*, ii (Cambridge, Mass.: Harvard University Press, 1984), 441–6 at 445.

truth of certain faith-claims. Maimonides, it will be shown here, adopted the second approach and in so doing introduced a new element into Judaism. Whatever his intent, one of the consequences of Maimonides' claim that Jews are defined first and foremost by their beliefs is, to my mind, unfortunate. This is the tendency to define Jewish 'legitimacy' in terms of the acceptance of certain abstract theological claims, which in turn involves the application of categories such as heresy and sectarianism to individuals and institutions. Once applied, the charge of heresy carries with it serious halakhic implications, notably the ostracism, vilification, and exclusion from the world to come of those deemed to be heretics. This is a fundamentally exclusivist approach. It also involves a certain amount of hubris, for those who brand others heretics are in doing so claiming that they themselves are virtuous and upright Jews, and determining for God, as it were, who gets into heaven.

This book has a clear polemical intent: I argue as a believing, Torah-observant Jew that the application of theological tests of Jewish legitimacy, so common today, reflects only one particular vision of Judaism, a vision first found in the writings of Maimonides. We can reject this Maimonidean innovation while remaining committed, mitzvah-observing Jews. My polemic is thus twofold, arguing against theological exclusivism and arguing for a more inclusivist vision of Judaism.

Beyond my polemical intent, I hope that this book also serves a second purpose: namely, to provide an examination of the place and nature of belief in Judaism. It is my analysis of the nature of *emunah* ('belief') in the Torah and Talmud which forms the foundation of my reservations about Maimonides' alternative understanding. Consequently, a person who could not care less about how contemporary Orthodoxy does and should view non-Orthodoxy can, I hope, profit from this book, learning from it about a little-known but crucial aspect of Judaism's self-understanding. Certainly my approach has raised not a little controversy in a number of circles, and I am therefore particularly grateful to the publishers for the opportunity to respond to some of my critics in the Afterword written for this new edition.

Must a Jew believe anything? If 'belief' is a matter of trust in God expressed in obedience to the Torah, my answer to the question is that a Jew must believe everything. If 'belief' is the intellectual acquiescence in carefully defined statements of dogma, the answer is that there is nothing that a Jew *must* believe.

ONE

Two Types of Faith

BELIEF in God was not an issue for the first generations of humanity as described in the Bible: God spoke to them, rewarded them, admonished them, all directly and without intermediaries.[1] By the time of Abraham, however, this immediate acquaintance with God had been destroyed. Abraham's family were idolaters and Abraham himself is depicted in the midrashic tradition as the first person for whom belief in God is a challenge, a question, a problem.

The Torah, however, ignores the issue altogether. God speaks to Abraham suddenly, almost literally 'out of the blue':

> Now the Lord said unto Abram: 'Get thee out of thy country, and from thy kindred, and from thy father's house, unto the land that I will show thee. And I will make of thee a great nation, and I will bless thee, and make thy name great; and be thou a blessing. And I will bless them that bless thee, and him that curseth thee will I curse, and in thee shall all the families of the earth be blessed.' (Gen. 12: 1–3)

What is Abraham's response to this? 'So Abram went,' the Torah continues, 'as the Lord had spoken unto him.'

This passage, perhaps more than most in the Torah, begs to be filled out midrashically. Had Abraham known God previously? What reason had he for accepting God's command? Did he ask any questions? Leaving one's tribe and striking out on one's own in the ancient Near East, not even knowing in advance where one was going, was, for a herder such as Abraham, an act little short of madness. Did he try to negotiate with God, buy time, fish for information about where he was going? As far as we can tell from the text, the answer to all these questions is simply no. The Lord had spoken to him and that was enough: 'So Abram went.'

[1] The title of this chapter is taken from that of Martin Buber's book *Two Types of Faith* (New York: Harper & Row, 1961). See further Louis Jacobs, *Faith* (New York: Basic Books, 1968).

Faith, Belief, and Trust

Abraham is presented as the archetype of the person of faith: God commands and Abraham obeys. As will become clear, it is significant that God's first recorded approach to Abraham is a command. What was the nature of Abraham's faith which led him to obey that command?

In our everyday conversation we distinguish between the expressions 'believe in' and 'believe that'. This is a distinction with a difference, and one that teaches us important things about Judaism. Consider two examples. First, a habitually heavy smoker, puffing on an unfiltered cigarette, discourses on the evils of smoking, stating with apparent sincerity: 'I firmly believe that smoking is a foul, disgusting, and dangerous habit.' Must we think that our smoker is disingenuous? Must we see her as insincere, trying to fool us or herself? Of course not. We all hold positions that clearly call for certain norms of behaviour while not always living up to those norms. I myself was grossly overweight for many years, all the while firmly believing that it was stupid and irresponsible not to take better care of myself (and thereby also of my family). Were my affirmations of that belief lies? Not at all. I really did believe it; I just did not act on it. That is called human frailty or laziness, not lying.

But consider a second case. A woman professes that she believes in her husband. We have no reason not to take her at her word and assume that she is speaking the truth. It then turns out that this same woman has been spending considerable sums of money to keep hired detectives dogging her husband's footsteps and reporting his every move, conversation, and meeting back to her. Do we still credit her claim to believe in her husband? We do not.

In each case a person affirms a particular belief. In each case the person acts inconsistently with that belief. In the first instance we dismiss the inconsistency as an example of (perhaps endearing) human frailty; in the second, we condemn the assertion as a lie. Why?

The obvious answer to this question is that in the two cases we are using the term 'belief' in different senses. These two different senses are indicated by the prepositions following the term. To say of a person that she believes *that* something is the case is to say that she affirms the truth of a proposition or set of propositions. It is a cognitive claim, about what a person holds to be true. To say that a person believes *in* something, on the other hand, certainly has cognitive implications (it would be hard to believe in something without affirming some factual claims about it, such as that it exists), but goes beyond affirmation or denial. Such a statement involves the relationship of the believer to that believed in, a relationship usually taken to be one of trust. It is a fact of everyday life that one can sincerely accede to cognitive claims (about the evils of smoking, for example) without that acceptance influencing one's behaviour in any noticeable way. It is equally true of everyday life that we expect protestations of trust and loyalty to find expression in concrete behaviour consistent with those protestations. If we do not find that behaviour we have good reason to suspect the sincerity of those protestations.

This distinction is crucially important. The prophet Habakkuk teaches that 'the righteous shall live by his faith' (Hab. 2: 4). If the righteous individual lives by his or her faith and is defined as righteous in terms of that faith alone, then one cannot hope to achieve or even understand righteousness without understanding faith. Is the faithful believer a person who affirms the truth of certain propositions or a person who steadfastly trusts in God and acts in accordance with that trust? In what follows I will try to show that the Torah and the Talmud see religious faith in terms of steadfast loyalty and trust which find expression in behaviour, and not in terms solely of intellectual acquiescence in certain propositions. It is this characteristic of classical Judaism which explains why systematic theology and dogma are so foreign to its spirit.[2]

[2] For a philosophical explanation of the difference between 'belief in' and 'belief that', see Kenneth Seeskin, 'Judaism and the Linguistic Interpretation of Jewish Faith', in Norbert Samuelson (ed.), *Studies in Jewish Philosophy: Collected Essays of the Academy for Jewish Philosophy, 1980–1985* (Lanham, Md.: University Press of America, 1987), 215–34. Some philosophers are unconvinced that the distinction between 'belief in' and 'belief that' is a real one, maintaining that all 'belief in' statements can be reduced to a series of 'belief that' statements. (On this issue, see H. H. Price, 'Belief "In" and Belief "That"', *Religious Studies*, 1 (1965), 5–28.) The matter is in fact irrelevant for my argument here. I argue in this section that the core meaning of *emunah* in biblical and rabbinic Judaism is a species of 'belief in' as opposed to 'belief that'. A much weaker claim would actually suffice for my needs, namely that biblical and rabbinic Judaism strongly emphasize belief expressed in behaviour over belief expressed in words, actions over declarations, non-verbal acts over verbal acts. On this view, *emunah* means or can be reduced to statements of 'belief that'; it was sufficient that a person hold correct beliefs implicitly, without necessarily expressing them in any clear-cut dogmatic fashion. While this sort of move would probably satisfy the criticisms of those philosophers who are convinced that all statements of the 'belief in' variety can be translated into statements of the 'belief that' variety, I am not willing to make it. I am convinced that the distinction is a valid one and that it teaches us important lessons about the nature of biblical and rabbinic Judaism. Kenneth Seeskin's discussion in 'Judaism and the Linguistic Interpretation of Jewish Faith' is extremely helpful in this respect. On the distinction between moral and intellectual virtues in Jewish thought, see Menachem Kellner, 'The Virtue of Faith', in Lenn Goodman (ed.), *Neoplatonism and Jewish Thought* (Albany: SUNY Press, 1992), 195–205.

Emunah in the Torah

The term *emunah*, which is rendered in English as 'faith' or 'belief', occurs for the first time in the Torah in connection with Abraham. After obeying God's command to leave his family and home, Abraham is led to the land which God promises to give to his descendants. Famine forces him to sojourn in Egypt, where his wife Sarah's beauty almost precipitates a tragedy. Back in the land promised by God, Abraham and his nephew Lot find that they cannot live together in peace, and each goes his own way. Lot is captured by enemies and then freed by Abraham.

'After these things,' the Torah tells us, 'the word of the Lord came unto Abram in a vision, saying: "Fear not, Abram, I am thy shield, thy reward shall be exceeding great."' Now, for the first time, Abraham questions God: 'O Lord God, what wilt Thou give me, seeing I go hence childless . . . to me thou hast given no seed.' God has repeatedly promised Abraham that the land to which he has been brought will be given to his descendants. But Abraham remains childless: what is the use of a 'great reward' if there are no children to whom it can be bequeathed? In response, God brings Abraham outside, and says: 'Look now towards heaven and count the stars, if thou be able to count them . . . so shall thy seed be.' What is Abraham's response to this new promise? '*Vehe'emin*, and he believed in the Lord; and He counted it to him for righteousness' (Gen. 15: 1–6).

What is the nature of Abraham's belief which God counted as 'righteousness'? It is quite clear that Abraham's righteous belief was not a matter of his accepting God's statements as true, or of having given explicit intellectual acquiescence to the truth of a series of propositions, such as:

1. God exists.
2. God communicates with individuals and makes promises to them.
3. God has the power to keep promises made.
4. God may be relied upon to keep promises.

No, the context makes it very clear: Abraham's act of righteousness was his demonstration of *trust* in God. There can be no doubt that, had he been asked, Abraham would happily have affirmed the truth of the four propositions listed just above. The Torah, however, gives us no reason for thinking that Abraham ever asked himself the sorts of questions to which our four propositions could be construed as answers. The *emunah* spoken of here is more than belief that certain statements about God are true; it is belief in God, trust and reliance upon God, all of which call forth behaviour consistent with that stance of trust and reliance.

The point I am making here about the meaning of *emunah* is neither new nor controversial; it is just not often noticed.[3] Yet perusing a concordance and examining the verses in context is enough to convince any reader that the basic, root meaning of *emunah* is trust and reliance, not intellectual acquiescence in the truth of certain propositions.[4] A few further examples should suffice to make the point clear. God is described as a God of *emunah* in the great poem 'Ha'azinu': 'The Rock, His work is perfect; for all His ways are justice; a God of faithfulness [*emunah*] and without iniquity; just and right is He' (Deut. 32: 4). God is not being described here as agreeing to the truth of certain statements. The verse itself teaches us which of God's characteristics make it possible to appeal to a 'God of faithfulness': God is free of iniquity, just and right.

Even in cases where the Hebrew can be construed in terms of 'belief that' as opposed to 'belief in', reading the verse in context almost always reaffirms the point being made here about the connotation of *emunah* in the Torah. In Deuteronomy 9: 23 Moses berates the Jews: 'And when the Lord sent you from Kadesh-Barnea, saying, "Go up and possess the land which I have given you"; then ye rebelled against the commandment of the Lord your God, and ye believed Him [*he'emantem*] not, nor hearkened to His voice.' This verse might be construed as saying that the Jews simply did not believe what God was telling them; i.e. they did not believe that God was speaking the truth. This, however, is an entirely implausible interpretation. In the first place, the parallel between 'believing' and 'hearkening' is clear; the Jews are being castigated for failing to

[3] For an analysis of the use of the root *a-m-n* in Torah and Talmud, see Norman J. Cohen, 'Analysis of an Exegetic Tradition in *Mekhilta de-Rabbi Ishmael*: The Meaning of *'Amanah* in the Second and Third Centuries', *AJS Review*, 9 (1984), 1–26. Compare further Isaac Heinemann, 'Faith' (Heb.), in *Entsiklopediyah mikra'it*, i. 426–8, and Gerhard Kittel, 'Faith', in *Bible Key Words from Gerhard Kittel's Theologisches Wörterbuch zum Neuen Testament*, 4 vols., vol. iii, trans. and ed. Dorothea M. Barton, P. R. Ackroyd, and A. E. Harvey (New York: Harper & Row, 1960), 10.

[4] My position here is supported by Moshe Halbertal and Avishai Margalit, *Idolatry* (Cambridge, Mass.: Harvard University Press, 1992), see e.g. pp. 22, 31. Compare further Lenn Evan Goodman's comment, 'Even the word "faith" in the Hebrew Bible does not have the sense that Augustine forged by merging Plato's *pistis* with Cicero's *fides*. It means steadfastness, trust and loyalty. It is more a moral than a cognitive term and never a form of knowledge.' See Goodman's *God of Abraham* (New York: Oxford University Press, 1996), 27.

do what God told them to do, not for their failure to believe in the truth of some statement or other. Why did they fail to do what God instructed? The Jews failed to trust God, and therefore they failed to obey God's command. God commanded the Jews to ascend to the Land of Israel and conquer it, promising that they would succeed. The lack of *emunah* in this verse relates to the Jews' failure to trust God to keep the promise made. Furthermore, what was the content of God's statement concerning which the Jews showed lack of *emunah*? It was the command to ascend to the Land of Israel. If one disobeys a command and is therefore accused of lack of *emunah*, it makes much more sense to say that one is being accused of lack of trust in the commander than of quibbling over the accuracy of statements made by or about the commander.[5]

Theology and the Torah

My claim here is that the Torah teaches belief in God, as opposed to beliefs about God. That is not to say that no specific beliefs are implied by or even explicitly taught in the Torah. The Torah obviously assumes God's existence, although it nowhere states simply that God exists, or, according to most interpreters, commands belief that God exists.[6] The Torah also clearly teaches that God is one: 'Hear, O Israel, the Lord our

[5] I should like to make it very clear that I am not seeking to read a version of religious existentialism into or out of the biblical text. Religious existentialists focus on the act of faith, interpreting it as the *response* of an entire human being (not just the faculty of reason) to some sort of call. Religious faith is presented as subjective, true for each individual in her or his own way. Religious existentialism is a response to and critique of medieval religious rationalism. These ideas, I think, and certainly the way in which they are expressed by thinkers like Martin Buber, are foreign to the world of the Torah. On all this, see Jacobs, *Faith*, 61 ff.

[6] My claim that few interpreters find in the Torah a commandment to believe in God's existence is strictly true. But since the main exponent of the view that Exodus 20: 2 ('I am the Lord thy God') contains an express command to believe that God exists was Maimonides, a few more comments are in order. To the best of my knowledge, Maimonides is the first authority to interpret the verse in that fashion, and, at least in the Middle Ages, one of the few who did so. (He was followed in this by the author of the *Sefer haḥinukh*, as Jolene Kellner pointed out to me; see commandment no. 25 in that work.) His decision to view this verse as a commandment to believe that God exists is a clear reflection of his understanding of Judaism (which will be described below in Chapter 4). His interpretation of the verse was rejected by, among others, Moses ben Nahman (1194–1270; also known as Nahmanides and Ramban), in his gloss to the first positive commandment in Maimonides' *Book of Commandments*, and R. Hasdai Crescas (d. 1412), in the introduction to his *Or hashem*. For texts and discussion, see Kellner, *Dogma*, 109–20. See also the discussion in R. Isaac Abrabanel's *Rosh amanah* (Ramat

God, the Lord is one' (Deut. 6: 4). It is significant that this verse is phrased as an exhortation, not as a commandment. But beyond these two core issues, there are many verses and ideas which make no sense whatsoever if we do not accept certain statements about God. The Torah teaches explicitly that God is 'merciful and gracious, long-suffering, and abundant in goodness and truth' (Exod. 34: 6 ff.). Isaiah (40: 18) implies that God is incomparable: 'To whom, then, will ye liken God? Or what likeness will ye compare unto Him?' and in the same chapter (verse 8) teaches God's eternity: 'The grass withereth, the flower fadeth; but the word of our God shall stand for ever.' If God's word stands for ever, how much more so the author of that word! God's power is emphasized in Job 42: 2, 'I know that Thou canst do everything', and God's ubiquity in Psalm 139: 7–12.

The Torah also teaches explicit beliefs about human beings as well as about God. Human freedom is the burden of Deuteronomy 30: 19: 'I call heaven and earth to witness against you this day, that I have set before thee life and death, the blessing and the curse; therefore, choose life, that thou mayest live, thou and thy seed.' If we are called upon to choose between life and death, it must mean that we can make the choice. Human behaviour is free, not determined.

Facts about history are also taught in the Torah. Many of these can be allegorized if one wishes; one can, for example, follow Maimonides in denying that Balaam's ass actually spoke (Exod. 22: 21–35).[7] Some, however, cannot be allegorized without destroying the Torah altogether. It would be difficult to allegorize away the claim that in some significant sense God created the cosmos; or, similarly, that God chose the Jews 'to be Mine own treasure from among all the peoples' (Exod. 19: 5). One can interpret the notion of chosen-ness in many ways; but one cannot deny that it is a specific, discrete belief explicitly taught in the Torah.

If, then, there are specific beliefs taught in the Torah, why can we not say that the *emunah* which the Torah both demands of a Jew and seeks to inculcate is belief that certain statements are true, as opposed to trust in God, trust which finds its expression in certain forms of behaviour? The

Gan: Bar Ilan University Press, 1993), chs. 4, 17. I have translated this book into English, under the title *Principles of Faith* (London: Littman Library of Jewish Civilization, 1982); see in this edition pp. 72–3, 152–5.

[7] For Maimonides' claim that Balaam's ass 'spoke' only in a subjective vision of Balaam's, see *Guide of the Perplexed*, trans. Shlomo Pines (Chicago: University of Chicago Press, 1963), ii. 42, p. 389.

answer to this question has to do with the Torah's understanding of itself and its understanding of the nature of human beings. To state part of the answer in summary fashion, before developing it in detail: the Torah teaches, occasionally explicitly, more often implicitly, certain beliefs about God, the universe, and human beings; notwithstanding this, the Torah has no systematic theology.

Judaism emerged through a struggle with idolatry, demanding loyalty to the one God, creator of the universe. This loyalty was to find expression in certain ways, pre-eminently through obedience to God's will as expressed in the Torah. So long as one expressed that essential loyalty in speech and (especially) in action, little attempt was made to enquire closely into the doctrines one affirmed; indeed, no attempt was even made to establish exactly what doctrines one ought to affirm. Furthermore, Judaism developed as a religion intimately bound up with a distinct and often beleaguered community. Loyalty to the community was a further way in which loyalty to God and God's revelation was expressed. Loyalty to God, Torah, and Israel, therefore, is the hallmark of the Jew: loyal behaviour, not systematic theology, is what is expected and demanded.

Systematic theology typically has two components. The first is an attempt to establish clearly what ideas a religion teaches; the second is an attempt to fit these ideas into a consistent framework of relationships, a system. Judaism lacks both. Let us take a look at a number of examples. In each case we will examine a belief that all would admit is central to Judaism; in each case we will see that what precisely is taught by the belief is anything but certain. It was simply never considered important enough to specify precisely what these beliefs entail.

Let us take as our first example the notion of providence, that God in some sense provides for, takes care of, is concerned for, all (or at least some) creatures. The Ba'al Shem Tov (Israel ben Eliezer, *c.* 1700–60, also known as the Besht), the founder of hasidism, is reported to have taught that a leaf does not fall in a forest without God ordaining the fall of that specific leaf in the time, place, and manner of its fall.[8] The Talmud makes much the same point: 'No one stubs his toe below without it having been ordained first on high.'[9] Maimonides rejects this doctrine explicitly in his *Guide of the Perplexed*: 'For I do not by any means believe that this particular leaf has fallen because of a providence watching over it.'[10] It is Maimonides' teaching that individual providence does not

[8] Probably based upon a comment in *Genesis rabbah* x. 6.

[9] BT *Ḥullin* 7*b*.

[10] Maimonides, *Guide*, iii. 17, p. 471.

extend beyond human beings. Nor are all human beings governed by that providence: only those who have perfected their intellects to one degree or another benefit from individual providence; and even those who have perfected their intellects are guided by providence in different degrees, depending upon each individual's level of intellectual attainment.[11]

The question of divine providence immediately raises three other questions, concerning God's knowledge, God's justice, and humankind's freedom. If God provides for us in some sense, rewarding our good deeds and punishing our infractions, God must know us in some fashion. If God's knowledge is perfect, as most religious believers would want to assert, does it then include the future, what we will do tomorrow? If it does, how can we be thought to be free and hence responsible for our behaviour? The typical response to this question in Judaism was not an attempt to work out the relationship between divine providence and knowledge on the one hand and the idea of human freedom on the other. Rather, the typical response was that of the second-century *tanna* R. Akiva, who made the famous statement in *Pirkei avot* ('Ethics of the Fathers') to the effect that even though God knows all, human freedom is preserved (iii. 19): a restatement of the problem, not its solution! The *tannaim* apparently agreed with the Yiddish saying, 'No one ever died from having a philosophical problem.'

Bible and Talmud alike, then, assume divine providence as a given (even Job never questioned God's providence; rather, because of his very acceptance of divine providence, he questioned God's justice). Yet they seek neither to define it nor to work out its systematic relationship to other givens assumed by Judaism.

One might be tempted to dismiss the example of providence since it is a belief assumed by the Torah, but not really explicitly taught by it. Let us admit the claim, just for the sake of argument (although it must be remembered that very few beliefs are explicitly taught as opposed to implied or assumed by the Torah), and turn to a belief concerning the explicit centrality of which in Judaism there can be no possible doubt: that there is a God. Judaism, as noted above, affirms God's existence and oneness; beyond these two issues, we find much disagreement in the tradition about the divine attributes. Two of the more blatant areas of dissension concern God's incorporeality and God's nature.

[11] For Maimonides' account of providence, see *Guide*, iii. 13–24, pp. 448–502. In this context it should be noted that the very term 'providence' (*hashgaḥah*) was an invention of the ibn Tibbon family; the Sages, it appears, had no term for the concept. See Ephraim Urbach, *The Sages*, 2 vols. (Jerusalem: Magnes, 1975), i. 256.

In a passage to which we will have occasion to return below, Maimonides asserts that anyone who claims that God has any physical characteristics or faculties whatsoever is a heretic, excluded from the community of Israel and barred entry to the world to come. It is important to grasp the full significance of this claim: Maimonides implies that a devoutly pious Jew who prays to God with fervour and devotion, but who conceives of God as having some aspects of corporeality, is actually performing an act of idolatry (praying to an entity other than the true God). This view, as we shall see below, aroused the ire of one of Maimonides' great contemporaries, R. Abraham ben David of Posquières. Individuals 'better and greater' than Maimonides, he insisted, had mistakenly affirmed God's corporeality without thereby becoming any less righteous or devout.[12]

Does God have a body or not? Both Maimonides and R. Abraham affirmed that the Master of the Universe is incorporeal; but Maimonides condemned as heretics those who made an innocent mistake on the issue, while R. Abraham lauded some of those very 'heretics' as being 'better and greater' than Maimonides. Neither Maimonides nor R. Abraham was ejected from the community of Israel: despite their contrary assessments of heresy and its implications, both men, and their disciples, are accepted (and even accept one another) as good and faithful Jews.

We can focus on another fundamental debate about God in Judaism by taking note of a question sent to R. David ben Solomon ibn Abi Zimra (1479–1573; also known as Radbaz), the noted halakhic authority and leader of sixteenth-century Egyptian Jewry. The question concerned a case in which 'Reuben' said forcefully and publicly of 'Simeon' that 'it is forbidden to pray with you! For you are a sectarian and heretic: others

[12] For the text of Maimonides' claim that believers in a corporeal God are sectarians and have no share in the world to come, see below, p. 58, and Kellner, *Dogma*, 22. For R. Abraham's reservations, see Kellner, *Dogma*, 89, 256. On R. Abraham generally, see Isadore Twersky, *Rabad of Posquières*, rev. edn. (Philadelphia: Jewish Publication Society, 1980). Twersky discusses R. Abraham's stricture on Maimonides on p. 282. R. Abraham's claim that individuals 'better and greater' than Maimonides believed in a corporeal God (and were thus heretics without a share in the world to come in Maimonides' eyes) was no mere rhetorical flourish. See Kellner, *Dogma*, 233; Harry Austryn Wolfson, *The Philosophy of the Kalam* (Cambridge, Mass.: Harvard University Press, 1976), 106–11; Bernard Septimus, *Hispano-Jewish Culture in Transition: The Career and Controversies of Ramah [R. Meir ha-Levi Abulafia]* (Cambridge, Mass.: Harvard University Press, 1982), 75–81. For a contemporary text, see Shem Tov ibn Falaquera, 'Letter on the *Guide of the Perplexed*' (Heb.), in J. Bisliches (ed.), *Minḥat kena'ot* (photo-edition, Israel, 1968), 183. See further the sources collected by Marc Shapiro, 'The Last Word in Jewish Theology? Maimonides' Thirteen Principles', *The Torah Umadda Journal*, 4 (1993), 187–242 at 191–4.

pray to the God of Abraham and the God of Isaac, while you pray to the god of Aristotle!' The question placed before Abi Zimra was: had Reuben thus violated the ban on shaming one's fellow in public?[13] Reuben's accusation that Simeon prayed to the God of Aristotle was seen as being prima-facie grounds for bringing Reuben to judgement before a rabbinic court. Why?

The distinction between 'the God of the philosophers', on the one hand, and 'the God of Abraham, Isaac, and Jacob', on the other hand, is deeply rooted in Western thought. The God of the philosophers is basically the conclusion to an argument, a philosophical hypothesis necessary to make sense of certain phenomena. The philosophers' God is aware only of itself and has no knowledge of changeable entities (such as you and me); extends no special providence; does not respond in any meaningful sense to prayer; indeed, beyond the creation of the cosmos (according to some but certainly not all systems), it does nothing whatsoever but exist and contemplate itself in a timeless and surprisingly un-self-aware state of pure intellectualism.

On this view of God, prophecy can be nothing more than a perfection of the prophet: the prophet is not actually sent by God to prophesy, but rather does so as a consequence of highly developed moral and intellectual capacities. Life after death becomes a consequence of philosophical, as opposed to religious or moral, excellence. Prayer, as anything beyond an opportunity for contemplation or the expression of communal solidarity, makes no sense. God neither rewards nor punishes specific actions.

The God of Abraham, Isaac, and Jacob, on the other hand, is wholly personal (in the sense of being self-aware and thus aware of others), knows us in all our individual particularity, creates, reveals, redeems, dispatches prophets, answers prayer (not always in the way we want), rewards and punishes, and, above all, actively and uninterruptedly loves all human beings.[14]

[13] See R. David ibn Abi Zimra, *Responsa* (Heb.), ed. Yitshak Sofer (Benei Berak: Et Vesefer, 1972), no. 191.

[14] In a variety of places throughout his works Abraham Joshua Heschel compares the God of the philosophers to the God of Abraham, Isaac, and Jacob. His discussion is useful for further refining the distinction. We may present his comparisons in the form of a table:

The philosophers' God	*The God of Abraham*
God = Being	God = Concern
God = Unmoved Mover	God = Most Moved Mover
Perfect person = philosopher	Perfect person = prophet
Man searches for God	God searches for man
We seek to define God	We seek to experience God
Concept of God	Presence of God

In view of the dramatic distinctions between the two views of the deity, it is no wonder that the seventeenth-century French scientist and philosopher Blaise Pascal is reputed never to have left home without a note pinned to the lining of his jacket: 'The God of Abraham, Isaac, and Jacob, not the God of the philosophers!'[15]

In the history of Jewish thought, the fourteenth-century Bible commentator, scientist, and philosopher Gersonides is notorious for having believed in the 'God of the philosophers' almost exactly as depicted above. Gersonides was hardly alone in this view. In most particulars on this issue he simply followed the greatest and most influential of all Jewish thinkers since the completion of the Talmud—Maimonides. Of course, Gersonides was much more open about his views than was Maimonides (which may account for the latter's more widespread acceptance and influence, since he could thus more easily be interpreted as teaching unexceptional views), but in most respects differed from the earlier scholar only in matters of detail.

Not all Jewish philosophers agreed with the views of Maimonides and Gersonides. Judah Halevi, for example, the philosopher and poet of eleventh- and twelfth-century Spain, rejected views like those of Maimonides and Gersonides as incompatible with authentic Judaism, and devoted much of his theological and philosophical work *Sefer hakuzari* to refuting them. In the century and a half after Maimonides' death in 1204 violent debates broke out repeatedly over the acceptability of Maimonidean teachings. Is God personal and intimately concerned with each one of us, as traditional rabbinic Judaism and later Jewish mysticism maintained? Or is God austere and aloof from us and our petty needs and concerns, as the philosophers insisted? Do we know God through nature (as Maimonides taught) or through history (as Halevi strongly held)? These and the other questions raised above, while they preoccupied a few philosophers, were simply never considered important enough by most of those concerned with the ongoing tradition of Judaism to demand clear-cut, once-for-all answers.

Judaism teaches that God exists and is one; it further teaches that God provides for all creatures. The Written Torah and the Talmud make no sense if we fail to affirm these teachings; they are absolutely central to the Jewish conception of the universe. That does not mean, as we have seen, that the tradition found it important to reach a normative, obligatory

[15] Having recounted the Pascal story endless times to my students over the years, I have finally found a written source for it. Lenn Goodman cites the source—'Memorial of 1654'—on the first page of his *God of Abraham*.

opinion concerning the actual, specific content of these teachings; it certainly made no effort to reach agreement on their implications and consequences.

The same situation obtains with respect to another question fundamental to Judaism: the meaning of the claim that Jews are God's chosen people. A typical expression of the idea is found in the following verses (Exod. 19: 3–6):

> And Moses went up unto God, and the Lord called unto him out of the mountain, saying: 'Thus shalt thou say to the house of Jacob, and tell the children of Israel: Ye have seen what I have done unto the Egyptians, and how I bore you on eagles' wings, and brought you unto Myself. Now therefore if ye will hearken unto My voice indeed, and keep My covenant, then ye shall be Mine own treasure from among all the peoples; for all the earth is Mine: and ye shall be unto Me a kingdom of priests and a holy nation. These are the words which thou shalt speak unto the children of Israel.

This and other passages clearly state a basic teaching of Judaism: the Jews enjoy a special relationship with God. But what is it that makes one a Jew? As we saw in the Introduction, the tradition seems to offer two alternative, indeed conflicting, answers to this question. According to certain midrashim, Judah Halevi, and the Zohar, Jews all have some kind of inborn, inherent characteristic by virtue of which they are 'essentially', not 'accidentally', distinguished from non-Jews. On the other view, which is that held by Maimonides, being Jewish is first and foremost a matter of commitment. On my understanding of Maimonides, that commitment involves intellectual acquiescence in certain doctrines.[16] An important aspect of the debate between Halevi and Maimonides is nicely captured in a distinction drawn by R. Isaac ben Judah Abrabanel (1437–1508): did God choose the Jews, or did the Jews choose God? Halevi would adopt the former view, Maimonides the latter.[17]

The difference between these two approaches is more than academic: it affects views about proselytes and proselytization, and about the nature of the messianic era; also, because the essentialist view often leads those who hold it to adopt an attitude of superiority over and distrust of non-Jews, it has had and continues to have actual policy implications for

[16] For the debate between Halevi and Maimonides on the nature of the Jewish people, see my *Maimonides on Judaism and the Jewish People*.

[17] On Abrabanel's distinction between God choosing the Jews (which calls to mind the old doggerel, 'how odd of God to choose the Jews'), and the Jews choosing God, see Shaul Regev, 'The Choice of the People of Israel in the Thought of R. Isaac Abrabanel' (Heb.), *Asufot*, 2 (1988), 271–83.

Israelis. And yet, despite its theoretical and practical implications, exactly what it means to be the 'chosen people' remains amorphous and hard to pin down. As with the nature of God and the nature of God's providence, Torah and tradition teach that God chose the Jews in some sense, without ever finding it important to establish in precisely what way.

Classical Judaism and the Absence of Dogma

All this being so (and it is), it is no surprise that classical Judaism has no dogmas. The term 'dogma' is often taken to mean a belief that one holds in the face of rational counter-evidence, and it is in that sense that we use the term 'dogmatic' in ordinary language. In theology, however, the term 'dogma' (from the Latin *dogma*, meaning 'opinion' or 'belief', deriving in turn from the Greek *dokein*, 'to think') typically means a belief ordained by a recognized religious authority, acceptance of which is a necessary condition both for membership in the faith community under discussion and for the achievement of personal redemption, however that may be defined. It is in this sense that we find dogmas, articles of faith, confessional statements, creeds, and catechisms in classical Christianity and later in Islam.[18]

Dogma is an outgrowth of systematic theology. If a religion demands acceptance of a body of specific doctrines, it is not surprising if it places some of these doctrines on a higher plane than others. Furthermore, if a religion teaches that personal fulfilment ('salvation' in Christian religious vocabulary) depends upon holding some or all of its doctrines correctly, it becomes very important to achieve absolute clarity on which doctrines have that status and what precisely they are. Given that classical Judaism has no systematic theology, and given that it sees personal perfection and fulfilment as growing out of a life rightly lived as opposed to one rightly thought, it is no surprise to discover that until the Middle Ages our religious tradition never sought to express itself in terms of a set of dogmas.

That the Torah explicitly teaches no articles of faith is clear (after all, there are no verses that begin, 'Thou shalt verily believe that . . .' or

[18] On dogma in Christianity and Islam, see e.g. Jaroslav Pelikan, *The Growth of Medieval Theology (600–1300)* (Chicago: University of Chicago Press, 1978); A. J. Wensinck, *The Muslim Creed* (Cambridge: Cambridge University Press, 1932). I do not mean to imply that Maimonides formulated dogmas for Judaism simply as a response to other religions (for details, see Kellner, *Dogma*, 34–49), nor do I think that he held that the classic version of Judaism was incomplete. Rather, Maimonides sought to make explicit matters which in his view had always been implicit in Judaism.

'Cursed be he who holds that . . .'); but is this true of the Talmud as well? In Chapter 2 it will be shown both that there are no explicit statements of dogma in the Talmud and that many talmudic passages and practices make sense only if we remember that Judaism defines *emunah* in the first instance as trust in God and only secondarily, if at all, in terms of specific beliefs held or rejected.[19] After that we can, in Chapter 3, seek to understand why this is the case and why it ceased to be so. That, in turn, will set the stage for Chapters 4 and 5, in which Maimonides' attempt to revolutionize Judaism by setting it on a firm dogmatic foundation will be examined. In Chapter 6 I introduce the explicitly polemical side of this book, criticizing current applications of Maimonides' approach. This opens the way for the last chapter, in which I attempt to sketch out an alternative view, one which emphasizes inclusion over exclusion, and commonalities over differences (without trying to hide those differences).

[19] Throughout my discussion in the early chapters of this book I will be trying to drive a wedge between theological formulations and behaviour. This is for polemical purposes, so as to state my case in the strongest possible terms. For a statement of what I take to be the correct relationship between the two, please turn to the section of Chapter 7 below entitled 'Maimonides and the Objectivity of Truth' (p. 119). For the moment, suffice it to say that, in maintaining that 'Judaism defines *emunah* in the first instance as trust in God and only secondarily, if at all, in terms of specific beliefs held or rejected', I do not mean to claim that what we affirm is irrelevant to what we do.

TWO

Rabbinic Thought

THE TALMUD and midrashim are simply not the sorts of works in which one can find explicit responses to questions such as: Does Judaism have a systematic theology? If not, why not? How does Judaism understand faith in God? It is not that answers to these sorts of questions cannot be found in talmudic literature; in some cases they can be. The questions themselves, however, are simply never raised. Systematic thinking and formulation, indeed, were foreign to the rabbis who constructed this literature, and it would be surprising if we were to find 'settled doctrines' about anything.[1] Jose Faur put the point pithily: 'The whole notion of a system, let alone systematic attention, was alien to them.'[2] We shall see below that later generations of Jews have looked back into the talmudic texts and found therein various ideas for which rabbinic authority is then claimed. This often leads to reading later systematic ideas back into rabbinic texts. Despite all this, examination of rabbinically ordained practices and rabbinic texts can help us in formulating answers to questions such as those raised above. In particular, what can we learn from rabbinic texts about Jewish conceptions of faith in God?

Testing for 'Required Beliefs'

It pays to put the question in the following way: assuming for the moment that the rabbis of the Talmud thought that faith in God was best expressed in a series of affirmations about God and God's universe (i.e. 'belief that' statements), in what contexts could we expect the rabbis to

[1] The Mishnah, Jerusalem Talmud, Babylonian Talmud, and allied midrashim constitute a vast body of literature composed over a period of at least 700 years. Moreover, it is a literature aimed at arriving at clear-cut canons of behaviour and inculcating values; it is not, as I have said, a collection of textbooks of systematic theology. Approached historically, therefore, it makes no sense whatsoever to seek after 'the attitude of the Talmud' on anything. I approach it here, however, as it has always been approached by traditionalist, believing Jews, as the embodiment of the Oral Torah.

[2] Jose Faur, 'Monolingualism and Judaism', *Cardozo Law Review*, 14 (1993), 1712–44 at 1724.

demand that one get one's beliefs in order, so to speak, and present them for inspection?

If we may use other monotheistic religions as a guide, then it seems that we should expect the rabbis to require specific statements on the exact content of one's beliefs at key junctures such as when one assumes the rights and responsibilities of full participation in the Jewish community; when one joins that community from the outside; and when one seeks admittance to the world to come. If Judaism is going to apply some sort of theological test, in other words, we should look for it when one celebrates reaching one's majority, when one seeks to convert to Judaism, and in discussions of what criteria one has to satisfy in order to achieve a share in the world to come.

While the terms barmitzvah or batmitzvah do not occur in the Talmud in their contemporary sense, there are many passages in which it is made clear that a young man becomes fully responsible for his actions at the age of thirteen years and one day. Up to this point the child is not actually obliged to fulfil the commandments of the Torah. This understanding of the nature of the transition is made clear by the name we give to it: 'barmitzvah', i.e. one who is obliged to fulfil the commandments.

What must one do in order to become bar- or batmitzvah? Contrary to popular belief, one need not spend a lot of money on a big party, one need not make a speech, one need not be called to the Torah, one need not even be aware of the day; all one needs to do is reach one's twelfth birthday if one is a girl, or one's thirteenth birthday if one is a boy. That is all there is to it. Just as one reaches one's majority in Britain and in most states in the USA by turning eighteen, so one reaches one's Jewish majority by turning twelve or thirteen. To become bar- or batmitzvah, then, one need not do anything—least of all pass a test on dogmatic theology.

The key focus is on behaviour. When one becomes old enough, one is held to standards of action which are too stringent for little children: one can be expected, for example, to fast on Yom Kippur and to observe the Sabbath. One also earns certain rights over property, for example, or the ability to enter into legally binding contracts. The question of when this happens is a practical one: at what age can most developing adults be expected to be able to do these things, and do them responsibly?[3] Nowhere in the tradition of Judaism is reaching a majority connected in

[3] It should be noted that in rabbinic literature the importance of reaching the age of majority focuses on issues like the binding character of vows (*nedarim*), not on matters of accepting theological teachings (see Mishnah *Nedarim* v. 6). For a valuable summary and analysis of classic texts dealing with barmitzvah, see Byron L. Sherwin, 'Bar-Mizvah', *Judaism*, 22 (1973), 53–65.

any fashion to the understanding and acceptance of specific beliefs. That is not to say that children reaching the age of bar- and batmitzvah are expected to be atheists or agnostics. On the contrary: it is expected that they will have been brought up in faith and trust in God so that they will want to behave as God wants them to behave and recognize their obligation to do so.

This situation may profitably be compared with the institution of confirmation as it is found in many Christian churches and as it was found in classical Reform Judaism, which, in this matter at least, explicitly sought to remodel Judaism in the light of Christian theological categories. A child is typically confirmed as a member of a particular religious community at the end of her formal religious education, at the point at which she will have achieved sufficient understanding of the tenets of her denomination to accept them in a mature, responsible fashion. One is confirmed, then, after demonstrating mastery (at some level) of the tenets (i.e. dogmas) of one's faith and after explicitly adopting them as one's own. By the time of bar- or batmitzvah, by contrast, few children are theologically sophisticated, fewer still have been taught any sort of catechism, and none has been tested on it in order to 'become' bar- or batmitzvah.[4]

If the Talmud gives no indication of a theological orientation in the context of bar- or batmitzvah, perhaps it does in the context of conversion to Judaism. The rabbis had no control over who was born Jewish, but they had total control over who was accepted as a proselyte. Is there any indication in their discussion of conversion to Judaism that they paid any attention at all to systematic theology (and its offshoot, dogma), or were even aware of the possibility that Judaism might be defined in systematic, dogmatic terms?

This issue, at least, is easily examined; there is only one text in the Talmud in which the process of conversion to Judaism is explicitly described:

[4] One might wish to argue (incorrectly) that the blessings recited over the reading of the Torah ('Who has chosen us from among all the nations and given us His Torah' and 'Who has given us a Torah of truth and [thus] planted in us everlasting life') reflect a kind of credo, involving belief that the Jews are God's chosen people and that acceptance of the Torah leads to life in the hereafter. But even if this is true (and there is no reason to think that it is), it has nothing to do with barmitzvah: anyone called to the Torah recites these blessings; boys under the age of thirteen are not called to the Torah. The recitation of these blessings, therefore, is in no way similar to a catechism, affirmation of which 'confirms' one into the Jewish faith.

Our rabbis taught: if at the present time a man desires to become a proselyte, he is to be addressed as follows: 'What reason do you have for desiring to become a proselyte? Do you not know that Israel at the present time are persecuted and oppressed, despised, harassed and overcome by afflictions?' If he replies, 'I know and yet am unworthy,' he is accepted forthwith and given instruction in some of the minor and major commandments . . . He is also told of the punishment for the transgression of the commandments . . . as he is informed of the punishment for the transgression of the commandments, so he is informed of the reward granted for their fulfilment.[5]

According to this text, which is the direct source for all the halakhot (discrete laws) of conversion, when a person comes before a rabbinic court in order to convert to Judaism the court seeks to dissuade the prospective proselyte, in effect testing his or her commitment to the process of adoption into the Jewish people. If the prospective convert passes this test, instruction in *some* of the commandments is given, and the person is then immersed in a ritual bath (*mikveh*) and, in the case of a man, circumcised. That is the whole story. The entire focus here is on two things: identification with the Jews and acceptance of the 'yoke of the commandments'. There is not a breath of a whisper of any sort of theological test. The issue simply does not come up.

I must make an important point here. I do not mean to imply that if a prospective convert sincerely affirmed his desire to become a Jew, but then added that he did so only out of identity with the historical fate of the Jewish people, or because he found the life of the Torah spiritually fulfilling, and did not really believe that God had given the Torah to Moses at Sinai, such a person would be accepted as a convert. Hardly. Similarly, if a person affirmed his desire to convert to Judaism because of his belief that God gave the Torah to Moses at Sinai, but then mentioned that in his view God was a pink elephant, it is likely that the court would turn him away.

It is not the case that classical Judaism adopted an 'anything goes' attitude towards matters of belief. The rabbis functioned in a context in which who was and who was not a Jew was relatively clear, and in which there was a broad consensus concerning matters of religious belief and very little attempt to pin down and codify the details of that religious belief. Persons who violated that theological consensus were probably considered up to a point as simply strange, and after some point as having placed themselves outside the community altogether. The attitude of the

[5] BT *Yevamot* 47*a*–*b*.

rabbis towards matters of theology, it would seem, was more *laissez-faire* than totally uninterested.[6]

I must re-emphasize, so as not to be misunderstood, that the Torah does have a theological message, and matters of belief are important in Judaism. The entire Torah, as Maimonides never tires of reminding his readers, revolves around the pole of the rejection of idolatry. Judaism without belief in reward and punishment of some sort is incoherent, as would be any attempt to ascribe to Judaism the denial of human freedom in some significant sense. But the Torah always emphasized the life rightly lived over the belief rightly held, and it never taught the specifics of these beliefs; for reasons which will be discussed in detail below, pre-medieval Judaism never found it necessary or important to hammer out the particulars of the beliefs implied by or generally taught in the Torah. At this point I am trying to prove that this is the case; in the next chapter I will seek to explain why it is so.

To return to the matter at hand, it should now be clear that in at least two crucial cases (barmitzvah and conversion) where we would have expected to find explicit attention paid to dogmatic theology had the rabbis defined faith in those terms, such attention is wholly lacking. Let us turn to the third case, admittance to the world to come.

While classical Judaism clearly teaches that right behaviour in this world is rewarded in the next, and wrong behaviour in this world is punished in the next, it typically never seeks to establish precisely what happens. The attitude seems to be: 'We'll die and then we'll see.' But what is clear—and for this one needs no texts—is that the criterion determining one's future fate is behaviour, not thought. In popular parlance, one is rewarded for one's good deeds and punished for one's evil deeds. With

[6] Even the case of Elisha ben Abuyah supports my claim here. Elisha, a *tanna* (i.e. an authority cited in the Mishnah), committed some offence. The exact nature of his sin was unknown to the rabbis of the Jerusalem and Babylonian Talmuds, who advanced several different theories about what he had done. According to some of the accounts he held that the cosmos was governed by 'two authorities'. In this he diverged from Judaic monotheism. For texts and studies on the case of Elisha ben Abuyah, see David Halperin, *The Merkabah in Rabbinic Literature* (New Haven: American Oriental Society, 1980), 71–2, 167–72, 176–7; Yehudah Liebes, *Elisha's Sin* (Heb.) (Jerusalem: Academon, 1990). One of the points which Liebes tries to prove is that Elisha's actual sin was hubris, overweening pride, and not the adoption of theologically obnoxious positions. Assuming that Liebes is right supports the general point I am trying to make here, but even Liebes admits that the *amoraim* (authors of the Jerusalem and Babylonian Talmuds) and later authorities all understand Elisha's sin as a theological deviation.

one possible exception, which will be discussed below, there are simply no biblical or rabbinic texts in which holding right beliefs is specified as the criterion for enjoying a share in the world to come.

Now, it is clear that some sorts of behaviour reflect or are the consequence of some beliefs. A person who on philosophical or theological grounds rejects monotheism may be led to idolatry. A person may admit the existence of one God, but deny reward and punishment, and thus be led to *perikat ol*, the throwing off of the 'yoke' of the commandments. But in all such cases, the individual's sin is the forbidden behaviour, not the forbidden thought. That is not to say that the Jewish tradition would actively welcome an extremely observant atheist or agnostic; but so long as the individual kept his or her unconventional thoughts private, no great attempt would be made to root them out.

Thus far I have examined three crucial transitions in the life of a Jew: from childhood to adulthood; from being a Gentile to being a Jew; and from this life to the next. Had the rabbis of the Talmud been interested in theology as such, these are the sorts of points at which we could reasonably expect to find them clearly laying out the basic teachings of Judaism in a dogmatic or at least theologically systematic fashion. But, in fact, we do not find them doing so. This I take as convincing evidence for my claim that pre-medieval Judaism did not express itself in terms which could be reduced to ordered theological formulations, formulations according to which the rabbis could clearly and neatly determine who was 'in' (a good Jew) and who was 'out' (a heretic).

This situation reflects the fact that in pre-medieval Judaism religious faith—*emunah*—was understood as a particular relationship with God, and not as a group of affirmations about God. There is one rabbinic text in which this point is made almost explicitly, and it repays examination here: 'R. Simlai expounded: "Six hundred and thirteen precepts were communicated to Moses, three hundred and sixty-five negative ones, corresponding to the days of the solar year, and two hundred and forty-eight positive ones, corresponding to the number of members of a human's body.' R. Simlai here tells us that the Torah contains precisely 613 commandments. We may skip the discussion which ensues, in which he proves his point. R. Simlai then continues his exposition, saying, 'David came and reduced them [the 613 commandments] to eleven.' Here R. Simlai cites Psalm 15, in which he finds eleven characteristics of the person who seeks to sojourn in the Lord's tabernacle and dwell in the holy mountain. The exposition continues: Isaiah is cited as having reduced the 613 to six, Micah to three, and Isaiah, again, to two. The passage ends as follows:

Amos came and reduced them to one, as it is said: 'For thus saith the Lord unto the house of Israel, Seek ye Me and live.' At this R. Nahman ben Isaac demurred, saying [Might it not be taken as meaning,] Seek Me by observing the whole Torah and live? But it is Habakkuk who came and based them all on one, as it is said, 'But the righteous shall live by his faith.'[7]

Here we have a passage in the Talmud in which the 613 commandments of the Torah are reduced to one statement: the righteous shall live by his faith. The *tzadik*, the righteous person, is defined as one who lives by faith (*emunah*); faith, in turn, it is clearly implied, finds its expression in the fulfilment of the 613 commandments of the Torah.

Faith, as apparently understood by Habakkuk and by R. Simlai, is meant to bring one to a particular kind of life, not to the affirmation of particular ideas, however important those ideas may be. Judaism prizes belief in God, trust in God, a life lived with God, over belief that certain statements are true of God. This does not mean that Judaism teaches nothing about God, or is open to any and all affirmations about God. It means that the room for discussion, debate, even divergence and error concerning these affirmations is broader than is often thought today. Systematic theology is simply not part of the focus of classical Judaism; theological questions as such were largely ignored by the Torah and Talmud and the answers to theological questions were not made central to the quest of learning how to live the life commanded by God. I must

[7] The talmudic text is found in BT *Makot* 23*b*–24*a*. The *amora* R. Nahman's comment here is noteworthy. The Talmud had said that the Prophet Amos had reduced all of the 613 commandments to one: 'For thus saith the Lord unto the house of Israel, Seek ye Me and live.' R. Nahman demurred, concerned lest the verse be interpreted to mean that only those who correctly fulfilled every single one of the 613 commandments are true God-seekers, and only they will live. This, as is well known, is the picture of Judaism presented by the apostle Paul. Paul replaced observance of the commandments with correct faith. If R. Nahman's comment is indeed part of an anti-Christian polemic, then my claim here that the faith spoken of by the prophet Habakkuk and recommended, as it were, by R. Nahman as a summary of the entire Torah could not possibly be the 'belief that' alleged by Paul. For an interpretation of this text precisely opposed to mine, see George Foot Moore, *Judaism in the First Centuries of the Christian Era*, 3 vols. (New York: Schocken, 1971), ii. 84. Moore seeks to identify the verse from Habakkuk 2: 4, 'But the righteous shall live by his faith', with Romans 1: 17 and Galatians 3: 11, 'The just shall live by faith.' The 'just' spoken of in these New Testament books obviously live without even trying to fulfil the 613 commandments of the Torah. For Moore's interpretation to make sense we must leave the last sentence out of the talmudic passage altogether.

emphasize again: theological views did find expression in classical Judaism; my point is that no attempt was ever made to systematize them, to compare them, to bring them into a consistent whole, or even to determine which were correct and how they were to be understood.

An Objection: Mishnah *Sanhedrin* x. 1

I maintained above that classical Judaism knows of no theological test for admission to the world to come. Readers familiar with the tradition will immediately object that there is at least one text in which such a test is applied. This same text, it has been argued, represents an attempt by the rabbis to set down the dogmas of Judaism. This latter claim has the authority of no less a figure than Maimonides behind it. If Maimonides' interpretation is to be rejected, the support for that rejection must be strong indeed.

Mishnah *Sanhedrin* x. 1 states:

> All Israelites have a share in the world to come, as it states, 'Thy people are all righteous, they shall inherit the land for ever' [Isa. 60: 21]. But the following have no share in the world to come: he who says there is no resurrection taught in the Torah, that the Torah is not from heaven, and the *epikoros*. Rabbi Akiva says: 'Even he who reads in the external books, and he who whispers over a wound, saying, "I will put none of the diseases upon thee, which I have put upon the Egyptians; for I am the Lord that healeth thee" [Exod. 15: 26].' Abba Saul says: 'Even he who pronounces the name according to its letters.'

What exactly does this mishnah teach? In the first place it takes as a given that all Jews (even, apparently, those whose execution was laid down in the preceding chapter of the Mishnah) will, other things being equal, enjoy a share in the world to come (the Jewish way of expressing what Christianity would come to call 'salvation').[8] Typically, the mishnah cites a proof text from the Bible to support its claim that Jews ('Israelites') will

[8] For background on the mishnah analysed here, see Lawrence Schiffman, *Who Was a Jew? Rabbinic and Halakhic Perspectives on the Jewish–Christian Schism* (Hoboken, NJ: Ktav, 1985), 41–6. Schiffman, I think, over-emphasizes the theological character of the mishnah, but is surely right in his claim that 'exclusion from a portion in the world to come does not imply exclusion from the Jewish people' (p. 42). This conclusion follows from the answer to a question which he poses on the previous page of his book: Can 'one be excluded from the Jewish people and lose his Jewish status as the result of any beliefs and actions[?] Indeed, it will be shown conclusively that this cannot occur and that only the criteria described above [birth or conversion] could serve to indicate who was or was not a Jew in the early centuries of this era.'

enjoy a place in the next world.[9] In that verse Isaiah says that the Jews are righteous (*tzadikim*) and will [therefore] inherit 'the land for ever'. The Hebrew term for 'for ever' (*le'olam*) connotes eternity. Since the righteous among us do not inherit anything in this world for all eternity, the mishnah apparently reasons, the 'land' which Isaiah assures us they will inherit for all eternity must be in another dispensation altogether. The righteous, therefore, can look forward to an eternal existence in another world, the 'world to come', i.e. the world we are not yet in.[10]

The presumption of this mishnah, then, is that righteousness is an absolute prerequisite for admittance to the world to come. It further teaches that with apparently very few exceptions (it says 'all Israelites') all Jews are sufficiently righteous to gain that end.[11]

But not quite all Jews. The author of our mishnah says that there are three types of Jew who are excluded from the world to come: those who deny that the Torah teaches resurrection, those who deny the divine origin of the Torah, and those who earn the label *epikoros*. The first two are tolerably clear, but what does the last mean? While it is highly probable that the term derives from the name of the Greek philosopher of the third and fourth centuries BCE—Epicurus—there is really no way of knowing what exactly the author of the mishnah meant. The Babylonian Talmud, however, in glossing this mishnah, is quite clear on its understanding of the term: the *epikoros* is that person who shows disrespect to the rabbis.[12]

[9] The Mishnah takes no stand on the question of whether non-Jews will also gain admittance to the world to come. This is a question treated in a parallel text (the *Tosefta* on *Sanhedrin*); the position which has become normative in Judaism is that 'righteous Gentiles' (*ḥasidei umot ha'olam*) will find their place in the world to come. For details, see Kellner, *Maimonides on Judaism and the Jewish People*, 29–32.

[10] The explanation of Isaiah 60: 21 offered here is drawn from Maimonides' 'Laws of Repentance', iii. 5.

[11] The assumption of Mishnah *Sanhedrin* x. 1, that by nature, so to speak, all Israelites are righteous and deserve a share in the world to come, should be compared with the orientation of classical Christianity (at least from the time of Augustine), according to which human beings are born stained with the original sin of Adam and Eve and are thus by nature anything but righteous and deserving of a share in the world to come. For discussion of this, see Elaine Pagels, *Adam, Eve, and the Serpent* (New York: Vintage, 1989), esp. ch. 6.

[12] For the talmudic understanding of *epikoros*, see *Sanhedrin* 96*b*–100*a* and JT *Sanhedrin* x. 1. The question of whether or not this amoraic understanding of the term properly reflects the way it was used by the *tannaim*, interesting in and of itself, is irrelevant for our purposes here. See further *Sanhedrin* 38*b*, where Gentile *epikoresim* are distinguished from Jewish *epikoresim*; if a Gentile can be an *epikoros* then the term can hardly refer to a heretic in any straightforward theological sense.

R. Akiva adds two further classes of people who exclude themselves from the world to come. The first of these consists of people who read 'external books' and the second comprises individuals who use biblical verses in what we would call a magical fashion to heal the sick. As with the term *epikoros*, so with 'external books': we do not know exactly what R. Akiva had in mind. He might mean those books later called apocryphal; but that seems unlikely, since in his day the biblical canon was still somewhat fluid (he is recorded as one of the authorities who helped establish it) and also because certain of the books we now call apocryphal were treated with respect by the authors of the Mishnah. Later interpreters are also divided over what R. Akiva meant: Maimonides took him to mean books of history and poetry, while R. Isaac ben Sheshet Perfet took him to mean works like Aristotle's *Rhetoric*.[13] Abba Saul's addition is clear: one loses one's portion in the world to come if one pronounces the tetragrammaton, God's four-letter name, as it is written.

This mishnah represents the only text known to us from classical Judaism which might serve as a counter-example to my claims that pre-medieval Judaism contains no statements of dogma and makes no theological test for admission to the world to come. But does it really? A number of points have to be made. First, it does not tell us what we have to believe. It is phrased negatively: all Jews have a share in the world to come, apart from those excluded under six headings. Instead of setting down criteria for achieving salvation, it assumes that all Jews will indeed earn it and then lists exceptions to that generalization, most of them phrased in terms of denials, not affirmations. Now, it is true that one can read an implied list of dogmas here: belief in resurrection, etc. Statements of dogma, however, do not typically instruct by implication.

This observation leads on to a second point: of the six issues raised in the mishnah, three (the additions of R. Akiva and Abba Saul) are actions, while a fourth, that of the *epikoros*, is interpreted by the Talmud as a species of behaviour. It is an odd statement of dogma which lists two things one is not supposed to believe in and then four species of

[13] Maimonides' explanation of the 'external books' is found in his commentary on the Mishnah. For R. Isaac ben Sheshet's discussion see Kellner, 'R. Isaac bar Sheshet's Responsum'. For a recent discussion of the term 'external books' see Gerald J. Blidstein, 'Rabbinic Judaism and General Culture: Normative Discussion and Attitudes', in Jacob J. Schacter (ed.), *Judaism's Encounter with Other Cultures: Rejection or Integration?* (Northvale, NJ: Jason Aronson, 1997), 1–56 at 21–3. Jose Faur suggested to me that the Mishnah means to forbid reading any extra-biblical book with the cantillation appropriate to the Torah.

prohibited behaviour. It is even odder when we consider that the mishnah literally says nothing about belief and talks only in terms of statements, excluding from the world to come 'he who *says* there is no resurrection taught in the Torah'. This would seem to indicate that the mishnah's primary interest is not so much in guaranteeing right belief as in extirpating dangerous talk. Its concern is more social than theological. It is interested in what one does *befarhesya*, in public, rather than in what one thinks in the privacy of one's head. This might be contrasted with the Church's injunction against Galileo, ordering him neither '*to hold* nor [to] defend' the Copernican theory.[14]

Thus we arrive at my third point. If this mishnah is meant to be a statement of Jewish dogma, it is odd not only for what it includes, but also for what it excludes. It makes no specific reference to belief in God, for example. (Maimonides, it should be noted, interprets the *epikoros* as one who denies God's existence, but we have no reason to suspect that that is the intent of the mishnah itself.)

Fourth, if we look at the mishnah in its historical context, the first part, at least, would seem to make excellent sense as part of a Pharisaic polemic against the Sadducees, as opposed to an attempt to lay down, once for all, in a succinct, self-conscious, and authoritative fashion, the normative dogmas of the Jewish religion. In their controversies with the Pharisees, which took place largely in the first century CE, the Sadducees denied life after death and the divine authorship of the Oral Torah. The first two excluded categories in our mishnah ('he who says there is no resurrection taught in the Torah, [and] that the Torah is not from heaven'), are clearly an anti-Sadducean polemic. Given that context, it probably makes more sense to see the *epikoros* as a Sadducee than anything else.[15]

[14] My source for the Church's injunction against Galileo is Maurice A. Finocchiaro (ed. and trans.), *The Galileo Affair: A Documentary History* (Berkeley: University of California Press, 1989), 147–8; see also ibid. 286–91.

[15] The definition of the *epikoros* as one who shows disrespect for the rabbis fits in very well here. J. N. Epstein also sees our mishnah as being an anti-Sadducean polemic. See his *Introduction to Tannaitic Literature* (Heb.) (Jerusalem: Magnes, 1957), 418. In this he is followed by Schiffman, *Who Was a Jew?*, 42. (See that page, including n. 8, for information on the textual history of the mishnah.) The Sadducean threat is taken in the Talmud less as a theological debate than as challenge to the authority of the rabbis. The Sadducees' insistence on performing ritual acts in a deviant manner is presented in the Talmud as more threatening than the theological justification offered for these deviations. See e.g. Mishnah *Yadayim* vi. 6–8 and Mishnah *Eruvin* vi. 2. It is noteworthy for our purposes that the Sages made no attempt to exclude the Sadducees from the community of Israel and turn them into a separate sect. On this, see Urbach, *The Sages*, i. 512.

The additions of R. Akiva and Abba Saul, for their part, ought to be seen in the context of the Talmud's readiness to pronounce exclusion from the world to come on people who exhibit all sorts of aberrant behaviour (such as shaming one's fellow in public), rather than as an attempt to lay down the principles of the Jewish religion. The expression 'such and such an action costs a person his or her share in the world to come' should be understood as a way of expressing strong disapproval of the behaviour rather than as a clear-cut eschatological claim.[16]

This last point raises a related issue, one which further strengthens my claim that our mishnah is not meant as a self-conscious statement of dogma. In the continuation of this text (namely, Mishnah *Sanhedrin* x. 2–4) a wide variety of people are said to have no share in the world to come. These include kings Jeroboam, Ahab, and Manasseh, and commoners Balaam, Doeg, Ahitophel, and Gehazi. Also included in this list (that is to say, excluded from the world to come) are the entire generation of the Flood, the generation of the Tower of Babel, the inhabitants of Sodom, and the entire generation of the Exodus (i.e. those who died during the forty years of wandering in the wilderness), as well as the followers of Korah. Aside from the 'three kings and four commoners', the mishnah records debates about the status of the other groups. These debates revolve around the midrashic exposition of various verses relating to the groups in question. There can be very little doubt that the expression 'so and so has no share in the world to come' in these texts is meant to express great disapproval of so and so; it is not meant as a straightforward eschatological assertion.

Even if the expression means exactly what it says, the three paragraphs which follow our text strengthen the claim that Mishnah *Sanhedrin* x. 1 is not put forward as a statement of dogma. It would take extremely creative readings of many biblical texts to support the claim that Jeroboam, Ahab, Manasseh, Balaam, Doeg, Ahitophel, Gehazi, the generation of the Flood, the generation of the Tower of Babel, the inhabitants

[16] For examples of other crimes which cost the perpetrator his or her share in the world to come, see *Pirkei avot* iii. 12; *Avot d'rabbi natan*, ch. 36 (where it is taught, for example, that 'scribes, elementary teachers, [even] the best of physicians, judges in their native cities, diviners, ministers of the court and butchers' are among many others who have no share in the world to come); Mishnah *Sanhedrin* x. 2–4; Tosefta *Sanhedrin* xii. 12; BT *Bava metsia* 59*a*; BT *Megillah* 28*a*; BT *Ketubot* 111*a* (those who die outside the Land of Israel, among others); and JT *Ḥagigah* ii. 1. On this tendency of the rabbis, compare the comment of Rabbi Shimon ben Tsemah Duran: 'in the Mishnah and the Baraita the Sages exaggerated in recording many things the doing of which cost one his share in the world to come.' This text is translated in Kellner, *Dogma*, 93.

of Sodom, the generation of the Exodus, and the followers of Korah all lost their share in the world to come because they held incorrect beliefs. Moreover, Balaam, those who perished in the Flood, the builders of the Tower of Babel, and the Sodomites were not even Jews! In other words, Mishnah *Sanhedrin* x. 2–4 (the clear continuation of x. 1) cannot by any stretch of the imagination be taken as a statement of dogma; that being the case, why should the first part of this unitary text (x. 1) be so taken?

This point is further strengthened if we consider texts parallel to our mishnah. Tosefta *Sanhedrin* xiii. 5 and BT *Rosh hashanah* 17*a* condemn the following to Gehinnom, the place of punishment after death: sectarians (*minim*), apostates (*meshumadim*), informers, *epikoresim*, deniers of the Torah, those who abandon the ways of the community, deniers of resurrection, those who sin and cause the masses to sin, those who cast their fear upon the land of the living, and those who stretch forth their hands upon the Temple. We have here a list of 'public enemies', so to speak; what we do not have is a statement of creed, or anything remotely resembling such a statement.[17]

Mishnah *Sanhedrin* x. 1, therefore, ought not to be seen as an attempt to lay down a self-conscious system of dogma for Judaism or set up a theological test for admission to the world to come. It does, however, represent part of what is the first recorded theological debate in Judaism, that between the Sadducees and Pharisees, and as such is certainly a harbinger of things to come.[18]

A Defence of Dogma

The position I have sketched out above is clearly controversial. Rabbi Dr J. David Bleich, for example, bluntly rejects the view I have been proposing here concerning the place of systematic theology (and its offshoot, dogma) in rabbinic thought as a misconception: 'one widespread

[17] Further on the passage cited from Tosefta *Sanhedrin* xiii. 5, see Schiffman, *Who Was a Jew?*, 46–9; Kellner, *Dogma*, 33.

[18] Note should be further made of the fact that the arguments in rabbinic literature against sectarians (*minim*) of various sorts are almost invariably midrashic and not theological. Even when challenged theologically, the rabbis tended not to respond in kind. For examples, see *Sifre* on Deuteronomy 32: 329; JT *Berakhot* ix. 1; *Exodus rabbah*, ii. 5; and BT *Sanhedrin* 38*b*. Ephraim Urbach, *The Sages*, i. 468, points out that arguments against *minim* in rabbinic texts tend to be grotesque and derisory; they were rarely reasoned responses to challenges over the intellectual content of religious faith. See also David Rokeah, *Jews, Pagans and Christians in Conflict* (Leiden: Brill, 1982), 76–8.

misconception concerning Judaism is the notion that Judaism is a religion which is not rooted in dogma.' Dogma, for Bleich, is a 'fulcrum of Judaism' and 'does not stand apart from the normative demands of Judaism but is the *sine qua non* without which other values and practices are bereft of meaning'.[19] Bleich's analysis rests upon the unarticulated assumption that the medieval Jewish philosophers (whom he cites) expressed views held by the *tannaim* and *amoraim* (whom he does not cite). In many ways, the argument of this entire book is directed against scholars like Bleich who, I will try to show, take a particular interpretation of the views of Maimonides as normative, read it back into classical Jewish texts, and then claim it to be authoritative for Jews today.[20]

It would certainly not be fair to leave my response to Bleich at this point, however, since his view is supported by a body of scholarship which ought not to be ignored. Max Kadushin, for example, has argued at length that 'in their own fashion, the Rabbis crystallized several of their beliefs into dogmas'. Kadushin immediately qualifies this claim, however, admitting that 'these dogmas differ widely in their character from the dogmas of medieval Jewish thought, and they do not constitute a creed'. They differ from medieval dogma, according to Kadushin, because of the 'indeterminate' nature of rabbinic beliefs and because 'a rabbinic dogma is a belief which the Rabbis have singled out as one to which all must subscribe. A dogma is a matter of belief, not a matter of daily, personal experience. Acknowledgment of God, on the other hand, involves daily, personal experience; hence it is not a dogma, notwithstanding the terminology.'[21] The dogmas of the rabbis are, according to Kadushin, belief in the Exodus from Egypt, in the Sinaitic Revelation, and in the resurrection of the dead.[22]

Kadushin bases his claims upon an analysis of rabbinic use of the terms *modeh* ('admit' or 'thank') and *kofer* ('deny'). This is not the place for a fully fledged critique of Kadushin's views; I will just note that in order to substantiate his claims, Kadushin is forced into the prima-facie odd position that belief in God is not among the dogmas of rabbinic Judaism, while belief in the historical truth of the Exodus, the Revelation at Sinai,

[19] These statements are drawn from J. David Bleich, *With Perfect Faith: The Foundations of Jewish Belief* (New York: Ktav, 1983), 1–2.

[20] Further on my disagreements with Bleich, see below, pp. 96–7, 99–104.

[21] Max Kadushin, *The Rabbinic Mind*, 3rd edn. (New York: Bloch, 1972), 340, 131–42, 347.

[22] Ibid. 348–66. Even Kadushin, however, admits that Mishnah *Sanhedrin* x. 1 is 'an anathema against sectaries . . . not a statement of the basic doctrines of Judaism' (p. 367).

and the future occurrence of resurrection are. He is furthermore forced to argue that the meaning of the term *modim* in the penultimate benediction of the Amidah prayer is 'we admit/acknowledge' rather than 'we thank'. This interpretation is, it seems clear (to me at least), very forced; the rest of the blessing clearly refers to things for which we owe thanks to God.[23]

Heretics and Sectarians

Another commonly adduced source for the claim that the rabbis understood themselves to some extent in what we today call theological terms is the twelfth blessing of the Amidah prayer, the *birkat haminim* (curse on *minim*): 'May the slanderers have no hope; may all wickedness perish instantly; may all thy enemies be soon cut down. Do thou speedily uproot and crush the arrogant; cast them down and humble them speedily in our days. Blessed art Thou, O Lord, who breakest the enemies and humblest the arrogant.'[24]

A number of scholars have argued that the meaning of *min* is 'heretic', with all that implies for notions of theological orthodoxy. The precise meaning of the term *min*, however, is hotly debated and certainly not at all clear. Stuart Miller refers to its 'nebulous and elusive nature'.[25] It is clear that it meant different things in different times and places; and it is certainly clear that the use of the term in rabbinic literature does not mean that most (or even any) of the rabbis of the Mishnah and Talmud

[23] The text of the benediction is as follows:

> We ever thank thee, who are the Lord our God and the God of our fathers. [Kadushin would have to translate: 'We acknowledge that thou art the Lord our God and the God of our fathers.'] Thou art the strength of our life and our saving shield. In every generation we will thank thee and recount thy praise—for our lives which are in thy charge, for our souls which are in thy care, for thy miracles which are daily with us, and for thy continual wonders and favors—evening, morning, and noon. Beneficent One, whose mercies never fail, Merciful One, whose kindnesses never cease, thou hast always been our hope.

I cite the translation of Philip Birnbaum, *Daily Prayer Book* (New York: Hebrew Publishing Co., 1949), 91. I ask the reader to decide whether it makes sense to claim that the use of *modim* in the first sentence means 'admit/acknowledge' while its use in the third sentence (*nodeh*) and the rest of the passage means 'we thank'.

[24] I cite the translation of Birnbaum, *Daily Prayer Book*, 88. Although the term *min* ('sectarian') is not found in this benediction in its current, censored form (in which *malshinim*, 'slanderers', replaces *minim*, 'sectarians'), it is referred to in the Talmud by that name (BT *Berakhot* 28*b*). See also Maimonides, 'Laws of Prayer', ii. 1.

[25] Stuart Miller, 'The *Minnim* of Sepphoris Reconsidered', *Harvard Theological Review*, 86 (1993), 377–402 at 401.

had a consciously developed and codified theology. While Reuven Kimelman translates the term both as 'sectarian' (with its social connotations) and as 'heretic' (with its theological connotations), he proves that the *birkat haminim*, at least, was actually directed against Jewish sectarians and not against heretics, and argues convincingly that 'in Palestine, the term *min* had a sectarian connotation'.[26] The key point for our present purposes is that even if modern scholars occasionally translate the word *min* as 'heretic', and even if in some contexts that translation is adequate, it is in no way proven that the rabbis had a clearly worked-out notion of theological heresy.[27]

It is appropriate to conclude this discussion with a further word about sectarians and heretics. In 'Rabbinism and Karaism: The Contest for

[26] Reuven Kimelman, '*Birkat ha-Minim* and the Lack of Evidence for an Anti-Christian Jewish Prayer in Late Antiquity', in E. P. Sanders, A. I. Baumgarten, and Alan Mendelson (eds.), *Aspects of Judaism in the Graeco-Roman Period*, vol. ii of *Jewish and Christian Self-definition*, 3 vols. (London: SCM, 1981), 226–44 at 231.

[27] Further on all this see Alan F. Segal, *Two Powers in Heaven: Early Rabbinic Reports about Christianity and Gnosticism* (Leiden: Brill, 1977), 4–7, and the survey of sources and studies in Ya'akov Sussmann, 'The History of *Halakha* and the Dead Sea Scrolls: A Preliminary to the Publication of the 4QMMT' (Heb.), *Tarbits*, 55 (1989–90), 11–76, n. 176 (53–5). Further support for my position may be found in another essay in Sanders *et al.* (eds.), *Aspects of Judaism*. Ephraim Urbach, in 'Self-Isolation and Self-Affirmation in Judaism in the First Three Centuries: Theory and Practice' (pp. 269–98), comments that *minim* 'are not condemned because of their teaching, but because of their infidelity towards their community' (p. 292). (On this last point, see also Schiffman, *Who Was A Jew?*, 4, 6, and 76–7.) Compare also in the same volume Ferdinand Dexinger, 'Limits of Tolerance in Judaism: The Samaritan Example', 88–114, esp. 111. For a striking example confirming Urbach's (and my) thesis that *minim* 'are not condemned because of their teaching, but because of their infidelity towards their community', note the following well-known passage from the Passover Haggadah: 'What does the wicked son say? "What is this service to you?" "To you," and not to him—since he excluded himself from the generality [of Israel] he denied the essential . . .'. The expression 'denied the essential' here translates *kafar ba' ikar*, an expression which in the Middle Ages came to mean 'denied an essential dogmatic teaching', but which here means 'excluded himself from the Jewish community'. For studies of this passage and its history, see Louis Finkelstein, 'Pre-Maccabean Documents in the Passover Haggadah', *Harvard Theological Review*, 36 (1943), 1–38, esp. 8–18; also D. Goldschmidt's edition of the Passover Haggadah (Jerusalem: Mosad Bialik, 1947), 25 n. 11, 28. On the expression *ikar*, see Isaac Abrabanel, *Principles of Faith*, ch. 6. In addition, as Jolene Kellner pointed out to me, it should be noted that Judaism recognizes three cardinal offences, which may never be committed, even to save one's life: idolatry, murder, and certain forms of sexual immorality (for details, see Maimonides, 'Laws of the Foundations of the Torah', ch. v). None of these, not even the first, which deals with forbidden behaviour, not the theology motivating it) is a strictly theological offence.

Supremacy', Daniel J. Lasker writes that the Karaite Jacob al-Kirkisani recorded a debate he had with a Rabbanite whom he described as maintaining that a 'manifestation of [complete] unbelief is more pardonable than the display of [petty] differences in the observance of holidays'.[28] On this Lasker comments: 'In other words, Rabbanite Judaism can co-exist with major doctrinal differences as long as they do not lead to substantial behavioral divergences. It is not able to abide ritual changes which involve, for example, the existence of a different calendar. Theological heresy is pardonable; observance of Passover on a different date is not.' Here we have a medieval discussion predicated upon the distinction between heresy ('the manifestation of unbelief') and sectarianism ('differences in the observance of holidays'). Lasker is absolutely correct: the rabbis of the Mishnah and Talmud tolerated the former with relative equanimity while being absolutely unwilling to countenance the latter. Sid Z. Leiman makes the same point in an interesting and compelling fashion:

> Books written in Hebrew and ascribed to the biblical period which challenged *central* halakic teachings of the rabbis were *ipso facto* excluded from the biblical canon. Thus, the book of Jubilees, which is predicated upon a calendar at variance with the rabbinic calendar, could not be considered a serious candidate for inclusion in the biblical canon . . . books which challenged central theological teachings of the rabbis, while problematic, were not necessarily excluded from the biblical canon. Ecclesiastes is a case in point. Its seemingly antinomian, pessimistic, and often contradictory sentiments left the rabbis nonplussed. Despite the theological problems it created for the rabbis, Ecclesiastes retained its position in the biblical canon precisely because it did not challenge central halakic practices in any substantive way.[29]

The entire point of this chapter could hardly be put in a clearer fashion!

Even if my discussion in this chapter should leave some readers unconvinced that systematic theology was foreign to rabbinic Judaism, at the very least it should be clear that for the rabbis matters of belief were not legally actionable. This is actually enough for my purpose, namely to show that Maimonides' approach (as will be seen in Chapter 4) represented an innovation in Judaism.

[28] Daniel J. Lasker, 'Rabbanism and Karaism: The Contest for Supremacy', in Raphael Jospe and Stanley M. Wagner (eds.), *Great Schisms in Jewish History* (New York: Ktav, 1981), 47–72 at 47.

[29] Sid Z. Leiman, 'Inspiration and Canonicity: Reflections on the Formation of the Biblical Canon', in Sanders *et al.* (eds.), *Aspects of Judaism*, 56–63 at 62.

A 'Theology' of Action

In this chapter I have defended the consistency of rabbinic with biblical thought. The Torah understands *emunah*, faith or belief, less in terms of propositions affirmed or denied by the believer ('belief that') and more in terms of the relationship (primarily of trust) between the believer and God ('belief in'). This faith expresses itself in terms of behaviour, rather than in terms of systematic theology.

We have seen that the Talmud, following the biblical precedent, gives no evidence, where it might reasonably be expected to be found, of being at all interested in systematic theology or dogma, both consequences of understanding faith in terms of its propositional content, i.e. in terms of precisely formulated statements which one affirms or denies. Moreover, in at least one text, the Talmud clearly connects faith with the observance of the commandments. Such a connection makes much more sense in the context of a 'belief in' orientation than in the context of a 'belief that' orientation.

But does this mean that Torah and Talmud teach us nothing about God and God's relationship with the world? Such a claim would be ridiculous. Judaism indeed affirms a large number of teachings of a theological nature. But it consistently focuses on the sort of life one is to lead in pursuit of those teachings, rather than on the teachings themselves. Two individuals can both be good Jews, fastidiously obeying the commandments, while disagreeing over fundamental matters of theology. This was certainly the case with Maimonides and the Ba'al Shem Tov.

If all this is true, why does Mishnah *Sanhedrin* x. 1 appear to lay down a set of dogmas and apply a test of theological orthodoxy? I have shown above that such was not, apparently, the intent of the mishnah. One must read the text in that fashion only if one assumes (as did Maimonides) that Judaism is a religion with a systematically theological base. Similarly, I have argued that rabbinic strictures against 'sectarians' are better understood in terms of social divisions than in terms of clear self-conscious theological division.

THREE

Why Judaism Acquired a Systematic Theology

IN the last chapter I showed that the mishnah beginning 'All Israelites have a share in the world to come . . .' ought not to be understood as a statement of dogma or as a test of theological orthodoxy. The present chapter is—in one sense—an argument to the effect that only an interpreter approaching that mishnah with the prior assumption that Judaism has a systematic theology like Islam or Christianity would read it as either a statement of dogma or a test of theological orthodoxy. I mean by this that there is nothing inherent in monotheistic faith which demands that it find expression in systematic theology. It is my contention that only if one assumes that such theology must underlie any monotheistic faith will one read Mishnah *Sanhedrin* x. 1 as an expression of systematic theology. But that very assumption is one which must come from outside Judaism. In other words, the question implicit in the title of this chapter is actually illegitimate. It is based upon the presupposition that all monotheistic religions have systematic theologies. But the fact that both Islam and Christianity express themselves in that fashion does not mean that all monotheistic faiths do so, or ought to do so.[1] As we have already seen, classical Judaism certainly did not!

Behaviour and Belief

In order to understand this situation, it must be remembered and emphasized that rabbinic Judaism understood itself first and foremost

[1] Islam and Christianity should really be distinguished from each other in this regard. For an accessible discussion, see Bernard Lewis, *Islam and the West* (New York: Oxford University Press, 1993), 155. As Lewis notes there,

> In accordance with a common but nevertheless misleading practice, outside observers often use words like 'sect' and 'schism' to describe . . . these Islamic differences. Some go even further and use such words as 'orthodox' and 'heterodox' or 'heretical' to describe Islamic religious disagreements. This is . . . inappropriate . . . in that the very notion of orthodoxy and heterodoxy is specifically Christian. It has little or no relevance to the history of Islam, which has no synods, churches, or councils to define orthodoxy, and therefore none to define and condemn departures from orthodoxy.

What Lewis writes here of Islam is even truer of Judaism.

as a system of commandments and values adhered to by a group of individuals defined in the first instance by shared descent. The Jews were a nation, a people, a family, bound together by a covenant with God; they were not a communion of true believers. Thus, as Lawrence Schiffman, a prominent historian of the period, comments,

> Although the Pharisees, Sadducees, Essenes, Dead Sea Sect, and others disagreed on fundamental issues of theology, law, biblical exegesis, and social and political matters, no sect ever claimed that the others were not Jews. Rather, all groups implicitly recognized the Jewish status of their competitors. Even in regard to the extreme Hellenists, the claim was never made that they had somehow left the Jewish people by their apostasy.[2]

Even groups competing with the Sages were recognized by the latter as Jews; whatever the fields in which the competition was carried out, they were not those of theology and dogma.

As we have established in Chapters 1 and 2, both Torah and Talmud see the *emunah* which defines the righteous person as steadfast trust in God expressed in action, and not as intellectual acquiescence in clearly defined teachings. In other words, classical Judaism has emphasized 'belief in' over 'belief that'.

The Torah, as both Maimonides and the Israeli Orthodox iconoclast Yeshayahu Leibowitz (1903–94) like to remind us, is not a present from God on a silver platter, designed to endow us with some precious gift without our lifting a finger. On the contrary, the Torah is a series of challenges. But these challenges can be met; and in meeting them a human being becomes better and earns a place in the world to come. In such a context, what is demanded of people is that they trust in God, secure in the faith that observing the commandments of the Torah is good for the Jew and good for the world, even if all the objective evidence seems to contradict this thesis. This is the sort of faith, *emunah*, which Judaism seeks to implant in the believer.

Individuals can earn their place in the world to come through fulfilment of the commandments because they are not, at the outset, entirely distanced from God. On this view, each of us is born pure; it is our job in living to remain pure, or at least pure enough not to destroy the connection with God. But no matter how bad a mess one makes of one's life, the doctrine of repentance teaches that God is always available to the *ba'al teshuvah*, the repentant individual. This is so because people are born like blank tablets on which a life is to be written. One can keep one's tablet clean, or one can sully it. But no matter how dirty the tablet

[2] Schiffman, *Who Was a Jew?*, 3.

becomes, it still remains there under all the filth. Cleaning the filth may be difficult, but it is not in principle impossible.

The upshot of all this is that Judaism is a religion which places a great deal of emphasis on correct behaviour. But Judaism is not simply a system of observances *per se* (a 'religion of pots and pans', as some of its detractors like to say). One observes the commandments of the Torah, ideally, because of one's relationship with God, out of love, with no thought of reward and punishment. The commandments are not an end in themselves, in other words, but an expression of the Jew's belief, *emunah*, in God. Trusting in God, and knowing what to do to give that trust concrete expression, the Jew has no need of subtle theological formulations and distinctions. In a works-orientated religion like Judaism, emphasis on 'belief in' makes more sense than an emphasis on 'belief that': Judaism has thus always been more concerned with knowing what to do than with knowing what to think.

Extrinsic Reasons for the Lack of Systematic Theology in Judaism

I have just argued that Judaism is a religion intrinsically uninterested in theology *per se*. But even such a religion might need to develop a systematic theology. Why was this not the case in pre-medieval Judaism? This question calls up another: namely, under what circumstances might a monotheistic religion lacking a home-grown theology feel the need to create one?[3]

Religions which need to defend themselves from outside attack, or which go on the offensive themselves, find it useful to be able to characterize themselves in terms understandable to their foes. When under siege, the first job of a good commander is to set his defences in order; and when one goes on the offensive, one surely wants one's forces

[3] In this section and elsewhere I refer to Judaism as a 'monotheistic' religion. I do so for the sake of linguistic convenience, but it should be noted that in so doing I injure my own case. The term 'monotheism' (from the Greek, *monos*, 'single', and *theos*, 'god') connotes certain philosophical and theological conceptions about God which were never explicitly expressed in pre-medieval Judaism. R. Bahya ibn Pakuda, and following him Maimonides, for example, were sure that to be a believer in one God a person had to understand certain ideas concerning the nature of that one-ness, ideas which derive clearly and directly from a philosophical universe of discourse. One of the points of this book is to argue that this universe of discourse is foreign to classical Judaism. Maimonides' position may easily be found in his 'Laws of the Foundations of the Torah', ch. 1.

arranged in the best possible manner. Thus, had the prophets of ancient Israel or the rabbis of the Talmud been interested in attracting non-Jews to Judaism, they would have been forced to organize Judaism in a clear, systematic fashion. Let us say that you are a rabbi in first-century Caesarea, trying to convince a pagan friend to embrace Judaism. Your friend will want to know what Judaism is, and will also expect to you to be able to trot out arguments in its favour acceptable to any rational human being. In other words, the pagan will expect some theology. Citing verses from a text which the pagan does not accept as holy will not be very convincing. Talking about the history of a people which he may regard with (probably at best) affectionate disdain is not going to cut any ice either. Had classical Judaism been an actively proselytizing faith, we would expect it to have developed a systematic theology. It was not, and it did not.[4]

Similarly, had Judaism been under attack from adversaries whom it took seriously and who had themselves developed systems of theology and dogma, then it too would have been forced to adapt itself to the theological model, if only to defend itself. The prophets struggled mightily against Canaanite idolatry. Given the nature of this response, it seems obvious that the prophets of Baal and other deities had not themselves developed sophisticated theologies. But overall, for a religion based upon the insight that God is one, while paganism may have been a challenge in cultural and social terms, it was not much of a challenge in

[4] I claim here that classical Judaism was basically uninterested in proselytism. That does not mean that Jews in the ancient world did not actively proselytize; very often they did. Judaism was not a proselytizing faith because it was more of a family affair than an organized religion; in the ordinary course of affairs, people do not go about trying to convert other people into their families. For surveys of what is known concerning the actual attempts of Jews to proselytize in the ancient world, see Louis H. Feldman, 'The Contribution of Professor Salo W. Baron to the Study of Ancient Jewish History: His Appraisal of Anti-Judaism and Proselytism', *AJS Review*, 18 (1993), 1–27; William G. Braude, *Jewish Proselytizing in the First Five Centuries of the Common Era: The Age of the Tannaim and the Amoraim* (Providence, RI: Brown University Press, 1940). In 'Proselytism by Jews in the Third, Fourth, and Fifth Centuries', *Journal for the Study of Judaism*, 24 (1993), 1–58, Louis Feldman proves that a considerable amount of proselytizing was undertaken by Jews throughout the ancient world. He fails to show, however, that this was sanctioned or encouraged by the talmudic rabbis. See also his *Jew and Gentile in the Ancient World* (Princeton: Princeton University Press, 1993). See further Rokeah, *Jews, Pagans and Christians in Conflict*, 42 ff., for a critique of scholars who over-emphasize evidence of proselytizing activity on the part of talmudic rabbis. In general, that Judaism was attractive to Gentiles does not mean that a conscious effort was made to attract them.

what we would call theological terms. Judaism did not teach that God was like the other deities, but that there was only one of them. Judaic monotheism is a complete rejection of the polytheistic world-view; there can be no shared universe of discourse between the two. (This might explain why so much of prophetic 'argument' against polytheistic idolatry is couched in terms of scorn, mockery, calumny, and simple denunciation.)

The rabbis of Palestine were confronted by versions of Greek and Roman polytheism (barely taken seriously by Greek and Roman philosophers themselves), Hellenistic philosophy, and, later, Christianity. The rabbis of Babylonia were, in addition, confronted by Zoroastrianism. It is hard to know to what extent these were viewed as posing serious dangers. It is tempting to explain the very scant argumentation against them found in rabbinic texts on the grounds that the rabbis did not find these competing religions threatening. It is surely likely that the rabbis were no more impressed by polytheistic idolatry than were the prophets, and felt no need to add their own contribution to the prophetic rejection of idolatry. Zoroastrianism was probably perceived as a form of polytheism, as early Christianity may have been.

But Christianity and Hellenistic philosophies may have been perceived as threatening without eliciting a theological response from the rabbis. It is noteworthy how little Hellenistic philosophical thought influenced the rabbis.[5] The few anti-Christian polemics we do have from this period are almost all midrashic, almost none strictly and systematically theological. This may reflect the fact that the controversy with early Christianity was perceived as an internal dispute, best carried on with traditional Jewish tools. When Christianity developed its own full-blown theology and also

[5] Not only does Greek philosophical thinking seem to have influenced the rabbis very little; there is also very little overt anti-Christian polemic to be found in the huge corpus of rabbinic literature. For the former, see the two studies by Saul Lieberman, *Greek in Jewish Palestine* (New York: Jewish Theological Seminary, 1942) and *Hellenism in Jewish Palestine* (New York: Jewish Theological Seminary, 1950). Rokeah, *Jews, Pagans and Christians in Conflict*, 201–2, takes Lieberman to task for exaggerating the extent of Greek influence in Jewish Palestine; but even Lieberman found very little evidence of rabbinic response to philosophical thought. For sources on the lack of clear anti-Christian polemic, see Cohen, 'Analysis of an Exegetic Tradition', 20. The rabbis seemed to have found Hellenistic and other forms of Gentile *behaviour* threatening and sought to extirpate its influence upon the Jews, primarily by restricting social intercourse between Jews and non-Jews as much as possible. The ideologies and theologies which lay behind the threatening behaviour were largely ignored. As Rokeah (p. 129) notes, 'the Jewish Sages were not particularly sensitive to philosophical assumptions'.

attacked Judaism (in the thirteenth to fifteenth centuries), it was met with a systematic theological defence. That is a story which will be taken up below.

Why Systematic Theology Developed among the Jews

In the next chapter I will analyse some of the writings of the individual who might be called the arch-theologian of Judaism—Maimonides. If everything I have said up to this point is true, then where did Maimonides come from? He certainly was not dropped into the midst of the Jewish world from a flying saucer. He also clearly saw himself as part of the ongoing rabbinic tradition. How, then, could an essentially non-theological tradition like Judaism give birth to a thinker as systematic as Maimonides?

I showed in the first section of this chapter that Judaism is a religious tradition which is inherently non-theological in orientation; I then argued that there were also extrinsic reasons for classical Judaism's lack of interest in systematic theology. I will now show how systematic theology did indeed arise among the Jews after the classical period. The reasons for this development are themselves historical accidents which did not change the inherent nature of the Jewish tradition. We will see below how, when these accidental factors disappeared, Judaism basically reverted to its pre-theological stance. But the situation at that juncture was complicated and made confusing by the fact that the attempt to 'theologify' Judaism had been made by some of its most prominent teachers.

The issue may be simply stated. With the rise of Islam from without and of Karaism from within, Judaism was confronted with challengers which it could not ignore. Islam was an aggressively proselytizing religion and Karaism denied the *Jewish* legitimacy of Rabbanite Judaism, relying for its authority solely upon the most sacred of all Jewish sources, the Written Torah. Conversion to Islam, moreover, a religion attractive to Jews because of its uncompromising monotheism, involved no overt acts which could be interpreted as idolatrous.

I would like to illustrate this last point with a personal experience. A number of years ago I had occasion to serve as academic adviser at Haifa University to an Israeli Muslim student. He himself was not particularly observant, but he had a room-mate in college who was a devout Muslim. He was told by his room-mate that Jews believed in a corporeal deity, as evidenced by many verses in the Torah, and were therefore not truly monotheists.[6] Turning to me as his 'expert' on all things Jewish, my student asked me if indeed Jews were not really monotheists. I, of course, explained to him how Judaism understands the anthropomorphic expressions in the Torah. The point of this story is that two intelligent, college-educated, Israeli Arab Muslims could believe that Judaism was less purely monotheist than Islam. This emphasizes the degree to which Islam understands itself and presents itself as a monotheist faith. The same was clearly true of Karaism, which, despite its allegedly exclusive reliance upon the Written Torah (i.e. the Hebrew Bible), taught the absolute incorporeality of God and which, in addition, preserved many easily recognized Jewish customs and ceremonials.

Islam in its early years was not only religiously attractive to medieval Jews, it also worked hard at attracting them, offering the carrot of complete acceptance into Muslim society for those who converted and brandishing the stick of oppressive discrimination for those who remained obdurate in their Judaism.

As it happens, both Islam and Karaism began, very early in their respective existences, to present themselves in a systematically theological fashion. In order to defend itself, Judaism was forced to present itself in a similar fashion, and to do this it had to begin to understand itself in theological terms. This is precisely what happened.

It is therefore no coincidence that the first systematic exposition of Jewish theology to be written by an accepted figure in the rabbinic tradition was authored by R. Sa'adia Gaon, who led Jewish communities in the heart of the Muslim world in the tenth century, and who moreover was a leading Rabbanite opponent of Karaism.[7]

The Importation of Theology

Judaism sees human beings as challenged to retain through their lives the purity with which they are born. In principle, therefore, one can earn

[6] My advisee's friend was apparently aware of the philosophical claim that a corporeal God is not truly one, since every corporeal entity has constituent parts or elements, or at least shares with other entities at least one feature, namely corporeality. On this, see Maimonides' discussion in 'Laws of the Foundations of the Torah', ch. 1.

[7] For more details on the influence of Islam and Karaism on the rise of systematic theology in Judaism, see Kellner, *Dogma*, 1–9. This should be supplemented with Haggai Ben-Shammai, 'Saadya Gaon's Ten Articles of Faith' (Heb.), *Da'at*, 37 (1996), 11–26. I do not mean to contradict the points cited in the name of Bernard Lewis (n. 1 above). The points I am trying to make about Judaism in this chapter are similar to the points Lewis was making about Islam.

one's share in the world to come. This task is aided by the Torah, which teaches how one should behave in a world full of temptations so as to avoid degeneration. Judaism, therefore, rather than focusing on questions of correct belief, has traditionally focused on questions of correct practice.

In addition to being inherently uninterested in systematic theology, pre-medieval Judaism also had no need for systematic theology: it was confronted by no competing theological system which it had to take seriously and did not itself actively seek to attract outsiders into the fold.

In the early Middle Ages this situation changed dramatically: confronted by the theological challenges of Islam and Karaism, Judaism responded in kind. It sought to define the specific beliefs which the Torah taught and which distinguished Judaism from other faiths, and further sought to organize these discrete beliefs into a systematic, coherent whole.

Once introduced, systematic theology found a home in Judaism and brought with it the propositional understanding of faith congenial to it. Defining religious faith as a series of affirmations or denials was a dramatic innovation in Judaism and one which carried with it far-reaching consequences, as we will see in the coming chapters.

One more point should be made here. Systematic theology was introduced into Judaism as a reaction to historical stimuli. But it also reflected an intellectual orientation to the nature of religious faith which many find attractive, even indispensable. We shall return to this idea in the last chapter of the book.

FOUR

Maimonides: Dogma without Dogmatism

IN the last chapter I showed that Judaism has no inherent need for or interest in systematic theology and its outgrowth, dogma. Systematic theology first appeared in normative Judaism (primarily in the writings of R. Sa'adia Gaon) as a response to historical stimuli. In the present chapter we will confront the most systematic, and certainly the most influential, of the medieval Jewish theologians: Maimonides.

Maimonides adopted the claim that Judaism was based upon a systematic theology and had the courage to face up to the consequences of that position, that Judaism therefore had dogmas. Here I will first analyse Maimonides' statement of dogma, showing that he meant his Thirteen Principles to be accepted as dogmas in the strictest sense of that word. I will then show that his position reflects a 'belief that' orientation. One of the most striking consequences of his position—one, moreover, that he did not hesitate to adopt—is that mistakes with respect to matters of dogma cannot in any sense be condoned. We will then see how Maimonides' position on dogma influences his views on how one becomes a Jew and ceases to be a Jew.

I then examine two assumptions crucial to Maimonides' view: that scientific knowledge and religious faith are ultimately the same thing; and that there is one objective, absolute standard of truth, in principle accessible to all. These two assumptions make it possible for Maimonides to insist that all Jews learn enough to know the truth of the principles of faith.

Maimonides' Dogmas

Once a religion specifies the distinct beliefs which constitute its theology, a new question must be answered: are all these beliefs equal in significance? Maimonides was the first Jew to raise this question and his answer is explicit: there are thirteen specific teachings of the Torah which stand on a plane all their own.

Maimonides makes this claim in his commentary on the mishnaic text that begins 'All Israelites have a share in the world to come.'[1] In doing so he makes clear that he views that text as a presentation of the dogmas of Judaism. Maimonides lays down thirteen discrete beliefs as the dogmatic foundation of the Jewish faith. These may be summarized as follows:

1. that God exists;
2. that God is one;
3. that God is incorporeal;
4. that God is ontologically prior to the cosmos;[2]
5. that God alone may be worshipped;
6. that prophecy occurs;
7. that Mosaic prophecy is superior to all others;
8. that the Torah was given from heaven;
9. that the Torah will never change nor be exchanged;
10. that God knows individuals;
11. that the righteous will be rewarded and the evil punished;
12. that the Messiah will come;
13. that the dead will be resurrected.[3]

Maimonides does not himself present a list (as I do here) but, rather, a discussion of these ideas. He cites proof-texts from the Torah, and in some cases sketches the outlines of a philosophical proof of the truth of the dogma. The entire discussion is a lengthy essay, written originally in Arabic *c.*1170. Maimonides' principles are better known in the Jewish world in the form of two poetic summaries, *Yigdal* and *Ani ma'amin*, found in most prayer-books.[4] The first of these has become part of the liturgy in many Jewish communities.

After he finishes presenting his principles, Maimonides makes the following statement:

When all these foundations are perfectly understood and believed in by a person he enters the community of Israel and one is obligated to love and pity him and to act towards him in all the ways in which the Creator has commanded that one

[1] Mishnah *Sanhedrin* x. 1. The text itself is quoted and discussed above, pp. 33–8.

[2] i.e. that God is cause, but not necessarily creator, of all that exists. For explanation, see my notes on the fourth principle in Appendix 2 below.

[3] The full text of Maimonides' Thirteen Principles is presented in Appendix 2 below. For detailed study of the principles, see Kellner, *Dogma*, 10–65.

[4] These two texts are reproduced in Appendix 3 below.

should act towards his brother, with love and fraternity. Even were he to commit every possible transgression, because of lust and because of being overpowered by the evil inclination, he will be punished according to his rebelliousness, but he has a portion [of the world to come]; he is one of the sinners of Israel. But if a man doubts any of these foundations, he leaves the community [of Israel], denies the fundamental, and is called a sectarian, *epikoros*, and one who 'cuts among the plantings'. One is required to hate him and destroy him. About such a person it was said, 'Do I not hate them, O Lord, who hate thee?' [Ps. 139: 21].

Maimonides' statement of his principles occurs at the end of a passage in which he defines the terms appearing in Mishnah *Sanhedrin* x. 1 ('All Israelites have a share in the world to come . . .'). One term alone remains undefined: 'Israelite'. He appears to have posited his principles here at least in part in order to define the term 'Israelite'. An Israelite is a person who affirms the Thirteen Principles.[5]

The text here, with which Maimonides closes his statement of the principles of the Torah, turns out, on close examination, to be quite remarkable. In the first instance, we see that Maimonides defines a Jew in terms of his or her acceptance of the principles: 'When all these foundations are perfectly understood and believed in by a person he enters the community of Israel.' That Maimonides took this theological answer to the question 'Who is a Jew?' seriously is evidenced by the fact that he immediately attaches to the acceptance of his principles the halakhic rights which Jews may demand of their fellows—to be treated with love, pity, and fraternity—and by the further fact that he here makes one's portion in the world to come—one's personal salvation—dependent upon the acceptance of the Thirteen Principles. Further still, Maimonides makes admittance to the world to come conditional solely on the acceptance of his principles, explicitly divorcing halakhic obedience from the equation ('even were he to commit every possible transgression').

Several points should be emphasized here. First, Maimonides makes unambiguous, conscious acceptance of the principles not only a necessary condition for being a Jew and enjoying a share in the world to come, but also a sufficient condition. In other words, in order to be counted as part of Israel, it is necessary that one accept the principles; that is also enough. If we take Maimonides at his word here, one need not do anything further.

Second, if one simply casts doubt upon any of the principles (without overtly denying them), one excludes oneself from the people of Israel.

[5] R. Isaac Abrabanel was the first to suggest that in his principles Maimonides was trying to define the term 'Israelite' in Mishnah *Sanhedrin* x. 1. See his *Principles of Faith*, ch. 6, pp. 82, 84; ch. 24, p. 204.

Such an individual must be hated and destroyed and loses his or her share in the world to come.

Third, Maimonides makes absolutely no provision for the possibility of inadvertence playing an exculpatory role when it comes to doubting or denying the principles of the faith. Even if one denies a principle of the faith because one thinks mistakenly that one is following the teaching of the Torah, one has excluded oneself from the Jewish community and lost one's share in the world to come.

Fourth, Maimonides presents his Thirteen Principles as dogmas in the strictest sense of the term. They are laid down as beliefs taught by the Torah, the highest ecclesiastical authority in Judaism, acceptance of which is a necessary (and sufficient) condition for being considered a member of the people of Israel, and acceptance of which is a necessary (and sufficient) condition for attaining a share in the world to come.

With respect to these four consequences of Maimonides' statement at the end of his principles, I would remind the reader that we are dealing with a theological text, not a halakhic one. This distinction is often fudged these days, and halakhic categories of decision-making are often—too often—applied to fundamentally aggadic (non-legal) issues.[6] Thus, it is not uncommon to hear the Thirteen Principles referred to today as if they comprised a *pesak halakhah*: a normative, authoritative halakhic decision. This would have surprised Maimonides' contemporaries, many of whom took issue with his principles, or rejected them altogether, without ever considering them a matter of halakhah.[7] For our present purposes, it must be noted that in making perfect and unquestioning acceptance of the principles the one necessary and sufficient condition for being a Jew, Maimonides was not trying to modify accepted halakhah, which defined a Jew as a person born to a Jewish mother or properly converted to Judaism.[8]

[6] Maimonides himself made much of this distinction. See his commentary on the Mishnah, *Sotah* iii. 5, *Sanhedrin* x. 3, and *Shevuot* i. 1.

[7] For details on the criticism to which the Thirteen Principles were subjected, see Kellner, *Dogma*, 66–199 (in other words, most of the book), and, very importantly, Shapiro, 'The Last Word in Jewish Theology? Maimonides' Thirteen Principles'. For a crucially important discussion of the misapplication of halakhic categories to aggadah, see Sacks, *One People?*, 100.

[8] For a suggestion concerning the messianic overtones of what Maimonides was actually trying to do, see Menachem Kellner, 'A Suggestion Concerning Maimonides' Thirteen Principles and the Status of Non-Jews in the Messianic Era', in M. Ayali (ed.), *Tura: Oranim Studies in Jewish Thought—Simon Greenberg Jubilee Volume* (Heb.) (Tel Aviv: Hakibuts Hame'uḥad, 1989), 249–60.

How has Maimonides arrived at this remarkable and—at the time he promulgated it—controversial stance? In the first place, it seems, he understands the verse from Habakkuk, 'the righteous shall live by his faith', as teaching that the righteous person is defined as righteous by his or her faith. He furthermore seems to understand the term 'live' in the verse as referring to life in the world to come. He also conflates the terms 'Israel' and 'righteous' (as Mishnah *Sanhedrin* x. 1 itself did, justifying the claim that 'all Israelites have a share in the world to come' by appealing to the verse, 'thy people are all righteous'). Finally, Maimonides understands the faith which defines the righteous Israelite, and through which he or she earns a share in the world to come, in terms of thirteen discrete beliefs which constitute that faith. In other words, Maimonides understands religious faith more as 'belief that' than as 'belief in'.[9]

This is, of course, a momentous development in the history of Judaism, one which was to have an impact on all subsequent attempts by Judaism to reflect upon itself, down to our day. This book is an attempt to resist some of the consequences of Maimonides' innovation.

Maimonides on Inadvertent Heresy

One of the most striking elements in Maimonides' formulation of his principles of faith is his apparent unwillingness to accept any excuses; put more formally, inadvertence is not exculpatory. I mean by this that for Maimonides a person who makes a mistake about matters of dogma is in no better shape than one who consciously and knowingly rejects one of the Thirteen Principles. The former, as well as the latter, is simply a heretic. This may not surprise all my readers: after all, if you are stopped for speeding, telling the police officer that you did not know that speeding was illegal is not going to get you very far. In Western legal systems, ignorance of the law is not generally considered a legitimate excuse for violating it.

Judaism, however, does recognize the category of *shegagah*, inadvert-

[9] For a textually based discussion of Maimonides' new definition of *emunah*, see Kellner, *Dogma*, 5–6. For an important (and technical) discussion of Maimonides' understanding of *emunah*, see Shalom Rosenberg, 'The Concept of *Emunah* in Post-Maimonidean Jewish Philosophy', in Isadore Twersky (ed.), *Studies in Medieval Jewish History and Literature*, ii (Cambridge, Mass.: Harvard University Press, 1984), 273–307. For a more accessible and very interesting discussion of *emunah* in medieval Jewish thought, see also pp. 353–8 in Charles Manekin, 'Hebrew Philosophy in the Fourteenth and Fifteenth Centuries', in D. H. Frank and O. Leaman (eds.), *History of Jewish Philosophy* (London: Routledge, 1997), 350–78.

ence, as mitigating guilt or even, in some cases, obliterating it altogether. The point is clearly made in a story told about the Hebrew poet Hayim Nahman Bialik (1873–1934), who in his youth was a student in the great yeshiva of Volozhin, Lithuania. Bialik and two of his friends, it is related, were sitting in a room one Sabbath morning and smoking. One of the rabbis happened by, glanced in the window, and to his shock and horror saw three of his students violating the sanctity of the Sabbath. Rushing into the room, he demanded to know what was going on. One student arose in confusion and embarrassment and stammered, 'Rebbe, I don't know how I could have been so stupid, but I entirely forgot that today was the Sabbath!' The second student then offered his explanation: 'Rebbe, somehow I forgot that it is forbidden to smoke on the Sabbath!' Bialik calmly rose, turned to the furious rabbi and said, 'Rebbe, I am terribly sorry, but I simply forgot to close the curtains.' The first two students were claiming that they had violated the law inadvertently, *beshogeg*, without conscious intent to sin. Bialik, on the other hand, affirmed that he had sinned *bemezid*, with 'malice aforethought'.

Persons who violate a commandment of the Torah inadvertently may have to perform some act of atonement in certain cases but they are certainly not considered in the same category as those who sin on purpose. Maimonides simply ignores this distinction, lumping the conscious and unconscious heretics together in one group: persons excluded from the community of Israel and the world to come.[10]

Why does Maimonides do this? In fact, because he has no choice: he has been locked into this position by a number of his previous decisions. If we interpret Habakkuk as defining the righteous in terms of faith, and if we further define faith in terms of its propositional content, then if one affirms an incorrect doctrine, or denies a correct doctrine, for any reason, one's faith is in actual fact deficient; and, therefore, so is one's righteousness. If righteousness is a criterion for being a member of the people of Israel, and for enjoying a share in the world to come, then the mistaken believer, however sweet, good, and pious in the conventional sense, is not righteous, and thus is not a Jew, and thus is not a candidate for a share in the world to come.

But perhaps I am wrong; perhaps Maimonides does in fact distinguish the purposeful heretic from the inadvertent heretic. This is not the place

[10] For proof that Maimonides does not, in fact, distinguish the purposeful heretic from the inadvertent heretic, see Menachem Kellner, 'What is Heresy?', in N. Samuelson (ed.), *Studies in Jewish Philosophy* (Lanham, Md.: University Press of America, 1987), 191–214, and idem, *Dogma*, 18–19.

to prove that such is not the case, but I would like to show that my exposition of Maimonides is supported by one of his most influential glossators and commentators, his younger contemporary R. Abraham ben David of Posquières.

R. Abraham composed a series of pithy and often caustic glosses on Maimonides' code of Jewish law, the *Mishneh torah* (*c.* 1180). Thus,

> The following have no portion in the world to come, but are cut off and perish, and for their great wickedness and sinfulness are condemned for ever and ever: sectarians . . . Five classes are termed sectarians: he who says there is no God and the world has no Ruler; he who says that there is a ruling power, but that it is vested in two or more persons; he who says that there is one Ruler, but that He is a body and has form . . .[11]

On this last sentence, R. Abraham writes:

> Why has he called such a person a sectarian? There are many people greater than, and superior to him, who adhere to such a belief on the basis of what they have seen in verses of Scripture, and even more in the aggadot which corrupt right opinion about religious matters.[12]

R. Abraham is not criticizing Maimonides for teaching the doctrine of God's incorporeality. Rather, he rejects Maimonides' claim that a Jew who makes a mistake about the doctrine is a sectarian. Persons 'greater than, and superior to' Maimonides have made that mistake without, according to R. Abraham, becoming thereby wicked and sinful, leaving the community of Israel and forfeiting their share in the world to come. In other words, R. Abraham attributes to Maimonides the claim that, in matters of heresy, ignorance or confusion is no excuse. An inadvertent heretic is a heretic like any other, and merits the punishment of all heretics.

Maimonides on Conversion and the Nature of Faith

Maimonides' view on sectarianism and heresy has a number of dramatic consequences. One has to do with how one joins the community of Israel, and another with how one leaves it. We have already quoted the talmudic text which serves as the basis for the laws of conversion (see

11 'Laws of Repentance', iii. 6–7.

12 For discussion of this text and its variants, see Kellner, *Dogma*, 256. In the same spirit, Isaiah of Trani the Elder (1232–79) criticizes Maimonides emphatically and at length. See Ya'akov Halevi Lipshitz (ed.), *Sanhedrei gedolah*, vol. v, pt. 2 (Jerusalem: Harry Fischel Institute, 1972), 116–20. I thank Marc Shapiro for drawing my attention to this text.

p. 29). In his *Mishneh torah*, Maimonides more often than not will simply translate the relevant talmudic passage from Aramaic into Hebrew. In a very few places, however, he departs from the talmudic source. One of those rare instances is his discussion of conversion, where he interpolates material of his own into the talmudic foundation. Let us look at the talmudic source, with Maimonides' additions in square brackets:

> Our rabbis taught: if at the present time a man desires to become a proselyte, he is to be addressed as follows: 'What reason do you have for desiring to become a proselyte? Do you not know that Israel at the present time are persecuted and oppressed, despised, harassed, and overcome by afflictions?' If he replies, 'I know and yet am unworthy,' he is accepted forthwith. [He should then be made acquainted with the principles of the faith, which are the oneness of God and the prohibition of idolatry. These matters should be discussed in great detail;] and given instruction [though not at great length] in some of the minor and major commandments . . . He is also told of the punishment for the transgression of the commandments . . . as he is informed of the punishment for the transgression of the commandments, so he is informed of the reward granted for their fulfilment.

We saw above how the talmudic discussion places all its emphasis on the willingness of the proselyte to be adopted into the Jewish family, so to speak, and on teaching him or her representative commandments. Through two small additions Maimonides turns the talmudic passage inside out. Where the emphasis in the talmudic source is entirely on *kabalat ol mitsvot* ('acceptance of the yoke of the commandments'), Maimonides makes the crux of conversion into a theological matter. The proselyte is instructed in detail on the principles of faith; we are explicitly instructed not to expatiate at length on the commandments.[13]

Why does Maimonides turn accepted notions concerning the process of conversion on their head? Because, once faith is defined in terms of its propositional content—in terms, that is, of the specific beliefs one affirms or denies—and if we expect Jews to be faithful, then we must demand of prospective Jews that they consciously and explicitly affirm those beliefs which constitute Jewish faith and deny those beliefs which

[13] For Maimonides' codification of the procedures governing conversion, see 'Laws of Forbidden Intercourse', xiii. 1–4. For further discussion of that text in the context of Maimonides' thought, see Kellner, *Maimonides on Judaism*, 49–57. For a discussion of Maimonides' departures from the text of the Talmud in his *Mishneh torah* see the sources cited in Menachem Kellner, 'The Beautiful Captive and Maimonides' Attitude towards Proselytes', in Stephen Benin (ed.), *Jewish–Gentile Relations through the Ages* (Detroit: Wayne State University Press, forthcoming).

contradict Jewish faith. Thus Maimonides is led to play down the importance in the process of conversion of teaching the technicalities of obedience to the commandments (the prospective convert is 'given instruction *though not at great length* in some of the minor and major commandments'). He is similarly led to place heavy emphasis on teaching the prospective convert the dogmas of Judaism, adding to the talmudic text the stipulation that 'He should then be made acquainted with the principles of the faith, which are the oneness of God and the prohibition of idolatry. *These matters should be discussed in great detail.*'

Maimonides is thus led by his understanding of the nature of faith to alter the accepted procedure of conversion.[14] That understanding also leads him to adopt strong and uncompromising positions concerning the way in which an individual leaves the community of Israel.

Maimonides on Leaving Judaism

As we saw above, Maimonides asserts that 'if a man doubts any of these foundations, he leaves the community [of Israel]'. Maimonides imposes harsh penalties on the heretic, sectarian, and *epikoros.* He defines a sectarian as one who denies any of the first five of his Thirteen Principles of faith. He affirms that 'Israelite sectarians are not like Israelites at all' and that it is forbidden to converse with them or return their greeting. He compares them to idolaters and says that even if they repent they are never accepted back into the community. The *epikoros* is defined as one who denies prophecy in general, Mosaic prophecy, and God's knowledge of each individual. Such a one is not considered part of the community of Israel; we are even bidden not to mourn them on their deaths. We are furthermore commanded to destroy them and told that they are no better than informers (individuals who hand innocent fellow Jews over to hostile authorities), the lowest of the low in Jewish estimation. The *epikoros,* of course, has no place in the world to come and it goes without saying that the testimony of such individuals is not acceptable in a Jewish court, since they are not Israelites.

The parallel is clear: one exits the community of Israel by denying certain teachings, just as one enters that community (through conversion, at least) by affirming certain teachings.[15]

[14] For further discussion, see Menachem Kellner, 'Heresy and the Nature of Faith in Medieval Jewish Philosophy', *Jewish Quarterly Review*, 76 (1987), 299–318.

[15] For the textual sources in this section, see Kellner, *Dogma*, 17–21. See further idem, *Maimonides on Judaism*, 59–64. Special attention should be paid to 'Laws of the Murderer', iv. 10, and 'Laws of the Rebellious Elder', iii. 2.

Maimonides' 'Non-dogmatic' Dogmas: Science and Religious Faith

It is important to understand that while Maimonides sought to base Jewish religious faith on a series of dogmas, this was not because he was 'dogmatic' in the accepted sense of the term. Maimonides did not urge Jews to accept as dogmas beliefs which ran counter to reason, or to accept them simply on his authority. On the contrary, he was convinced that the core beliefs of Judaism were true, where 'true' means rationally demonstrable.

That God exists, is one, is incorporeal, and precedes the world are beliefs which one need not accept 'on faith', according to Maimonides. These beliefs can be proven using the tools of philosophy. That God alone may be worshipped is a consequence of the first four beliefs, since worshipping another impugns God's unity. That prophecy occurs was a fact not disputed by any religious believer and, in Maimonides' day, was accepted by all educated persons. In his *Guide of the Perplexed* Maimonides proves to his satisfaction that the Torah really was given by God;[16] this being so, it is not susceptible to change. Since the Torah was the content of Moses' prophecy, and since the Torah will never change, Moses' prophecy must of necessity be superior to that of all other prophets. That God knows the deeds of human beings is, again, something which Maimonides was convinced could be proved to be true. A good and powerful God, Maimonides held, guides human beings through reward and punishment; the coming of the Messiah and resurrection are examples of such recompense. Thus, all thirteen of the principles are beliefs which any rational person—at least, any rational person in the twelfth century—could be expected to accept, at least after he or she was shown their truth.

Maimonides, then, not only understood religious belief in terms of its intellectual, propositional content; he was also convinced that the beliefs of Judaism, at least, were basically equivalent to the teachings of true philosophy.[17] This underlying approach to religious faith comes out

[16] For a discussion of Maimonides' proof of the divine origin of the Torah, see Menachem Kellner, 'Revelation and Messianism: A Maimonidean Study', in Dan Cohn-Sherbok (ed.), *Torah and Revelation* (New York: Edwin Mellen Press, 1992), 117–33.

[17] On the relationship between religious belief and philosophy in Maimonides' thought, as expressed here, see the discussion in Kellner, *Maimonides on Judaism*, 65–79. See further idem, 'Maimonides' Allegiances to Torah and Science', *The Torah Umadda Journal*, 7 (1997), 88–104.

clearly in the very first sentence of Maimonides' *Mishneh torah*, at the beginning of 'Laws of the Foundations of the Torah', where he writes: 'The foundation of all [religious] foundations and the pillar of [all] the sciences is to know that there exists a Prime Existent.' Remember, please, that this is the first sentence of a systematic exposition of halakhah, Jewish law. In this sentence Maimonides teaches that religion and science share a common axiom: God's existence.[18]

This may sound odd to contemporary ears, but the science Maimonides was dealing with was Aristotelian; the most foundational of all the sciences for any Aristotelian was metaphysics; and the fundamental teaching of metaphysics was God's existence. Thus, one who was confused on that issue was confused at the broadest and most foundational level of scientific truth. The basic axiom of all the sciences is God's existence; the basic axiom of religious faith is God's existence. At their very heart, then, religion and science do not teach the same thing; they are the same thing.

Science must be based on knowledge, not 'blind' faith (the very opposite of Maimonidean faith!) or wishful thinking. Similarly, to know that God exists one must be able to know it scientifically. Since such knowledge is possible, Maimonides can make it the first of his Thirteen Principles; he can also make it the first commandment: 'Knowledge of this [God's unconditional existence, uniqueness, and mastery of the cosmos] is a positive commandment.' In Maimonidean terms, to know something means to be able to show why it is so; in other words, to offer rational proof for it. For Maimonides, therefore, to fulfil the very first commandment, to accept the first principle of faith, one must be sufficiently sophisticated to prove God's existence.

The importance of scientific knowledge to religious faith is further underscored by Maimonides in the four chapters of the *Mishneh torah* following his emphatic opening assertion concerning the identity of the basic axioms of religion and of science. In these chapters Maimonides gives a quick course in two sciences, physics (including astronomy) and metaphysics, maintaining that it is through the study of these sciences that one can be brought to the love and fear of God.[19]

[18] Maimonides makes knowing that God exists the first commandment in his *Book of Commandments*, and in 'Laws of the Foundations of the Torah', i. 6.

[19] For a discussion of the physics and astronomy presented in the first four chapters of the *Mishneh torah*, see Menachem Kellner, 'Maimonides on the Science of the *Mishneh torah*: Provisional or Permanent?', *AJS Review*, 18 (1993), 169–94.

Maimonides on Truth

Maimonides' position as outlined in the previous section reflects an idea of his which we will have to examine again below. For Maimonides, truth is one and objective: there is an absolute standard of truth and falsity, and that standard is discoverable by human reason. In a subsequent chapter we will have to ask to what extent that position is acceptable to us today. There can be little doubt, however, that Maimonides held it. He gives clear expression to this view in his introduction to his commentary on *Pirkei avot* ('Ethics of the Fathers'):

Know that the things about which we shall speak in these chapters and in what will come in the commentary are not matters invented on my own nor explanations I have originated. Indeed, they are matters gathered from the discourse of the Sages in the Midrash, the Talmud, and other compositions of theirs, as well as from the discourse of both the ancient and modern philosophers and from the compositions of many men. *Hear the truth from whoever says it.* Sometimes I have taken a complete passage from the text of a famous book. Now there is nothing wrong with that, for I do not attribute to myself what someone who preceded me said. We hereby acknowledge this and shall not indicate that 'so and so said' and 'so and so said', since that would be useless prolixity. Moreover, the name of such an individual might make the passage offensive to someone without experience and make him think it has an evil inner meaning of which he is not aware. Consequently, I saw fit to omit the author's name, since my goal is to be useful to the reader. We shall explain to him the hidden meanings in this tractate.[20]

Let us recall that this passage opens a commentary on a portion of the Mishnah, the first clearly halakhic text of Judaism. Maimonides here tells us that in order to explain the Mishnah to his fellow Jews, he must make use of the works of the rabbis, of course, but also of the 'ancient [Greek] and modern [Muslim] philosophers and . . . the compositions of many men'. This is really quite remarkable: Maimonides feels that, in order to make the 'Ethics of the Fathers' clear, he must use the writings of, as it turns out, Aristotle and al-Farabi (*c*.870–950)—a Muslim Aristotelian philosopher![21] Aware of the fact that this is likely to arouse the antagon-

[20] I cite the text from 'Eight Chapters', Maimonides' introduction to his commentary on *Pirkei avot*, as it is in *Ethical Writings of Maimonides*, trans. Raymond Weiss and Charles Butterworth (New York: Dover, 1983), 60. Emphasis added..

[21] For Maimonides' use of Aristotle and al-Farabi in 'Eight Chapters', see Herbert A. Davidson, 'Maimonides' *Shemonah Peraqim* and Alfarabi's *Fusul al-Madani*', *Proceedings of the American Academy for Jewish Research*, 31 (1963), 33–50.

ism of some (probably many) of his readers, Maimonides immediately adds: 'Hear the truth from whoever says it.'

Truth is truth, Maimonides is telling us, made no more and no less true by the identity of its speaker. If there is truth to be learned from Aristotle and al-Farabi, then the fact that one was an uncircumcised heathen and the other a member of the oppressive master class was no obstacle for Maimonides; he used the truths they taught.

Maimonides, however, was no fool, and could predict the outraged response of many of his contemporaries: 'What? You cite Greeks and Arabs in commenting on the Mishnah! What sort of free-thinking heretic are you?' Therefore, Maimonides tells us, he will not cite his sources: 'Moreover, the name of such an individual might make the passage offensive to someone without experience and make him think it has an evil inner meaning of which he is not aware.' Since it is Maimonides' aim to be useful to his readers, he uses the writings of Greek and Muslim philosophers to explain 'the hidden meanings' in *Pirkei avot*, without explicitly citing his sources each time he uses them.

The Logic of Righteousness: Reason and Faith

Apparently taking the prophet Habakkuk at his word, Maimonides believed that righteous individuals are both defined by their faith and achieve life in the world to come because of it. Because of his understanding of faith as 'belief that', Maimonides was led to ask which specific beliefs constitute the faith of the righteous Jew and grant that Jew access to the world to come. The answer to that question he phrased in terms of the Thirteen Principles.

A person whose faith is deficient, for any reason, is, in cold, hard fact, not righteous. Maimonides can thus not allow *shegagah* (inadvertence) with respect to matters of faith. For this he was taken to task by R. Abraham ben David of Posquières.

Defining a Jew in terms of her or his beliefs, Maimonides was forced to codify as halakhah a process of conversion in which matters of theology are given pride of place and to exclude altogether from the Jewish community in this world and from the world to come individuals who hold false views on (in Maimonides' eyes) crucial issues of dogma, no matter how devout their behaviour, and no matter why they hold those views.[22]

[22] My claim here is an interpretation of Maimonides. His son R. Abraham makes the point explicitly: 'Idolaters deny God's Torah and worship other gods beside Him, while

But Maimonides did not simply posit his principles of faith in a 'dogmatic' manner. He was convinced that reason supported him. In fact, reason had to support him in this enterprise, since in the final analysis the teachings of the Torah and the teachings of science are and have to be the same: there is only one truth.[23] This leads to a point which will be emphasized in the following chapter: what Maimonides demands is not belief in his principles (in the sense of 'blind' acceptance) but knowledge of them —or at least, of those involving God. Maimonides does not tell us, that is, to accept the Thirteen Principles because he tells us to, nor even because the Torah teaches them, but because they are in and of themselves true.

Maimonides sought to set Judaism on a new course altogether: he sought to establish it as a religion based upon systematic theology, a religion in which doctrinal orthodoxy was the key to everything. The Thirteen Principles are an outgrowth of this attempt, not its cause. To a considerable extent, Maimonides failed in his project. Certainly, the Thirteen Principles soon achieved near normative status in the eyes of many (but by no means all) Jews in the Middle Ages and today; but the theological substrate, the reason why Maimonides formulated them, is barely understood within the tradition and has certainly not taken it over as Maimonides hoped. It is to an elaboration of this issue that I turn in the next chapter.

one who, in his stupidity, allows it to enter his mind that the Creator has a body or an image or a location, which is possible only for a body, does not know Him. One who does not know Him denies Him, and such a person's worship and prayer are not to the Creator of the world. [Anthropomorphists] do not worship the God of heaven and earth but a false image of Him . . .'. See David Berger, 'Judaism and General Culture in Medieval and Early Modern Times', in Jacob J. Schacter (ed.), *Judaism's Encounter with Other Cultures: Rejection or Integration?* (Northvale, NJ: Jason Aronson, 1997), 57–141 at 93. For strong support of my interpretation of Maimonides himself, see the text from *Guide of the Perplexed*, i. 36, cited below at pp. 84–5.

[23] On the structural similarity of the Torah to the sciences, see Menachem Kellner, 'The Conception of the Torah as a Deductive Science in Medieval Jewish Thought', *Revue des études juives*, 146 (1987), 265–79; idem, 'Maimonides and Gersonides on Astronomy and Metaphysics', in Samuel Kottek and Fred Rosner (eds.), *Moses Maimonides: Physician, Scientist, and Philosopher* (Northvale, NJ: Jason Aronson, 1993), 91–6, 249–51.

FIVE

Maimonides: Impact, Implications, Challenges

THIS chapter addresses Maimonides' impact on his contemporaries and upon subsequent generations of Jewish thinkers and halakhic authorities. Maimonides' position on the nature of Judaism and the centrality of dogma in it enables, indeed necessitates, the application of theological tests of Jewish legitimacy. Nevertheless, I will show that while many other thinkers accepted Maimonides' claim that Judaism has dogmas, almost none accepted the theological substrate of that position. Medieval critiques of Maimonides are also addressed here. The chapter concludes with a discussion of an apparent inconsistency in Maimonides' treatment of heresy.

The Impact

The impact of Maimonides' position—that Jewish faith is a matter of believing that certain things are true; that it is thus crucial to get clear on the theological substrate of Judaism; that correct appreciation of that substrate is both a necessary and a sufficient condition for becoming a Jew, remaining a Jew, and achieving a share in the world to come; that mistakes concerning the fundamental beliefs of Judaism cost an individual his or her membership in the community of Israel and share in the world to come; that, in short, Judaism has dogmas in the strictest sense of the word—was monumental and pervasive while at the same time negligible.

The impact of Maimonides' innovation was monumental because since his time Jews have taken it as a matter of course that the Jewish religion has dogmas; and it was negligible because the theoretical substrate on which Maimonides built his dogmatic system (summarized in the previous paragraph) was not accepted as part of the Jewish tradition.

The pervasive influence of Maimonides' innovation cannot be denied. Not only have his principles of Judaism entered the liturgy; stop any halfway Jewishly literate person on the street and ask if Judaism has dogmas and you will get the answer, 'Of course—Maimonides' Thirteen Principles.' More than that, the impact of Maimonides' formulation of dogmas for Judaism finds expression in the attempt by contemporary Jews, discussed later in this chapter, to apply theological tests for religious legitimacy.[1]

No one, I think, would deny the profound influence Maimonides' principles have had in Judaism. But what of my paradoxical claim that despite this influence the impact of Maimonides' attempt to re-establish Judaism on dogmatic grounds is actually negligible? This claim must strike most readers as bizarre; it is, none the less, true.

That Maimonides' attempt to ground Judaism in dogmatic theology had only a superficial impact may be seen in several ways. First, Maimonides is the only halakhist to include principles of faith in the 613 commandments of Judaism. In claiming that Judaism had commandments relating to belief, Maimonides tried to slide a major innovation past his readers. The Catalonian Jewish leader R. Hasdai Crescas (d. 1412) was one of the few subsequent halakhists to reject the claim outright. The others simply rejected it in practice.

A comparison of Maimonides' *Mishneh torah*—which opens with 'Laws of the Foundations of the Torah' and contains a summary of the Thirteen Principles in 'Laws of Repentance'—with the various codes written in response to it, such as the *Arba'ah turim* of R. Jacob ben Asher (*c.*1270–1340) and the *Shulḥan arukh* of R. Joseph Karo (1488–1575), which ignore theological matters entirely, makes the point clearly. Similarly, just glancing at the layout of the pages of most printed editions of the *Mishneh torah* confirms the claim that subsequent halakhists ignored Maimonides' attempt to present Judaism as a religion with a clear dogmatic base. Almost every word of the text is elaborated on in commentaries and supercommentaries—so much so, that on most pages of the work only a few lines of text appear, surrounded, island-like, by seas of commentary. On those pages, however, where Maimonides presents his principles and their corollaries, his words stand in lonely splendour.[2]

[1] For an excellent example of the profound influence of Maimonides' attempt to put Judaism on a firm dogmatic basis, see the comments made by David Bleich quoted above (p. 39) and below (p. 95).

[2] I came across a fascinating parallel to this situation with respect to the reception of Copernicus' *De revolutionibus orbium celestium*. In book 1 he describes his revolutionary, 'Copernican' view of the cosmos.

> The remaining five books . . . describe geometrical models for each of the planets and tell how to compute tables. These constructions represent an enormous advance in technique and simplicity over anything previously available . . . The working astronomer of those days was involved in

Even more decisive is the fact that the responsa literature, from his own time to the present day, is almost entirely innocent of discussions of Maimonides' principles of faith.

By not including matters of dogma in their statements of halakhah, Maimonides' successors were, consciously or unconsciously, rejecting his claim that Judaism had commandments relating to belief, a claim which lay at the very heart of his understanding of the Torah as consisting of a mass of laws built upon a solid and unchanging base of explicit, detailed, systematically arranged and obligatory theological teachings.

Second, with only two exceptions that I have been able to find, none of the many halakhists and philosophers who engaged Maimonides in theological discussion concerning his principles of faith accepted his claim that one who makes a mistake concerning them is a heretic in the same sense as one who purposefully rejects them. This is as true of our contemporaries as it is of Maimonides: even the Hazon Ish (R. Abraham Karelitz, 1878–1953), considered by many to be one of the most important formulators of what might be called post-Second World War 'hard-line' Orthodoxy, is careful to distinguish between heretics who consciously and knowledgeably reject the teachings of Judaism and the vast majority of non-Orthodox Jews, who are to be considered 'babes fallen into captivity' and thus neither responsible nor culpable for their non-Orthodoxy.[3] And yet rejecting the possibility of *shegagah*, of non-culpable inadvertence, is a crucial consequence of Maimonides' position

producing almanacs for agriculture and casting horoscopes for births, christenings, marriages, medical treatments, and the erection of buildings. He had no more inclination to ponder the conceptual foundations of the system than a modern automotive mechanic has to think about the thermodynamics of combustion.

I quote here from David Park, *The How and the Why: An Essay on the Origins and Development of Physical Theory* (Princeton: Princeton University Press, 1988), 146. On this passage, Park writes in a footnote: 'Professor Owen Gingerich tells me he has examined nearly every extant copy of *De revolutionibus* and that while the pages of the technical sections of most copies are darkened with the grime of many fingers, those of Book 1 are mostly as white as snow.' Copernicus' practically minded readers were interested in his planetary tables and paid little or no attention to the new astronomy underlying them. Similarly, Maimonides' rabbinic readers were interested in the practical halakhah in the *Mishneh torah*, not in the theological substrate so important to Maimonides. Thus the substrate was neither rejected nor accepted by his successors; it was simply ignored.

[3] The only two medieval thinkers who follow Maimonides in disallowing *shegagah* with respect to heresy are R. Abraham Bibago and R. Isaac Abrabanel. For details, see chs. 7 and 8 in Kellner, *Dogma*; also idem, 'What is Heresy?' and 'Heresy and the Nature of Faith'. With respect to the Hazon Ish, see below, p. 116.

that *emunah*, faith, consists in the unquestioning acceptance of specific beliefs. If we admit the possibility of *shegagah* with respect to dogma, we reject the definition of faith which forms the foundation of the entire Maimonidean project.

Third, Maimonides was both the first and the last formulator of principles of Judaism to use them as a test for Jewish legitimacy. Subsequent discussions of dogma dealt with the subject as a way of distinguishing Judaism from Christianity, not as a way of distinguishing legitimate Jews from heretics.

In refusing to make principles of faith commandments, in allowing *shegagah* with respect to matters of faith, and in refraining from adopting a clear-cut theological test for Jewish 'orthodoxy', post-Maimonidean Judaism turned Maimonides' principles of faith from a statement of the unchanging dogmas of Judaism into a literary device, a convenient way of summarizing some widely accepted teachings of the Torah.[4]

Further support for my claim concerning the superficial impact of Maimonides' principles on Judaism may be found in the fact that the principles themselves, in the way in which Maimonides presented them, are almost entirely unknown in the Jewish tradition. By and large, they are known only through two poetic summaries, *Yigdal* and *Ani ma'amin*.[5] While these poems preserve the spirit of Maimonides' ideas, they reduce a long, detailed, complex, and philosophically sophisticated text to thirteen rhymed stanzas. As such, they represent an extreme simplification of Maimonides' original ideas. Understanding the principles in their poetic format is not much of a challenge; following the arguments in the original is another matter altogether. Thus, not only were Maimonides' principles accepted without the theological substrate which gave them coherence and which made of them something more than an elegant literary device for teaching Jewish ideas; they were not even accepted in the form in which Maimonides presented them, but, rather, in a simplified, even debased, fashion.

The history of the response to Maimonides' principles also supports my assertion. After their promulgation, the principles were at first largely ignored. In the two centuries or so after Maimonides published his commentary on the Mishnah, only half a dozen Jewish thinkers—not

[4] It is precisely and only as a literary device that Abrabanel defends Maimonides' principles in the twenty-third chapter of his *Principles of Faith*.

[5] On the textual history of these poems (reproduced in Appendix 3 below), see Alexander Marx, 'A List of Poems on the Articles of the Creed', *Jewish Quarterly Review*, 9 (1919), 305–36.

of the first rank—discussed them at all, and none of them did so in halakhic contexts. The question of the dogmas of Judaism became a live issue again only in the fifteenth century and only in Iberia. There and then it was taken up almost exclusively by figures defending Judaism against the onslaught of Christianity. With the expulsion of the Jews from Spain in 1492, the issue once again disappeared from the Jewish agenda, remaining unconsidered until the Haskalah (the Jewish Enlightenment) at the end of the eighteenth century, and the rise of Reform Judaism.

The conclusion to be drawn from this historical sequence is that by and large Jews sought to express Jewish faith in dogmatic terms only when forced to do so by Christian interlocutors. In the disputations and apologetics of the fifteenth century it was the Christians who set the agenda and the ground rules. Left to their own devices, as it were, Jews did not naturally turn to dogma as a way of expressing the authentic character of Jewish faith.[6]

My claim here about the superficial impact of Maimonides' attempt to place Judaism on a firm dogmatic footing echoes Isadore Twersky's assessment of the impact of the *Mishneh torah*:

> It may be proposed that Maimonides' revolution remained primarily 'literary'; there was maximum dissemination of the *Mishneh Torah* itself but more limited acceptance of its premises and goals; it did not basically transform modes of thought or redirect the course of codification, but it impinged, directly and indirectly, on methods of study and norms of observance and provided a nearly universal referent for discussion of halakhah.[7]

As I have tried to argue in this book, the actual impact of Maimonides' innovation remained 'literary' and certainly did not 'transform modes of

[6] For details on all this see Kellner, *Dogma*, 66–9, 80–2, 200–17. A fascinating and unusual responsum of R. David ibn Abi Zimra (on whom see above, p. 20) throws further light on this matter. He was asked (*Responsa*, part I, no. 344) which account of the principles of religion he accepted—that of Maimonides, that of Crescas, or that of Albo. In his answer, ibn Abi Zimra cited Abrabanel's *Principles of Faith* (ch. 23) to the effect that since all of the Torah was given by God we have no right to distinguish some elements as more fundamental than others. Every part of the Torah is a principle of faith. (Compare further responsum iv. 187, in which he holds that error in theological matters may be excusable in that one who so errs may be considered *anus*, 'forced'.) As noted in the text, theological issues in general and Maimonides' principles in particular are almost never brought up in the responsa literature, a fact which may be confirmed by a glance at Louis Jacobs' *Theology in the Responsa* (London: Routledge & Kegan Paul, 1975).

[7] Isadore Twersky, *Introduction to the Code of Maimonides* (New Haven: Yale University Press, 1980), 536.

thought'. Authorities since Maimonides' time have adopted the shell of his position, leaving the meat uneaten, indeed almost entirely unknown. In this, they have not followed in the footsteps of the second-/third-century *tanna* R. Meir, who, as the Talmud recounts, ate the meat (i.e. the permitted portions) of his apostate master Elisha ben Abuyah's teachings, while rejecting the shell (BT *Ḥagigah* 15*b*).

The Implications

While the impact of Maimonides' claims may have been superficial, their implications are profound. In the first place, as I have been at pains to demonstrate in this book, a Jew who fails to accept the Thirteen Principles has certainly excluded him- or herself from the world to come—or, more precisely, has failed to do that which makes it possible to enter the world to come. Furthermore, such a person, according to Maimonides, has also excluded him- or herself from *kelal yisrael*, the community of Israel. Is such a person a Jew? I think the only possible answer to this question, for Maimonides, is that such a person is required to fulfil all the obligations that devolve upon those of Jewish descent (i.e. the mitzvot: the commandments of the Torah) but will receive none of the rewards that follow from that status, be they in the world to come or in this world (in the sense that the obligations upon other Jews to love, cherish, and succour their fellow Jews do not apply in respect of such a person). These individuals remain Jews in a halakhic sense but in no other sense. They are indeed Jewish, I think Maimonides would be forced to say, but only 'on a technicality'.

Norman Lamm raises this very issue forcefully: 'If we take [Maimonides] literally, we reach the astonishing conclusion that he who observes *mitzvot* but has not reflected upon their theological basis would also be excluded from the Children of Israel.'[8] I think that we have to take Maimonides literally, but that the consequence is exclusion from the world to come, not from the Jewish people in this world.

To put the matter bluntly, Maimonides sought to make of Judaism an ecclesiastical community—what other religious traditions call a church of true believers. Maimonides' position reflects a particular philosophical understanding of human nature, according to which (*a*) no human being is born with a fully developed soul—we are, rather, born with the

[8] Norman Lamm, 'Loving and Hating Jews as Halakhic Categories', *Tradition*, 24 (1989), 98–122 (at 115), based upon idem, 'Love of Israel and Hatred of Evildoers', in his *Laws and Customs* (Heb.) (Jerusalem: Mosad Harav Kook, 1990), 149–59.

potential to acquire what can be called a soul—and (*b*) the only way in which an individual can possibly actualize his or her potential to acquire a soul is through intellectual activity.[9]

On the one hand, this theory commits one to an extremely parochial stance: namely, that only the intellectually gifted and energetic can ever really fulfil themselves as human beings. This form of intellectual élitism leaves most of the human race out in the cold. On the other hand, the theory also forces one to adopt a very non-parochial stance: anyone born with a measure of intelligence and a willingness to apply him- or herself to the exacting demands of intellectual labour can achieve some measure or other of spiritual advancement. Race, creed, sex, or national origin are quite simply irrelevant to one's potential achievement.

Turning Judaism into a series of truth-claims is simply a reflection of this broader position. Such an understanding of Judaism also forces a kind of universalism on Maimonides: being Jewish is a matter of what you believe, not of who your parents were. It is, to repeat the metaphor suggested earlier, a matter of software, not hardware.

Maimonides does not specify in his statement of the Thirteen Principles whether they are to be understood or simply believed (i.e. accepted on the basis of traditional authority without necessarily understanding why they are and must be true). But in his parallel statement in 'Laws of the Foundations of the Torah', at the beginning of the *Mishneh torah*, he clearly states that it is knowledge of God's existence which is the 'foundation of all foundations'. He further states there that knowing that God exists is the first of all the commandments of the Torah. It makes considerable sense, therefore, to interpret the Thirteen Principles (or at least the first five of them, which deal with God) as involving knowledge rather than belief.[10] Indeed, Maimonides cannot be interpreted in any

[9] For details on Maimonides' psychology (theory of the human soul), see Kellner, *Maimonides on Judaism*, 9–15. According to Maimonides human beings are born, *contra* Plato, without innate knowledge but with a capacity or potential to learn. This capacity is called, depending on the specific version of the theory which one encounters, 'hylic intellect', 'material intellect', or 'potential intellect'. If one takes advantage of one's capacity to learn and actualizes one's potential for study, then one will have acquired what Maimonides came to call 'an intellect in actu', more often called the 'acquired intellect'. To the extent that immortality is affirmed, it is the acquired intellect which is seen as immortal. Since one can actualize one's potential intellect to different degrees, it follows that one's perfection, and thus one's share of immortality, depends on the degree to which one has perfected oneself intellectually.

[10] For studies concerning Maimonides' attitude towards knowledge and belief, see Kellner, *Dogma*, 244 n. 268.

other fashion. This will turn out to be crucial for understanding his position. It will also help us to understand why contemporary authorities end up adopting only the shell of his teaching, while ignoring, rejecting, or, most likely, being ignorant of its essence.

For Maimonides, as for philosophers generally, the distinction between knowing and believing is crucial. Knowledge, as Maimonides understands it, corresponds to reality and must therefore be true (the expression 'true knowledge' is thus tautologous). Belief is what we represent to ourselves as corresponding to reality, irrespective of whether or not in fact it actually does so correspond. Human beings are distinguished from all other creatures on earth by their ability to achieve knowledge. In fact, being born with that ability is precisely what it means to be born with human potential, and becoming truly human means realizing that ability to one extent or another.

Note carefully what I have just written: the child of human parents is born as a *potential* human; only the individual who achieves knowledge actually becomes a fully fledged human being. Immortality, a share in the world to come, is something to which only humans can aspire. It is Maimonides' settled doctrine that only human beings, i.e. only those individuals, born to human parents, who have also achieved knowledge ('perfection of the intellect' in the sort of language Maimonides used), have a portion in the world to come.[11] This is a position which grates painfully on the ears of many people today, but there is no point pretending that it isn't there. It is a position which Maimonides adopts and which, in fact, given his understanding of human psychology, he must adopt.[12]

It is important to understand that one corollary of this stance is that the only key to earning a share in the world to come is intellectual perfection, in varying degrees. Good deeds are not enough; nor is correct belief in the sense that one accepts true teachings on the basis of authority as opposed to rational conviction. A further upshot of this theory is that just

[11] Maimonides' theory that human, religious, Jewish perfection involves the acquisition of philosophical truths is summarized in Menachem Kellner, *Maimonides on Human Perfection* (Atlanta, Ga.: Scholars Press, 1990), 1–7. Since this statement is likely to surprise many of my readers here, and since it is crucial for any understanding of Maimonides, I have defended it in detail in Appendix 1 below.

[12] It ought to be noted, emphatically, that many of Maimonides' positions on philosophical and theological matters follow from his acceptance of the definition of human beings as rational animals. This point is crucially important. All that we share with animals (bodily needs, feelings, even emotions) is not truly human; that which makes us human is our rationality and only our rationality.

as one cannot be a little bit pregnant, one cannot be a little bit eligible for the world to come: either you are pregnant or you are not; either you are eligible for the world to come or you are not. But, just as one can be in an early or advanced stage of pregnancy, one can have earned a smaller or larger share of the world to come. There remains an important difference between the two situations, however, in that a pregnant woman advances from early to later stages of pregnancy; the share in the world to come one earns through one's intellectual endeavours is the share with which one is stuck for all eternity.

What sort of knowledge must we acquire in order to establish our humanity and thereby earn a share in the world to come? On this medieval Jewish scholars were divided, some saying that all knowledge counted, others that only knowledge of God and the angels qualified. In the language of the Middle Ages, the question was: does knowing mathematics and the physical sciences get one into the world to come, or must one also know metaphysics? Maimonides comes down heavily for the second alternative. To become an actual human being, to earn a share in the world to come, one must acquire knowledge of metaphysical matters—namely, of God and the angels.[13]

It is not enough to be able to recite things by heart like a parrot. One must be able to understand what one is saying. For Maimonides, then, one cannot even fulfil the first of the 613 commandments until one can properly prove to oneself that God exists. Furthermore, since acceptance of the Thirteen Principles is a key to enjoying a share in the world to come, and only those who have achieved knowledge gain entry into the world to come, it follows that believing the Thirteen Principles is not enough: one must know that God exists, is one, is incorporeal, etc.

I once heard my esteemed colleague Rabbi Dr J. David Bleich, speaking at a conference, explain Maimonides' view of immortality in the following terms. Let us say that a person of moderate intelligence and no formal training in mathematics and physics applied for admittance to a doctoral programme in theoretical physics. It would be no favour to that person to admit her to the programme, since there is no way she could succeed; it is a recipe for frustration. Similarly, even if an intellectually unprepared individual managed to wriggle his way into life in the hereafter, he would not be happy there.

[13] See Menachem Kellner, 'Gersonides on the Role of the Active Intellect in Human Cognition', *Hebrew Union College Annual*, 65 (1994), 233–59. The reader interested in the contemporary scholarly debate on Maimonides' attitude towards immortality will find references to the relevant studies there.

Bleich was speaking facetiously, but the analogy is apt. On the face of it, Maimonides' position might appear strange, but it can be phrased so as to sound much less outlandish. Compare the following passage from George Schlesinger's *New Perspectives on Old-time Religion*:

> According to classical theologians, one who has spent one's life as a passionate servant of the Lord will have developed and perfected one's soul adequately to have acquired the capacity to partake in the transmundane bliss that awaits in the afterlife. The suitably groomed soul, when released from its earthly fetters, will bask in the radiance of the divine presence and delight in the adoring communion with a loving God.[14]

This is precisely Maimonides' position. In his hands, however, the development and perfection of the soul are a matter of achieving understanding of and insight into metaphysical matters.

We are now in a position better to understand why Maimonides cannot allow for *shegagah* with respect to his principles. Well-intentioned but poor philosophers do not achieve knowledge; their mistakes exclude them from the ranks of actual (as opposed to potential) humans and thus keep them out of the world to come. The outcome is similar for well-intentioned but confused or mistaken Jews: their mistakes in metaphysics (i.e. mistakes concerning at least the first five of Maimonides' Thirteen Principles) exclude them from membership in Israel and from the world to come.

In Chapter 4 I noted that *shegagah* with respect to matters of religious belief renders that belief incorrect and thus not really belief at all as far as Maimonides is concerned. I said there that this reflected Maimonides' claim that *emunah* is defined in terms of intellectual affirmations. Now we can understand why. Maimonides defines belief in this fashion because of his theory of knowledge. If one holds incorrect beliefs (i.e. makes mistakes in metaphysics), then one has not achieved full humanity and thus is not even a candidate for admission to the world to come.

The entire structure of Maimonides' conception of Judaism as a religion constructed upon a dogmatic base depends upon the theory sketched here. Many people today are happy to accept the consequence of that theory, that Judaism has dogmas, and that it is therefore incumbent on us to apply theological tests of Jewish legitimacy; and yet no one I have met or heard of in today's world accepts the theory itself, as promulgated by Maimonides.

[14] George Schlesinger, *New Perspectives on Old-time Religion* (Oxford: Clarendon Press, 1988), 160.

This point cannot be overstressed, even though contemporary Maimonideans tend to ignore it. The issue was well stated in a comment made to me by Kenneth Seeskin:

> No single proposition like 'God is one' can be understood in isolation. To know what we are talking about, and not just be mouthing words, we need to be responsible for the whole (Neoplatonic) system of metaphysics that explains what 'one' means [for Maimonides]. Note, for example, that for Maimonides, unity cannot be explicated without a lot of detailed work on related subjects like existence, attribute, subject, predicate etc. . . . How many Orthodox rabbis who cite Maimonides . . . want to take a pop quiz on the essentials of medieval logic and metaphysics?[15]

Remember that the ontology underlying Maimonides' first principle of faith is derived from the Neoplatonic Aristotelianism which Maimonides regarded as the correct vision of the structure of the universe. That ontology has been succinctly summarized by Elliot R. Wolfson:

> One of the basic tenets of [Neoplatonism] is the insistence on the unknowability, indescribability, and ineffability of the One, the ultimate ground of all being. In the standard Neoplatonic ontology the One cannot be delimited in any way without undermining its status as the One, i.e. the absolute simple unity that comprehends within itself all being even though it itself is beyond being. Insofar as the One is unlimited all terms used in reference to it cannot be taken referentially.[16]

This is the philosophical position which underlies Maimonides' principles of faith. To be a consistent Maimonidean today means to accept the whole system of logic and metaphysics which undergirds Maimonides' articles of faith. On Maimonides' terms, that is the only way to earn a share in the world to come.

It should further be noted that Maimonides was not optimistic that rabbis of his own generation would understand the philosophy behind his principles. Thus he 'determined not to teach these basic truths in the idiom of inquiry, since examination of these roots requires skills in many fields, of which, as I pointed out in the *Guide*, the learned in Torah know nothing'.[17]

15 Personal communication.

16 Elliot R. Wolfson, 'Negative Theology and Positive Assertion in the Early Kabbalah', *Da'at*, 31–2 (1994), pp. v–xxii at p. v.

17 See Maimonides' 'Essay on Resurrection', in *Crisis and Leadership: Epistles of Maimonides*, trans. A. S. Halkin, discussions by David Hartman (Philadelphia: Jewish Publication Society, 1985), 212. The entire passage repays close study in the context of this present issue.

The point made here bears clear and forceful restatement: Maimonides did not expect to meet many of his rabbinic contemporaries in the world to come.

Challenges to Maimonides

Maimonides' innovation (and that, as I have tried above to show, it certainly was) did not go unchallenged.[18] Given that, as I have shown in earlier chapters, classical Judaism understood *emunah* in a different way from Maimonides, i.e. as a matter of trust in God expressed through obedience to the commandments, it is not surprising that his ideas concerning the nature of Jewish faith were not clearly understood in their own terms and thus earned neither applause nor reproach but were—largely—simply ignored.

Maimonides' innovation did spark off some discussion in the Middle Ages, especially in the fifteenth century. As I have shown elsewhere, of the two dozen or so Jewish thinkers who addressed the issue at all, none followed Maimonides' definition of articles of faith. Rather, in almost all cases, the principles of faith were deployed not as a theological but as a literary device, or as part of an anti-Christian apologetic in cases where Jews were forced to present Judaism in terms laid down by their Christian interlocutors. This claim may easily be proved: medieval Jews debated the principles of Judaism, but in no case did any of those involved in the debate denounce as heretics others who disagreed with them over what these principles actually were. But that is precisely what Maimonides was doing.[19]

However, while medieval Jewish thinkers did not, in general, engage directly with Maimonides' claims about the nature of faith, his assertion that the Torah includes commandments to know or believe certain things was subjected to incisive and, I think, convincing criticism. This criticism is still relevant today.

R. Hasdai Crescas, the great leader of fourteenth-century Iberian Jewry, rejected the idea that the Torah contains commandments con-

[18] Maimonides was indeed the first Jewish thinker to affirm both that Judaism had core 'faith-commitments' (to borrow an expression of Bleich's from a text I will discuss in Chapter 6) and that Jews were expressly commanded to believe that these tenets were true; he was not, however, the last. His clear influence is seen, for example, in the *Sefer haḥinukh*, on which see above, p. 16.

[19] For details, see Kellner, *Dogma*, 201–17. My position here is supported by Joseph M. Davis, 'Philosophy, Dogma, and Exegesis in Medieval Ashkenazic Judaism: The Evidence of *Sefer Hadrat Qodesh*', *AJS Review*, 18 (1993), 195–222, esp. 215, 222.

cerning matters of belief and knowledge. For a commandment to have any significance, Crescas argues, we must be able to accept it or reject it. It makes no sense whatsoever to command someone to do something over which he has no control. It is, he says, a matter of both common sense and common experience that we cannot control our convictions. We cannot will to believe or not to believe, to be convinced of the truth of something or to be convinced of its falsity. How can we then be commanded, Crescas asks, to know (or even believe) that God exists, is one, and is incorporeal?[20]

Abrabanel responded to Crescas' criticism of Maimonides in his analysis of Jewish dogma, *Principles of Faith* (completed in 1494). Abrabanel grants Crescas' point that we have no control over our beliefs and convictions; but, he maintains, we do have control over the processes that lead to belief and conviction. These processes are study and learning.

Take, for example, Pythagoras' theorem. Let us say that someone shows me a right-angled triangle and tells me that the square of the hypotenuse is equal to the sum of the squares of the other two sides. I cannot be commanded to believe that that claim is true. I can, however, be commanded to measure the three sides of the triangle, which will rapidly convince me of the truth of the theorem with respect to this particular triangle at any rate.

Let us say further that I examine dozens of right-angled triangles and find that the theorem holds for every one of them. Even then, it makes no sense to command me to accept the truth of the theorem. After all, the theorem is meant to hold for all right-angled triangles, and no matter how much time I devote to the project, I will never be able to examine more than a small number of all possible right-angled triangles. I have no reason to accept the theorem; I certainly have not been shown anything which would convince a reasonably sceptical person that it holds for all right-angled triangles; how, then, can I be commanded to believe it?

Let us say yet further that I am by nature a pleasant, amiable fellow who likes to make people happy. Let us then posit that the person commanding me to believe that Pythagoras' theorem is true is someone for whom I have profound respect and deep affection, someone who has never lied to me, and someone who has proved to have nothing but my best interests at heart. For all these reasons. I might very much want to obey the command to believe that Pythagoras' theorem is true, but I simply cannot choose to believe it. Either I believe it or I don't.

20 For the details of Crescas' critique of Maimonides' claim that Judaism has commandments addressed to the intellect, so to speak, see Kellner, *Dogma*, 108–39.

I cannot be commanded to be convinced of the truth of Pythagoras' theorem. I can, however, be commanded to study geometry. If I am reasonably intelligent and apply myself, I will ultimately become convinced of the truth of the theorem. At some point, the proverbial light will flick on and I will say, 'Ah, now I see it!' And once I have 'seen it' no command will be able to force me to deny the truth of the theorem.

Thus, Abrabanel says, 'Maimonides did not count as a positive commandment the form of the belief and its truth, but, rather, knowledge of those things which bring one to acquire beliefs.[21] According to Abrabanel, when Maimonides codifies as commandments the obligation to accept that God exists, is one, and is incorporeal, he means that we are commanded to apply ourselves to the study of physics and metaphysics so as to become convinced of the truth of the claims that God exists, is one, and is incorporeal.

Although this is not the place investigate it in detail, Abrabanel's proposal has much to recommend it, and it may very well be an accurate interpretation of Maimonides' intent. But does it help us in today's world? I think not.

Maimonides could reasonably write that the Torah commands us to know that God exists and mean that the Torah commands us to study enough science and philosophy to be able rationally to demonstrate God's existence. What is acceptable for Maimonides, however, is not satisfactory for our contemporaries. Medieval science and philosophy (or physics and metaphysics, as Maimonides would have said) could be used by a reasonable person to demonstrate that God exists, is one, and is incorporeal. Maimonides' predecessors and contemporaries in the Jewish, Muslim, and Christian worlds were unanimous in agreeing that such proofs were available. Any intelligent person in Maimonides' day who denied the existence of God could be faulted for not studying science and philosophy diligently enough. To all intents and purposes no one denied the basic postulates of Aristotelian science; and, once accepted, these postulates, it was very widely agreed, led directly to the proofs of God's existence, unity, and incorporeality.

Today, however, the situation is very different. Contemporary science and philosophy cannot prove to the satisfaction of reasonable persons that God exists, is one, and is incorporeal. I suppose that some over-enthusiastic religious people today might sincerely believe that they can rationally prove the existence not only of the God of the philosophers but

[21] For Abrabanel's response to Crescas, see *Principles of Faith*, ch. 11. The passage quoted from Abrabanel is found on p. 155.

of the God of Abraham, Isaac, and Jacob. If they were correct, however (without going into the details of the argumentation), then anyone who denied or questioned God's existence would be guilty of stupidity, irrationality, or wilfully ignoring the evidence. That is so strong a claim, and so unlikely on the face of it to be the case, that I can surely say safely and reasonably that the burden of proof rests not on me, but on those who think they can prove that the God of Abraham, Isaac, and Jacob exists.[22]

That God does not exist cannot be proved either, of course, but that does not help us very much. Even those individuals who believe (mistakenly, in my view) that God's existence can be proven must admit that reasonable people applying themselves to the study of science and philosophy will not without exception arrive at the conviction that God exists, is one, and is incorporeal.

The upshot of all this is that Abrabanel's interpretation of Maimonides, namely that commandments of belief really relate to the study necessary to arrive at belief, may save Maimonides from Crescas' criticisms but does not help make possible commandments relating to beliefs today. Anyone today who maintains that the Torah commands belief that certain statements are true must explain how the Torah can command things over which we have no conscious control.

As I have shown above, the claim that Judaism has dogmas is new with Maimonides and reflects his view that *emunah* consists of specific affirmations of truth and falsity. In fact, there were other medieval authorities who shared this basic approach, but refused to go to the extremes that he did. Let us examine this point first.

R. Sa'adia Gaon (in the tenth century) and R. Bahya ibn Pakuda (in the eleventh century) agreed that the Torah teaches specific, discrete beliefs.

[22] A number of recent thinkers (R. Samson Raphael Hirsch, the saintly and martyred R. Elhanan Wasserman, and R. Elia Lapian) have made a similar claim, to the effect that the principles of faith are self-evident to all but the corrupted. While there are differences of emphasis among these three thinkers, they all share the idea that 'all non-believers . . . are to a greater or lesser degree, immoral or at best weak of character. To put it another way, there is no legitimate disbelief, only chosen lifestyles that jam the wavelength of faith.' I quote from pp. 34–5 of Joseph Grunblatt, 'Confronting Disbelievers', *Tradition*, 23 (1987), 33–9. For a similar position, one apparently typical of the Musar movement, see Eliyahu Dessler, *Letter from Elijah* (Heb.), 5 vols. (Benei Berak: Committee for the Publication of the Writings of Rabbi E. L. Dessler, 1983), i. 171–6. According to Rabbi Dessler, the secularist suppresses what he actually knows, in his heart of hearts, to be the truth. This position is, of course, impossible to prove. It also makes a mockery of the lives of highly sophisticated, morally sensitive, deeply thoughtful atheists and agnostics. Were Sartre and Camus weak of character?

Sa'adia, in fact, is the first Jew in the rabbinic tradition to have made this claim explicitly: he structured his famous *Book of Beliefs and Doctrines* around a series of these teachings. The point of this book was to transform the 'beliefs' of Judaism (ideas accepted on the basis of traditional authority) into 'doctrines' (these same ideas, after they have been rationally proven to be true). Are Jews obliged to transform their beliefs into doctrines? Sa'adia's answer is simple: they are not. He wrote his book only for those Jews who were troubled by the fact that they had not achieved a state of intellectual certainty concerning traditional beliefs. It is not that they doubted the truths of Judaism; they just wanted these truths to have the same epistemological status as the teachings of science.

But what of a Jew who is content to accept the teachings of the Torah on the basis of traditional authority, or is unable to understand the arguments proving their truth? Is such a person in any sense an inferior Jew to one who has succeeded in proving to herself or himself that God exists, created the world, etc.? Here again, Sa'adia's answer is simple: no. There is no obligation whatsoever to transform one's simple beliefs into doctrines. If one is comfortable in observing the Torah without being able to prove that its teachings are true, fine.

Note well, please, that the question arises only if we adopt the view that the Torah has explicit and clearly defined teachings of a theological nature. There is no doubt that Sa'adia adopts that view, but he nowhere insists that a person should find out exactly what those teachings are and come to understand them; nor does he use them to define who is and who is not a Jew, or threaten dire punishments for the person who rejects or even makes a mistake about them.

Bahya takes the issue a step further. For him the Torah includes *ḥovot halevavot*, 'obligations of the intellect'. These obligations are commandments, and are every bit as normative as the 'obligations of the limbs' (*ḥovot ha'evarim*), such as observing the laws of kosher food. But among the differences he identifies between intellectual obligations (what Bahya calls 'obligations of the intellect') and obligations of the limbs is the following: all Jews are required to obey the obligations of the limbs; but only those Jews who are capable of it are required to obey the intellectual obligations. Anyone can keep kosher. But not every person can rationally understand the proofs for God's existence. It would not be fair if intellectual obligations devolved upon those who were incapable of observing them. Bahya, a fair man, and, I might add, one who appears to have had a warm and loving personality, does not demand from the simple Jew what he or she cannot perform.

Bahya, then, goes a step beyond Sa'adia. The latter makes the intellectual affirmation of the teachings of the Torah entirely a matter of *reshut*, something permitted but not obligatory; Bahya makes their acceptance (which means understanding) obligatory, but only for those capable of it. Jews unable to prove that God exists are still good Jews. In addition to Bahya, Rabeinu Hananel (eleventh century), as cited by Bahya ben Asher in his commentary on Exodus 14: 31, and Abraham ibn Ezra (*c*. 1089–1164), in his long commentary on Exodus 20, anticipate Maimonides' claim that Judaism has commandments addressed to the intellect.

It was up to Maimonides to take the next step: namely, to state that knowing God's existence, unity, and incorporeality is obligatory for all Jews, even, as Maimonides says in *Guide of the Perplexed*, i. 36, for women and children. Individuals who are not capable of this, or make mistakes about it, are not simply inferior Jews, they are not really Jews at all. That is Maimonides' position. How many of his followers today are willing to accept that assertion? How many of them even qualify as Jews on Maimonides' criteria? The answer to both questions is, I think, few if any.

Was Maimonides Inconsistent? The Karaites

There are good reasons for asking how consistent Maimonides was in applying his theory. This issue has direct implications for the way in which Maimonides' positions are used today. As the discussion proceeds we will see that while Maimonides was indeed a 'Maimonidean' (i.e. he actually held the theory which undergirds his system of dogma), his true position was somewhat different from his public stance, in that he distinguished decisively between those who doubted or rejected any of the first five of his Thirteen Principles and those who doubted or rejected any of the others.

One area in which Maimonides appears to be inconsistent with respect to the application of his principles is in his attitudes. This has to do with his stance regarding Karaites. Karaites reject part of the eighth principle in that they deny the divine origin of the Oral Torah; with respect to all the other principles they are fully 'orthodox'.[23] In his first public statement concerning the Karaites, in his commentary on the Mishnah,

[23] For an excellent and brief explanation of Karaism, see Lasker, 'Rabbanism and Karaism'. On the development of 'Rabbanites' are those Jews who upheld the validity of the rabbinic tradition, denied by the Karaites. For important discussions of the development of Maimonides' views on Karaites, see Ya'akov Blidstein, 'Maimonides' Attitude towards Karaites' (Heb.), *Teḥumin*, 8 (1988), 501–10; Daniel J. Lasker, 'The Influence of Karaism on Maimonides' (Heb.), *Sefunot*, 5 (1991), 145–61.

Maimonides adjudged them to be heretics and called for their execution where possible. In the course of time Maimonides moderated his stance, distinguishing between, on the one hand, the founders of Karaism and Rabbanite Jews who joined them, and, on the other, their descendants. Descendants of Karaites, Maimonides avers in the *Mishneh torah*,

> misguided by their parents, [and] raised among the Karaites and trained in their views, are like a child taken captive by them and raised in their religion, whose status is that of an *anus* [one who abjures the Jewish religion under duress], who, although he later learns that he is a Jew, meets Jews, observes them practice their religion, is nevertheless to be regarded as an *anus*, since he was raised in the erroneous ways of his fathers. Thus it is with those who adhere to the practices of their Karaite parents. Therefore efforts should be made to bring them back in repentance, to draw them near by friendly relations, so that they may return to the strength-giving source, i.e., the Torah.[24]

As we shall see below, this more moderate position, that contemporary Karaites are not to be killed but, rather, treated like 'straying brethren' and returned to the fold through 'ways of pleasantness' (Prov. 3: 17), undergirds the position adopted by most halakhic decisors today that Jews who fail to satisfy theological tests of orthodoxy are heretics, but inadvertent heretics and therefore not fully culpable. The full rigour of the law concerning heretics (that they be killed where possible and that no relations be allowed with them whatsoever where killing them is not feasible) is therefore not imposed upon them.

I personally am fully in support of the idea that Orthodox Jews may not kill their Reform, Conservative, Reconstructionist, and secular brethren. I certainly have no interest in casting doubt upon the wisdom of the policy of not calling for their deaths. But how can Maimonides justify the claim? After all, we have seen how he disallows *shegagah* with respect to heresy; now we see him allowing it!

The answer to this question saves Maimonides from the charge of inconsistency, but, as will become evident as we proceed, only deepens the crisis of those who wish to use him as an authority for the imposition of theological tests of Jewish legitimacy. The founders of Karaism rejected part of the eighth principle of faith, but they accepted all the others. In particular, they were in full agreement with the first five, those which deal with God. That turns out to be significant.

Let us recall that acceptance of principles of faith is supposed to lead to

[24] 'Laws of Rebellious Elders', iii. 3. I cite the translation of A. M. Hershman in *The Book of Judges* (New Haven: Yale University Press, 1949), 143–4.

a share in the world to come. This acceptance, I pointed out above, involves more than learning the principles by rote: it involves some level of understanding of them. This is so because Maimonides, on his own philosophical grounds, can only get people into heaven, so to speak, if they have made themselves full human beings, individuals with a certain amount of intellectual advancement. One achieves that level of advancement only through an understanding of basic metaphysical teachings. (Correct) knowledge concerning God is the only key to immortality. Essential elements in this knowledge are taught and explained in the first five principles.

Maimonides' first five principles, then, teach metaphysical truths. Understanding those truths constitutes enough intellectual advancement to guarantee a share in the world to come. The other principles also teach truths, of course, but of a type different from the first group. These latter truths relate to certain historical events (concerning the giving of the Torah), to the way God relates to us, and to certain future events (the coming of the Messiah and resurrection). Rejection of these truths excludes one from that community constituted by their acceptance (the community of Israel), but does not and cannot in and of itself lead to exclusion from the world to come.

Maimonides' claim that all his principles are dogmas in the strict sense that perfect acceptance of them is a necessary and sufficient condition for being part of the community of Israel, and for having a share in the world to come, is thus seen to be exaggerated: it is only the first five principles that are dogmas in that sense. No mistakes can be tolerated concerning them, and none is. Innocent mistakes concerning the other principles can be tolerated to the extent that those who make these mistakes need not be subjected to the full rigour of the law concerning heretics—as is clear from the treatment of Karaite descendants prescribed in Maimonides' writings.

But is it indeed the case that Maimonides himself distinguished between the first five principles and all the others, as I here claim? It turns out that—fortunately for my case—he makes the point explicitly in the *Guide of the Perplexed*. In part 1, chapter 36 of that work Maimonides raises the question of the status of a person who mistakenly (i.e. with no intention to rebel against God and the Torah) attributes corporeality to God. This is what he says:

> What then should be the state of him whose infidelity bears upon His essence, may He be exalted, and consists in believing Him to be different from what He really is? . . . If, however, it should occur to you that one who believes in the

corporeality of God should be excused because of his having been brought up in this doctrine or because of his ignorance and the shortcomings of his apprehension, you ought to hold a similar belief with regard to *an idolater*; for he only worships idols because of his ignorance or because of his upbringing: *They continue in the custom of their fathers*. If, however, you should say that the external sense of the biblical text causes men to fall into this doubt, you ought to know that *an idolater* is similarly impelled to his idolatry by imaginings and defective representations. Accordingly there is no excuse for one who does not accept the authority of men who inquire into the truth and are engaged in speculation if he himself is incapable of engaging in such speculation. (pp. 84–5)

A person has been brought up to believe in a corporeal God. This person might even (mistakenly) believe that God has material characteristics because of his or her misunderstanding of the Torah (the last verses of Deuteronomy, for example, speak of God's 'mighty hand and outstretched arm'), or even because of the misunderstanding of a parent or teacher. Such a person holds incorrect beliefs about the deity because of 'his ignorance and the shortcomings of his apprehension', not out of any desire to be a bad Jew. Can we excuse these mistakes? Only, Maimonides insists, if we are willing to excuse outright idolatry. There is no excuse for mistakes concerning God, whether made by Jews or by idolaters. The truth is ready to hand; if you can't work it out yourself, go to an appropriate teacher who can help you.

Karaites did not reject God's existence, unity, or incorporeality; they did not reject the creation of the universe; and they did not pray to intermediaries. Persons raised as Karaites, in other words, are not 'infidels' in the sense described here by Maimonides. They reject a true teaching concerning the Torah, but they do not misconstrue or misrepresent the nature of God. As such, they do not commit fatal metaphysical mistakes, and are not, therefore, automatically excluded from the world to come.[25]

The founders of Karaism (and Rabbanite Jews who joined it later) consciously rebelled against the authority of the Sanhedrin, a capital offence; thus, they deserved death. Their descendants have not so rebelled and can therefore be treated with greater leniency. By maintaining correct beliefs about God, Karaite descendants remain within the essen-

25 For important support of my interpretation that according to Maimonides Karaites do not deny the first five principles and are not *minim* in the strict sense, see R. Joseph Kafih's new Hebrew translation of Judah Halevi's *Sefer hakuzari* (Kiryat Ono: Makhon Moshe, 1997), 1 n. 3.

tial fold of Judaism (if not within the Jewish community); their disagreement is largely about matters of 'detail', so to speak.

Maimonides, then, attached cardinal importance to the first five of the Thirteen Principles, somewhat less importance to the others. Rejection of or mistakes concerning the first group truly exclude one from the community of Israel and from the world to come. Mistakes concerning the latter group do not actually exclude one from the community of Israel (we are, after all, bound to make efforts in respect of those who err 'to bring them back in repentance, to draw them near by friendly relations, so that they may return to the strength-giving source, i.e., the Torah') and certainly do not, in and of themselves, exclude one from the world to come.[26]

Maimonides' willingness to extend Jewish identity to contemporary Karaites, and not call for their extinction, is therefore not evidence of inconsistency. The founders of Karaism deserve death as rebels; their descendants accept those principles of faith about which Maimonides cannot compromise (those the acceptance of which gain one entry into the world to come) and therefore are mistaken, not heretical.

[26] Further on Maimonides' distinction between the first five principles and the last eight, see Kellner, *Dogma*, 34–49.

SIX

Heresy-hunting

ONE of the most difficult and painful problems facing contemporary Orthodoxy is the question of how to relate to non-Orthodox versions of Jewish religiosity. One of the reasons why the issue is so complex is that the tradition really presents very little guidance on how to deal with the problem. Orthodoxy today is faced with something new and unprecedented: expressions of Judaism which claim to be the legitimate, normatively correct versions of the Torah while at the same time rejecting the divine origin and obligatory character of halakhic obedience (Reform Judaism) or understanding the nature and character of the halakhic process in new and unprecedented ways (Conservative Judaism).

Moreover, what came to be called 'Orthodoxy' was faced with these new problems against the background of the development of the modern world, with its dizzying variety of non-religious versions of Jewish identification, and the ever-present possibility of simply melting away in a usually painless and often unconscious process of assimilation. It is no surprise that bulwarks were thrown up, fortifications built, and positions entrenched.

Orthodoxy and Heresy

Part of the typically Orthodox response to the challenge posed by non-Orthodox versions of religious Judaism is to brand the followers of other varieties of Judaism (or at least their leaders) as heretics. Heretics are beyond the pale, not to be associated with, lest that association lend them legitimacy. Heretics, it should be further noted, have no share in the world to come. This position was made possible by what might be called Maimonides' 'theologification' of Judaism. I have my doubts about the wisdom of this response, but that is not what concerns me here. Rather, I am interested in its coherence: is it internally consistent, and does it cohere with classic forms of Jewish self-understanding? In this and the following chapter I will try to show that the answer to both questions is no.

I would like first, however, to fill in some of the background to our problem. Orthodoxy is unwilling to do anything which might be construed as conferring legitimacy upon Conservative, Reform, and Reconstructionist Judaism.[1] The reason for this is quite simple: non-Orthodox Judaism is heresy. This comes out very clearly in the many responsa of the late Rabbi Moses Feinstein (1892–1986), in which the subject comes up directly or indirectly. He forbids, for example, an Orthodox service in a Conservative synagogue building (not just in the main sanctuary, but in any room in the building), since 'it is well-known that they [Conservative Jews] are deniers [*koferim*] of many Torah laws'. Most Conservative and Reform rabbis can be assumed to be 'deniers of God and His Torah'. All the people buried in Reform cemeteries are 'evil-doers who have denied our holy Torah'.[2]

Maimonides' influence in all this, though rarely stated explicitly, lurks prominently in the background, as is evidenced, for example, by Bleich's comment on the matter: 'Halakhah is remarkably tolerant, nay accepting, but only within certain clearly defined parameters. These parameters involve matters of dogma primarily.' Bleich then goes on, more or less paraphrasing Maimonides' statement at the end of his principles: 'Judaism has always distinguished between those who transgress and those

[1] With respect to the fear of conferring legitimacy upon non-Orthodox Judaism, see the very clear statement of the Orthodox position in J. David Bleich, *Contemporary Halakhic Problems*, 4 vols. (New York: Ktav, 1989–), iii. 82–111. As Rabbi Bleich puts it, 'the issue in the United States is not that of possible negative influence [of non-Orthodox Judaism upon Orthodoxy and Orthodox Jews] but of legitimization' (p. 90).

[2] The three quotations of Rabbi Feinstein's are from *Responsa* (Heb.) (New York: n.p., 1996), *Oraḥ ḥayim*, ii. 50, iv. 91, and *Yoreh de'ah*, iii. 149. Rabbi Feinstein, of course, is the single most influential halakhic decisor of the second half of the twentieth century. Further on his attitudes towards non-Orthodox Judaism see J. Chinitz, 'Reb Moshe and the Conservatives', *Conservative Judaism*, 41 (1989), 5–15; Y. Levin, 'The Conservative Movement as Reflected in the Responsa of R. Moshe Feinstein', in Y. Raphael (ed.), *Aviad Memorial Volume* (Heb.) (Jerusalem: Mosad Harav Kook, 1986), 281–93; on the modern world in general, see Ira Robinson, 'Because of Our Many Sins: The Contemporary World as Reflected in the Responsa of Moses Feinstein', *Judaism*, 35 (1986), 35–46. Levin points out that Rabbi Feinstein does not distinguish between Conservative and Reform Judaism and that he characterizes Conservative and Reform rabbis as 'deniers, sectarians, heretics, evil-doers, enticers [to sin] and corrupters' (p. 287). See further the comments by Louis Jacobs, 'Theological Responsa', *Judaism*, 16 (1967), 345–52 at 346. For the history of Orthodox attitudes towards the non-Orthodox in the last few centuries, a history which serves as the backdrop for Rabbi Feinstein's approach, see Judith Bleich, 'Rabbinic Responses to Nonobservance in the Modern Era', in Jacob J. Schacter (ed.), *Jewish Tradition and the Nontraditional Jew* (Northvale, NJ: Jason Aronson, 1992), 37–116.

who renounce. Transgression is to be deplored, but transgression does not place the transgressor beyond the pale of believers. Renunciation—even without actual transgression—is a matter of an entirely different magnitude.' It is this different order of magnitude which makes co-operation in religious matters, membership in community-wide organizations (such as the Synagogue Council of America and local boards of rabbis), and any act which implies recognition or the conferring of legitimacy, or which might give 'the appearance of dealing with Conservative and Reform leaders with deference and dignity' wholly unacceptable in the Orthodox world today.[3]

[3] The quotations from David Bleich are from his *Contemporary Halakhic Problems*, iii. 85, 86. The *Jewish Observer*, the official organ of the Agudat Yisrael of the United States, took Rabbi Norman Lamm, president of Yeshiva University, to task for giving the impression that he treated Conservative and Reform rabbis with 'deference and dignity' (June 1988, p. 13). In general, see the exchange between Lamm and Professor Aaron Twersky in the *Jewish Observer*, April 1988, pp. 6–9, and June 1988, pp. 13–16, 17–26. Twersky's position clearly reflects his dependence upon Maimonides:

> Should one who preaches vile *kefira* [heresy] be allowed to travel throughout the United States as a consultant to over three score Jewish Federations preaching 'pluralism' and heresy in the name of Orthodox 'Centrism'? Isn't it essential that someone declare that 'the field' begins and ends with unquestioning *emuna*, and that denial of *Ikrim* (basic tenets of faith) *does not* render someone 'left wing' but totally out of the ballpark? (June 1988, 20–1)

Twersky's ire here was aroused by rabbis Yitzchak Greenberg and Emmanuel Rackman. See further the *Jewish Observer* editorial, January 1985, pp. 37–9, and, very importantly for our purposes, 'Council of Torah Sages Declares: No Rabbinic Dialogue with Conservatives', *Jewish Observer*, April 1985, p. 21: 'The classic tenets of Judaism are not negotiable nor are they the subject matter for dialogues with those who are purveying to an unwary public a "Judaism" that tears down fundamentals of our ancient heritage—all in the name of Halachah.' One can multiply statements such as these almost without end. I shall, however, cite only a few more examples. The first is a text which clearly illuminates the tendencies I am trying to describe here. Rabbi Chaim Dov Keller quotes a remark made at his [Keller's] wedding in 1962 by his 'sainted Rebbe, Reb Elya Meir Bloch zt'l, Telshe Rosh Yeshiva', to the effect that 'We no longer have to fear Conservatism—that is no longer the danger. Everyone knows that it is *avoda zara*. What we have to fear is Modern Orthodoxy.' See Chaim Dov Keller, 'Modern Orthodoxy: An Analysis and a Response', *Jewish Observer*, June 1979, pp. 3–14, repr. in Reuven Bulka (ed.), *Dimensions of Orthodox Judaism* (New York: Ktav, 1983), 233–71 at 253. Conservative Judaism is *avodah zarah* (lit. 'foreign worship', i.e. idolatry)—'everyone knows' that; Reform Judaism is presumably worse. Rabbi Keller enthusiastically endorses his rebbe's position and explicitly ties it to Maimonides. The reader should be reminded that idolatry is one of the three cardinal sins. A Jew is commanded to sacrifice her life rather than perform *avodah zarah*. It is the very antithesis of Torah.

I must emphasize that this approach is not restricted to 'ultra' Orthodoxy. For an interesting example of the way in which the heretical nature of non-Orthodox

Theology and Halakhah: A Category Mistake

My argument against those who wish to pose a theological test to determine Jewish legitimacy is based in part on the claim that those who seek to turn theology into halakhah are making a category mistake. It is not a halakhic issue and halakhic authorities are not adequately trained to deal with it. Leaving aside Maimonides (and those who think that they accept his views), there is no classic authority to support the application of halakhic categories to theology. Moreover, as I will show, those who seek to impose tests of theological orthodoxy upon other Jews cannot really be said to be adopting Maimonides' position, even though they are convinced that they are. Rather, they are adopting the shell of his position (that Judaism has dogmas) while rejecting the meat—that is, the philosophical and theological basis for that position. Further-more, there are very few Jews alive today who actually subscribe to Maimonides' principles as he formulated them. And finally, as we saw in the last section of the previous chapter, Maimonides himself was, on the face of it, inconsistent in the way in which he applied his principles. That apparent inconsistency may be sufficient to indicate that it was not his intent that they should be used in the way which has become prevalent today.

movements in Judaism is taken for granted (by a spokesperson for 'modern' or 'centrist' Orthodoxy) see Mayer Schiller, '*Torah Umadda* and *The Jewish Observer* Critique: Towards a Clarification of the Issues', *The Torah Umadda Journal*, 6 (1995–6), 58–90 at 83 and esp. n. 14 (p. 88): 'In 1986, before an audience comprised largely of Jews affiliated with *heretical* movements, Dr Lamm declared . . .' (emphasis added). This is an article devoted to defending the philosophical bases of 'centrist' or 'modern' Orthodoxy, and its major contemporary spokesperson (Rabbi Dr Norman Lamm), from criticisms voiced in the more or less official journal of what is variously called 'right-wing', '*ḥaredi*' or 'yeshiva' Orthodoxy, the *Jewish Observer*. The author, Rabbi Schiller, a distinguished and personally open-minded Talmud instructor of long standing in Yeshiva University High School for boys, takes it as a given that Conservative and Reform Judaism constitute heresy and that his readers will take it for granted that such is the case.

It has become a commonplace in the contemporary Orthodox world to view Reform Judaism as a new religion altogether. For an example, see Rabbi Yisrael Rozen, a strident and influential spokesperson in (Israel) National Religious Party circles, in *Shabat beshabato*, no. 622 (parashat Eikev, 23 Aug. 1997). Rabbi Rozen is important both for reflecting widely held views and for helping to shape them. Rabbi Rozen sees Reform Jews as Jews who have converted to a new religion without losing their identity (and halakhic obligations) as Jews (in the same way, I might add, that Jews for Jesus are still seen as halakhically Jewish). Rabbi Zvi Elimelekh Halberstam, leader of the Zanz hasidim, and a highly respected individual, was reported in the Israeli newspaper *Ha'arets* (15 Aug. 1997, p. 6*a*) as having publicly affirmed that Reform Jews have not only removed themselves from the Jewish religion, but have also removed themselves from the people of Israel and thus have no rights in the Land of Israel.

It is obvious that Orthodoxy cannot leave matters as laid down by Maimonides and implemented by rabbis Feinstein and Bleich: the penalties for idolatry and heresy are severe, and treating non-Orthodox (and Modern Orthodox) Jews as idolaters and heretics would make it impossible to live with and among them.[4] The way in which Orthodox spokesmen get around this problem will be taken up in the next chapter. Here, I want to illustrate the strategy I plan to follow by drawing a parallel with another difficult problem facing the halakhically observant world. As I have been writing this book, Israel and the Palestinians have been taking hesitant steps towards mutual recognition and, perhaps, ultimate reconciliation. It has become a commonplace in the so-called 'national religious' camp to argue that it is halakhically forbidden to surrender territory in the Land of Israel to non-Jewish authorities. Some voices in this camp even insist that territorial compromise is forbidden in the same way that murder, idolatry, and sexual immorality are forbidden: one must sacrifice one's life before committing one of these forbidden acts. More moderate voices say that it is forbidden, just as it is forbidden to violate the Sabbath or eat non-kosher food. In both cases, it is agreed that the issue is a halakhic one, and that the halakhah on the matter is clear: one may not give up portions of the Land of Israel. The religious legitimacy of persons holding opposed views is, typically, rejected.

The argument against this position, as voiced from within the 'national religious' world, is usually presented in two stages. First, it is argued that the issue is not subject to halakhic determination at all. The late Rabbi J. B. Soloveitchik (1903–93), former head of Yeshiva University, for example, is widely reported to have held that questions concerning the disposition of territory should be asked of generals and political leaders, not rabbis. But even if one rejects this view, a second point requires attention: namely, that even if the disposition of parts of the Land of Israel is deemed subject to halakhic determination, it is still the case that the halakhic issue is debated. There is no lack of reputable rabbis who hold, on halakhic grounds, that surrender of territory in the Land of Israel is not in every case forbidden. Once the issue becomes a matter of halakhic debate between recognized authorities, then the classic category of 'these and these are the words of the living God' (i.e. both are legitimate) comes into play and neither side has the right to rule the other illegitimate.

I here adopt the first half of the two-pronged strategy of those who

[4] A consequence quite explicitly adopted by the Satmar hasidim; on this see Allan Nadler, 'Piety and Politics: The Case of the Satmar Rebbe', *Judaism*, 31 (1982), 135–52.

defend the halakhic legitimacy of the politically 'dovish' position in Israel. That is, I take the view that the question who should and should not be counted a member of the legitimate Jewish community, the question with whom we may have social, intellectual, and religious intercourse, the question whether or not we ought to cooperate with this or that institution or movement—all these are questions which transcend halakhah as it has been received in our day. Especially given the unprecedented existing circumstances of Jewish life in the modern world, these are questions for which halakhah has no ready answers; and they are questions which traditionally trained *posekim* (halakhic decisors) have not proved themselves particularly well equipped to answer.

I hasten to clarify my position: I am not saying that halakhah cannot clearly answer questions concerning such matters as whom we may or may not marry, or who can offer testimony in a Jewish court. These are technical questions and have technical answers. Who or what is a Jew (especially in today's fractured world) is a meta-halakhic question.

Let us look at the issue in a historical fashion. The question of who is and who is not a Jew, or a 'good' Jew, simply does not come up in the Torah, and receives little if any explicit attention in the Talmud. Clear-cut answers to the question were developed in the Middle Ages—by Maimonides, facing Islam and Karaism, and by later halakhic decisors facing the *anusim*, the forced converts of fifteenth-century Iberia. The answers they developed were important in their day and made a signal contribution to the continued existence of Jews and Judaism. That does not mean that those answers should be applied blindly in today's world.[5]

I should offer one more caveat before proceeding further: as will become clear, my claim that turning theology into halakhah is a category mistake is not identical with Rabbi Jonathan Sacks' important and painfully true insight that many contemporary Jews seek to apply halakhic categories to the realm of aggadah.[6]

Three Contemporary Orthodox Statements

I will here focus on three statements of what I take to be Jewish Orthodoxy in the spirit of Maimonides' principles of faith. The first was published in a journal sponsored by Yeshiva University, a journal dedicated

[5] For an important discussion of many of the relevant texts, see Gerald J. Blidstein, 'Who is Not a Jew: The Medieval Discussion', *Israel Law Review*, 11 (1976), 369–90.

[6] See Sacks, *One People?*, 99–100. Further on this whole problem see Norman Solomon's discussion of what he calls 'pan-Halakhism' in his *The Analytic Movement: Hayyim Soloveitchik and his Circle* (Atlanta, Ga.: Scholars Press, 1993), 223–40.

to exploring and explicating the intersection between Torah and science (in the broadest sense of both terms). The second was published by a scholar of vast erudition and profound insight who holds two professorships at Yeshiva University, one in Talmud and the second in law. He is, moreover, one of the very few Orthodox scholars who consistently attempts constructive and respectful intellectual intercourse with non-Orthodox intellectuals, both rabbinic and lay. Moreover, this article was published in a collection of essays edited by Jonathan Sacks, the Chief Rabbi of Great Britain, a man deeply committed to openness towards the entire Jewish world. The third text is Rabbi Sacks' own attempt to argue for a policy of Orthodox inclusivism towards non-Orthodox Jews.

Put simply, if we are to find texts expressing authoritative Orthodox opinion which do not take it to be a matter of course that all non-Orthodox expressions of Judaism are entirely without legitimacy and have nothing of value to say to the Jew, then these texts are the place to look. In the first two of these texts, however, the spirit of Maimonides' principles of faith leaves its clear and, to my mind, unfortunate impression. With respect to the third text, Chief Rabbi Sacks wrote his book in order to make possible a policy of inclusivism and openness towards non-Orthodox Jews and Judaism. His acceptance of Maimonides' understanding of Judaism, however, handcuffs him from the very start, and makes it impossible for him to get to where he seems to want to go.

I must emphasize at the outset that by citing the writings of rabbis Parnes, Bleich, and Sacks together I am not seeking to imply that they form a unified school or that they would even necessarily agree with each other. Furthermore, I am not seeking to criticize them; while I do not know Rabbi Parnes beyond the articles of his which I cite here, I have nothing but the deepest respect and admiration for the writings and persons of rabbis Bleich and Sacks. Indeed, it could not be otherwise, since both represent for me the finest expression of what Orthodoxy can accomplish in seeking a positive relationship with non-Orthodox Jews, given the tools currently available. It is the point of the present book to suggest that these tools (the application of the category of heresy to non-Orthodox Judaisms) are not the only or indeed the best ones available to an Orthodox Jew.

Freedom of Enquiry

The first issue of *The Torah Umadda Journal*, published in 1989, contains a brief article by Rabbi Yehudah Parnes entitled 'Torah Umadda and

Freedom of Inquiry'. Starting from the supposition that being 'involved in the intellectual and cultural experience of mankind' is a positive good, one that leads to an enriched Jewishness, Parnes asks if there are any areas of enquiry which are out of bounds for the Jew. Using as his source a passage in Maimonides' *Mishneh torah*, Parnes bans free intellectual enquiry 'in areas that spark and arouse ideas which are antithetical to the tenets of our faith'. These tenets, not surprisingly, he identifies as Maimonides' Thirteen Principles. 'Torah u-Madda can only be viable', he concludes, 'if it imposes strict limits on freedom of inquiry in areas that may undermine the Thirteen Principles of Faith.'

Parnes' article sparked considerable debate in the pages of the journal, and its author was given an opportunity to rebut his critics in a subsequent issue. His second piece, published in 1990, amplifies and clarifies some of the ideas put forward in the first. Here he makes clear that, in his eyes, he has

> raised a halakhic issue essentially no different than a *she'elah* [halakhic enquiry] in *kashrut* [the laws of kosher food]. In fact, this is a *she'elah* of *kashrut* [here, legitimacy] in the sphere of intellectual activity. Consequently, this mandates a response by great *poskim* [halakhic decisors] and *morei hora'ah* [authoritative teachers] as is wont in other areas of *halakhah le-ma 'aseh* [practical halakhah].

This is as succinct a statement of the position I wish to criticize as one could wish for.

Parnes' own intellectual honesty is evidenced by his next sentence, in which he refers to one of the positions I defend in this book: 'Of course, there has been previous mention of the possibility that freedom of inquiry is not an halakhic issue.' This view had been attributed to the late Rabbi J. B. Soloveitchik by one of Parnes' critics. Parnes then goes on: 'If this is so, then it should be spelled out in the classical format of a *she'elah u-teshuvah* [halakhic enquiry and responsum].' In other words, Rabbi Parnes' last word on the issue is that the halakhic status of questions concerning matters of belief and enquiry is itself a halakhic question.

This last point smacks of an odd kind of circularity; but whether Rabbi Parnes' reasoning is circular or not is irrelevant here. What is at issue are his claims that Maimonides' Thirteen Principles constitute the tenets of Jewish faith and that the determination of 'kosher thinking' is a halakhic determination precisely parallel to the determination of whether or not a particular chicken is kosher.[7]

[7] *The Torah Umadda Journal* is edited by Rabbi J. J. Schacter and published by Yeshiva University. Parnes' articles are in the first and second volumes (1989 and 1990) of

The Illegitimacy of the Non-Orthodox

Parnes limits his discussion to permitted fields of study. In an important statement of Orthodox views concerning the illegitimacy of non-Orthodox approaches to Judaism, David Bleich applies a similar attitude and approach to the question of theological *kashrut*. 'With a sense of pain and anguish', Bleich confronts the problem of 'Orthodoxy and the Non-Orthodox: Prospects of Unity' in a volume of essays called *Orthodoxy Confronts Modernity*.[8] Building heavily upon Maimonides, Bleich maintains that certain deviations from accepted behaviour are 'repugnant and . . . odious', not because of the behaviour they entail, but because they are 'manifestation[s] of intellectual renunciation of fundamental beliefs posited by the Torah'. With respect to idolatry (the issue discussed by Maimonides in the texts quoted and analysed by Bleich), it is not the act of bowing down to idols which forces the idolater beyond the pale and out of the world to come; it is, rather, 'his denial and renunciation of the basic faith-commitments of Judaism that serve to bar such an individual's entry into the world-to-come'.

Bleich continues in his Maimonidean vein, affirming that 'all transgressions of commandments addressed to the intellect are, in this respect, the functional equivalent of idolatry'. It follows from this that 'it is necessary to us to be cognizant of this basic principle, and to be cognizant of the centrality of faith-commitments in Judaism in order to recognize that there are issues which cannot be compromised in any manner'. 'Compromise', Bleich continues,

> is entirely out of the question with regard to any of the fundamentals of our faith. It is for this reason that in seeking the unity of *Klal Yisrael* [the community of Israel], in reaching out with 'calm patience' to draw back our separated brethren with 'words of peace', one must carefully distinguish between conduct that is directed toward individual fellow Jews and conduct that is directed towards institutions, movements, or streams, lest we be drawn into a situation involving intellectual compromise or into legitimization, either actual or perceived, of alien ideology.

the journal. For an important response to Parnes see Shapiro, 'The Last Word in Jewish Theology?' With vast erudition, Shapiro documents the mixed reception accorded Maimonides' dogmas in medieval and early modern Judaism. Parnes' position, it should be noted, is considerably more open and liberal than many found in the world of contemporary Orthodoxy. See e.g. the statements of the (martyred) R. Elhanan Wasserman, cited by Solomon on p. 28 of *The Analytic Movement*.

[8] Jonathan Sacks (ed.), *Orthodoxy Confronts Modernity* (Hoboken, NJ: Ktav, 1991); Bleich's article appears on pp. 97–108. I do not know whether or not Bleich would approve of Parnes' attempt to limit freedom of enquiry. I suspect not.

Let us try to establish clearly what is being said here. Non-Orthodox interpretations of Judaism are 'alien' ideologies; those who follow them are 'separated brethren'. With two important restrictions, every effort must be made to draw these brethren away from their alien ideologies and back into the fold. These restrictions are that no act may be performed which might involve compromise on any of the intellectual commandments of Judaism, and that no act may be performed which might be perceived as granting legitimacy to the alien ideologies.

What brings Bleich to adopt this stance? He makes two crucial assumptions, or, I should say, accepts two Maimonidean teachings which lock him into his position. The first concerns the 'centrality of faith-commitments in Judaism' and the second the idea that Judaism recognizes a category of 'commandments addressed to the intellect'. If there are commandments addressed to the intellect and these concern the central faith-commitments of Judaism, then those who violate these commandments have separated themselves from the community of Israel and have adopted alien systems of thought. Compromise with such individuals or with such ideologies cannot be countenanced, since it means compromising the essential nature of true Judaism. Cooperating with their institutions, even on matters relating to the community of Israel, is forbidden, lest such cooperation be misperceived as the legitimization of such institutions. Addressing the clergy of non-Orthodox Judaisms by the title 'rabbi' is similarly problematic and holders of Bleich's position try to avoid it.

Bleich, in short, is proposing a theological litmus test to distinguish legitimate from illegitimate Jews and Judaism. As it turns out, in his hands the test is applied with sensitivity, tact, and good humour; in the hands of many others it deteriorates into heresy-hunting.

It is important to note that Bleich's argument here depends for its cogency upon an earlier discussion of his in the introduction to his anthology *With Perfect Faith* (referred to in Chapter 2 above). He there interprets Maimonides as holding that 'basic philosophical beliefs are not simply matters of intellectual curiosity but constitute a branch of *Halakhah*' (p. 2) and that matters of dogma are decided like other areas of halakhah. Bleich has recently reiterated this position. In an article published in 1996 he insists that 'Matters of belief are inherently matters of halakha. It is not at all surprising that disagreements exist with regard to substantive matters of belief, just as is the case with regard to other areas of Jewish law. Such matters are subject to the canons of halakhic decision-making no less than other questions of Jewish law.'[9]

[9] J. David Bleich, 'Reply', *Tradition*, 30 (1966), 100–2 at 101.

A number of things must be said in response to this. First, I think that Bleich here misunderstands Maimonides: basic philosophical beliefs are neither simply matters of intellectual curiosity nor a branch of halakhah. They are attempts to understand the true nature of the universe to the greatest extent possible. *Ma'aseh bereshit* equals physics; *ma'aseh merkavah* equals metaphysics; and Maimonides calls these two sciences the 'roots' (Arabic: *uṣul*) of the specific halakhot (*gufei torah*) in his commentary on Mishnah *Ḥagigah* ii. 1. These roots being either true or false absolutely, it is literally inconceivable that Maimonides could have held that their truth status depends upon rabbinic *pesak* (decision), as Bleich avers.

This leads to my second point: can we seriously credit the idea that Maimonides would have held that, for example, before he 'paskened' (decided halakhically) that Moses was superior to all the other prophets before and after him, the question was undecided in Judaism? Of course not; and the same point applies with respect to the other twelve of the Thirteen Principles.

Third, even were Bleich correct in his understanding of Maimonides, the latter's position is quite clearly an innovation in Judaism, as I have been at pains to argue in earlier chapters of this book, and it is simply incorrect to read it back into rabbinic texts.[10]

Inclusivism

Jonathan Sacks explicitly seeks to be as 'inclusive' as possible. He is interested in building bridges between Jews, in erasing boundaries to the greatest extent possible. This overall approach reflects his deeply held commitment to 'the idea of "one people" [which] forms the very core of Jewish faith in the covenant between God and a chosen nation'.[11] Sacks summarizes his position as follows:

> Inclusivism, then, uses classic halakhic strategies—variants on the themes of *minhag avoteihem beyadeihem* (habit, not belief) and *tinok shenishbah* (excusable ignorance)—to include within the covenantal community those whose beliefs and practices would, if taken at their face value, place them outside. It is an extraordinarily powerful device, capable of neutralizing the schismatic impact of almost any Jewish ideology at odds with tradition. Its method, considered as a

[10] For discussion of Maimonides on the relationship between philosophical truths and halakhah, see Kellner, 'Maimonides' Allegiances to Torah and Science', *The Torah Umadda Journal*, 7 (1997), 88–104.

[11] Sacks, *One People?*, 212.

formal halakhic device, is to isolate the liberal or secular Jew from his beliefs. The beliefs remain heretical, but those who believe them are not heretics, for they do not ultimately or culpably believe them. Liberal and secular Jews remain Jews, even though neither liberal or secular Judaism is Judaism.[12]

Sacks' position relies upon the idea that '[Orthodoxy] is a boundary, defined by halakhah and *the principles of Jewish faith.*'[13] Yet once Orthodoxy is defined in terms of principles of faith, the notion of heresy becomes operational. With all the goodwill in the world, Sacks cannot get away from that point. Nor is he unaware of it. He, too, is trapped by the language of legitimacy and illegitimacy. The furthest his basic universe of discourse allows him to go is well expressed in the following passage:

> Attaching no significance to liberal Jews' description of their own actions and intentions allows Orthodoxy to include individuals within the halakhic community while excluding their ideologies. In so doing, it bypasses the conflict between communal unity and doctrinal integrity. It is, as we have seen, a device that allows enormous inclusivity. But it does so by devaluing the legitimacy of any interpretation of Judaism that lies outside the parameters of traditional faith. It is a strategy of which non-Orthodox Jews might understandably not wish to avail themselves. Explicitly or implicitly, they will feel that it assaults their authenticity.[14]

Sacks cannot escape his Maimonidean basis, and in the final analysis adopts the position stated more bluntly by Bleich: non-Orthodox Jews and Judaism are illegitimate and inauthentic.[15] Is that the only way Orthodoxy can relate to them? Is it the best way? These questions will be taken up below in Chapter 7. Here I want to turn to a brief critique of the positions of Parnes, Bleich, and Sacks.

[12] Sacks, *One People?*, 133.

[13] Ibid. 216 (emphasis added); see also p. 218.

[14] Ibid. 252.

[15] For a position similar in its basic intent to that of Rabbi Sacks, see Norman Lamm, 'Seventy Faces', *Moment*, June 1986, pp. 23–8. Rabbi Lamm, the president of Yeshiva University and the *bête noire* of many Orthodox Jews to his 'right' (witness the discussion between him and Aaron Twersky, cited in n. 3 above), starts from the perspective that 'Orthodox rabbis consider those movements not bound by the traditional *halacha* as heretical'. But, despite that, he seeks to be as non-confrontational as possible: 'As an Orthodox Jew, I not only have no trouble in acknowledging the functional validity of non-Orthodox rabbinic leadership, but also in granting that non-Orthodox rabbis and laypeople may possess spiritual dignity.' There are, of course, limits: 'But neither functional *validity* nor spiritual *dignity* are identical with Jewish *legitimacy*.' (All these passages are from p. 24 of the article.) I would like to thank Rabbi Lamm for his kindness in providing me with copies of many of his publications on this subject.

The Three Statements: A Critique

The positions affirmed by Parnes, Bleich, and Sacks depend upon the truth of two separate claims. The first is that *emunah* in Judaism is defined in terms of the intellectual affirmation of certain claims (what Bleich calls 'faith-commitments'); the second is that the Torah commands matters of belief or knowledge. It is important to understand that the two are distinct. The Torah could teach certain claims about God, the universe, and the Jewish people, and condemn as lacking in faith those Jews who doubt or reject those claims, without there being any explicit commandments to acknowledge the truth of those claims.

The Torah, for example, teaches that God exists and is one, created the world, and revealed the Torah. Nowhere, however, does it command us to accept the truth of these claims. That is not to say that a Jew is free to accept them or reject them. It is, rather, to say that the acceptance of these claims is taken as a matter of course, not subject to explicit commandment. We could, in theory, accept the idea (nowhere in fact taught in the Torah or Talmud) that to be a *ma'amin*, a faithful person, one must affirm these (and other) Torah teachings without at the same time affirming that the acceptance of these teachings is a matter of explicit commandment. This is precisely the position of classical Judaism. In fact, in the long history of pre-modern Judaism, the first authoritative figure clearly to affirm both assertions (that Judaism taught specific theological tenets and that there were specific mitzvot, commandments, to believe them) was Maimonides.

Jews today who use Maimonides' authority to impose theological tests of legitimacy upon other Jews choose parts of Maimonides' position, not all of it, ignore the alternative attitudes of Sa'adia and Bahya (discussed in the previous chapter), and certainly ignore the fact that the position shared by Sa'adia, Bahya, and Maimonides, that the Torah has a clear-cut systematic theology, is an innovation in Judaism, with no historical or textual basis before the Middle Ages.

From a traditionalist perspective, I have no right to disagree with Maimonides on my own, as it were, and any attempt to reject one of his teachings based only on analysis of the issues would be considered illegitimate. Let me therefore remind the reader that the claim that Judaism has dogmas in the sense proposed by Maimonides was rejected by his contemporary, R. Abraham ben David of Posquières, as we saw above, while Maimonides' understanding of the nature of dogma was rejected by R. Shimon ben Tsemah Duran (1361–1444) and by R. Isaac Arama

(1420–94), among many others. The claim that Judaism has dogmas at all was rejected by Abrabanel. The claim that Judaism has dogmas and that they have halakhic standing has been ignored by almost every halakhic decisor from Maimonides' time to our own.

It is Maimonides' claim that one becomes a Jew through the unconditional acceptance of the Thirteen Principles as promulgated in the commentary on Mishnah *Sanhedrin*. Having accepted the principles, one becomes part of that 'Israel' which is considered 'all righteous'. Members of that 'Israel' are guaranteed a share in the world to come. That is the positive side of the coin; the other side is that any Jew who doubts or makes a mistake concerning the principles is excluded from *kelal yisrael* (the 'community of Israel') and loses his or her share in the world to come.

These claims are theological, not precisely halakhic. Maimonides did, in fact, accept many of the halakhic consequences of these claims. We can, however, leave that complex issue aside for the moment and focus on the theological point. Maimonides here distinguishes theological orthodoxy from halakhic obedience, making membership in the Jewish community and the enjoyment of a share in the world to come dependent on the former, not the latter. In short, it is Maimonides' claim that to be a Jew, and to get into heaven, one must minimally accept correct teachings; once one has accepted those teachings, one is a Jew and has a share in the world to come, no matter what one actually does.

Is there anyone alive today who would maintain that Judaism teaches theological orthodoxy as the fundamental criterion for being Jewish? Taking Maimonides at his word, a category of persons born as Gentiles, who become Jews by conviction but not by conversion, becomes possible. Remember that Maimonides says,

> When all these foundations are perfectly understood and believed in by a person he enters the community of Israel and one is obligated to love and pity him and to act towards him in all the ways in which the Creator has commanded that one should act towards his brother, with love and fraternity.[16]

Maimonides gives us no reason not to take him literally here. (By this I mean that the logic of his position should lead him to adopt this stand, not that he actually and self-consciously did.) But how many of our contemporaries who use the authority of Maimonides to impose theological

[16] See below, p. 151.

tests of legitimacy upon their fellow Jews would be willing to accept the consequences of his position in this matter?[17]

Thus far I have been concerned with the positive side of Maimonides' position. But there is also the negative side: the claim that rejection of the principles, or even mistakes concerning them, exclude a person from the Jewish community and from the world to come. On this understanding, remember, any person who fails to satisfy the criterion of correct 'faith-commitments' is simply not Jewish. Every single secular, Reform, Conservative, and Reconstructionst Jew is thus found not to be Jewish at all. Even ostensibly Orthodox Jews who in their heart of hearts wonder if the dead will be literally resurrected in the flesh, while still punctiliously observing every commandment, are to be excluded from the Jewish community in this world and have no share in the world to come. Similarly, Jews who address prayers to angels,[18] or who naïvely see their hasidic masters as intermediaries between themselves and God, are not really Jews and certainly have no share in the world to come.

The issue gets even more complicated, and, on many readings, the circle of acceptable Jews—of Jews *per se*— shrinks even further. Let me explain how. In 1982 I heard a lecture given by Avraham Shapiro, then a member of the Israeli Knesset, representing what was then called the Agudat Yisrael party. This was shortly after the massacres of Palestinians in the Sabra and Shatila camps, and Shapiro was arguing against the demand to institute a governmental commission of inquiry (what

[17] For a stimulating discussion of the claim that a consequence of Maimonides' position is that unconverted Gentiles might have to be considered Jews if they adopt correct theological views, see Steven Schwarzschild, 'J.-P. Sartre as Jew', *Modern Judaism*, 3 (1983), 39–73, repr. in M. Kellner (ed.), *The Pursuit of the Ideal: Jewish Writings of Steven Schwarzschild* (Albany: SUNY Press, 1990), 161–84. For an argument to the effect that Maimonides expected this state of affairs actually to obtain in the messianic era (but, *contra* Schwarzschild, not before it), see Kellner, 'A Suggestion Concerning Maimonides' Thirteen Principles and the Status of Non-Jews in the Messianic Era', in M. Ayali (ed.), *Tura: Oranim Studies in Jewish Thought—Simon Greenberg Jubilee Volume* (Heb.) (Tel Aviv: Hakibuts Hame'uḥad, 1989), 249–60.

[18] For indications of Metatron worship in rabbinic times, see BT *Ḥagigah* 15*a* and BT *Sanhedrin* 38*b*. On prayer to the (kabbalistic) *sefirot*, see Gershom Scholem, *Origins of the Kabbalah* (Princeton: Princeton University Press, 1987), 194–7. Further on this, see Moshe Idel, 'Kabbalistic Prayer in Provence' (Heb.), *Tarbits*, 62 (1993), 265–86. For citations from relevant texts which surprised me, see Daniel Abrams, 'The Boundaries of Divine Ontology: The Inclusion and Exclusion of Metatron in the Godhead', *Harvard Theological Review*, 87 (1994), 291–321, esp. 315 and 320.

ultimately became the Kahan commission). Shapiro led his listeners through the following argument:

1. Acceptance of the Oral Torah commits one to *emunat ḥakhamim* (trust and faith in Torah Sages).
2. *Emunat ḥakhamim* commits one to accept the authoritative pronouncements (*da'at torah*) of Torah Sages.
3. The Council of Torah Sages of Agudat Yisrael authoritatively expresses the opinion of the Torah (*da'at torah*) on all issues.
4. The Council of Torah Sages opposed the creation of a commission of inquiry into the massacres in Sabra and Shatila.
5. In consequence, anyone who supported the establishment of such a commission rejected the authority of the Oral Torah and was a heretic according to Maimonides.

Had Shapiro been entirely consistent, and aware of the actual teachings of Maimonides, he would have been forced to add the following phrase to the conclusion of his argument (5): 'and therefore no Jew'.

Similarly, the leaders of so-called Lithuanian ultra-Orthodoxy and of Habad hasidism would not only be able to deny the legitimacy and even sanity each of the other, as they do now; they could also deny each other the very status of being a Jew. After all, each claims to represent *da'at torah*; those who reject *da'at torah* are heretics (so Avraham Shapiro argued); according to Maimonides, heretics have no share in the world to come and are not even Jews.

In the eyes of most contemporary Jews, even the most 'ultra-Orthodox', this argument is a *reductio ad absurdum* of the claim that we must adopt Maimonides' views concerning dogma and the status of Jews who deny or question the Thirteen Principles.

Let us recall that for Maimonides *shegagah*, inadvertence, is no defence in matters of dogma. We have seen that Maimonides is himself not entirely consistent on this matter, but here let us restrict ourselves to a consideration of what Maimonides says, not what he does. If we take Maimonides at his word (and those who follow him on the issues under discussion have no reason and, in their eyes, no right not to), then any Jew who makes a mistake about any one of the Thirteen Principles excludes her- or himself from the Jewish people and loses her or his share in the world to come.

This judgement rules out all of the various moves on the part of contemporary halakhic authorities who want to adopt Maimonides' conception of Judaism as a religion defined by a body of dogma while holding fast to traditional Jewish conceptions concerning the unity of the Jewish people, not to mention the exculpatory character of *shegagah*. Those who deny the basic 'faith-commitments' of Judaism (in Bleich's words) are 'straying brethren' but are still brethren, because they are *tinokot shenishbu* (children taken into captivity and thus not trained in the ways and beliefs of Judaism) or *anusim*, 'forced' to abandon traditional Judaism by the tribulations and dislocations of the modern era. (Maimonides' own discussion of this issue was taken up in the last section of Chapter 5.)

I do not mean to criticize these attempts to hold fast to Maimonidean orthodoxy while not accepting its more extreme consequences. I simply want to show that the position is inconsistent: a true Maimonidean is forced to admit that even sweet-tempered, well-intentioned, Jewishly committed Reform and Conservative Jews are heretics and have no share in the world to come. It should also be remembered that on Maimonides' account, fervently Orthodox Jews who are confused about the nature of God's incorporeality, or who believe that Joshua wrote the last few verses of Deuteronomy,[19] or who pray to the angel Metatron, or who use photographs of great rabbis as good-luck charms, are all heretics and have no share in the world to come. A heretic is a heretic is a heretic, and heretics have no share in the world to come. It is as simple as that.

This point must be emphasized. As argued above in connection with the Karaites, Maimonides does *not* apply the category of *tinokot shenishbu* ('children carried off by heathens', i.e. Jews who cannot be expected to know of their halakhic obligations—a category to which we shall return in the next chapter) to heretics, i.e. people who deny, doubt, question, or are ignorant of at least the first five principles of faith. For a Maimonidean this is not an available escape clause.

Many contemporary Conservative and Reform Jews, probably many secular Jews, and maybe even some followers of Rabbi Mordecai Kaplan (1881–1983), the founder of Reconstructionism, accept the first five of Maimonides' principles. From an Orthodox perspective, the major prob-

[19] It turns out that there are not a few kabbalists who deny divine authorship of the Book of Deuteronomy altogether, attributing the book to Moses, not to God. This is a clear violation of Maimonides' eighth principle. Despite this, I know of no one who has ever been labelled a heretic for holding this position. For details, see Yaakov Elman, 'The Book of Deuteronomy as Revelation: Nahmanides and Abrabanel', in Elman and Jeffrey Gurock (eds.), *Hazon Nahum: Studies Presented to Norman Lamm* (New York: Yeshiva University Press, 1997), 229–50.

lems relate to the other principles, dealing with revelation and with reward and punishment. It is with respect to these principles, rarely with respect to the first five, that tests of theological legitimacy are usually applied. It is ironic that today's heresy-hunters, not a few of whom could not themselves pass the actual Maimonidean test of knowing, not just believing, God's existence, unity, and incorporeality, use his authority to exclude from the Jewish community and from the world to come individuals for whom Maimonides himself may have had greater tolerance.

In sum, Maimonides was a Maimonidean with respect to the question of dogma, but not the sort of Maimonidean many of his present-day supporters think that he was. Maimonides was a Maimonidean because he truly accepted and applied the theory of human nature which underlay his system of dogma. I would venture to say that very few of the people who today use his system of dogma to exclude heterodox Jews from the community of Israel and from the world to come are even aware of the philosophical foundation of that system. Were they to become aware of it, they would most likely be horrified: for on that theory, many of them would themselves be excluded from the world to come.

Maimonides' position negates any tendencies in Judaism towards nationalist triumphalism or downright racism. That is good. Unfortunately, Maimonides' position also enables, in fact demands, theological tests for Jewish legitimacy. Searching out and condemning heretics (to exclusion from the community, not to the stake!) becomes a possibility. That is bad. In the next chapter I will sketch out a vision of Judaism which remains true to the biblical and rabbinic understanding of *emunah* (which demands strict halakhic obedience coupled with a relatively *laissez-faire* approach to theology) and at the same time seeks to take advantage of the positive aspects of Maimonides' emphasis on intellectualism.

Why has Maimonides' Position become Dominant?

Before turning to that vision, however, I think I owe my readers an explanation of why Orthodoxy in the modern world has chosen to define itself so emphatically in Maimonidean, dogmatic terms. This explanation is necessary as I have consistently argued here that classical Judaism is not Maimonidean in this sense and that the Jewish tradition did not have to (and today should not) define itself in that fashion. If it is true that Judaism was not always like this, what happened to make it so?

One could, I am sure, look for answers to this question in broader sociological discussions concerning, for example, the rise of fundamentalism in the modern world,[20] or the need members of any religion feel to find unimpeachable sources of authority in the face of the attacks of modernity (witness the way in which papal infallibility became a dogma of the Catholic Church); one could also use psychology to examine whether there is a connection between the rise of dogmatic Orthodoxy in Judaism and Jewish reactions to the Holocaust; or, in a polemical vein, one could (mistakenly in my view) see this phenomenon as an example of the sheer momentum of halakhah working itself into an ever narrower corner.

To my mind, however, it is not necessary to go so far afield in search of an explanation. The answer to our problem lies in the dynamics of Jewish history. I noted above that Maimonides' innovation was largely ignored in the first centuries after his death. This is true for the two centuries after the publication of the Thirteen Principles in the commentary on the Mishnah, but not for the century beginning with the murderous anti-Jewish riots of 1391. As I have described in greater detail elsewhere, the Jews of Iberia were challenged by the contemporary Church to defend Judaism.[21] The Church set the parameters for the debate; the presentation of Christianity in dogmatic terms made it necessary for the Jews to reply in kind.

Furthermore, the Jews who were forced to defend their ancestral faith were the religious leaders of their communities, the communal rabbis and heads of rabbinical academies. Their dogmatic presentations of Judaism (pre-eminently but by no means only R. Joseph Albo's *Sefer ha'ikarim*) were thus written by and for religious Jews, not by and for philosophers. These books became very popular and quickly achieved a level of acceptance and authority never reached by the more straightforwardly philosophical works written by Jewish thinkers in the generations immediately after the death of Maimonides. Thus the dogmatization, theologification, Maimonidesification of Judaism is not a twentieth-century phenomenon, but a fifteenth-century one. In a world in which almost all Jews accepted the authority of tradition, it really made relatively little difference. Once the traditional world began

[20] For discussions of fundamentalism in the modern world in general, and the Jewish world in particular, see Martin Marty and R. Scott Appleby (eds.), *The Fundamentalism Project*, 5 vols. (Chicago: University of Chicago Press, 1991–5).

[21] For the rise of Jewish dogmatics in the fifteenth century, see Kellner, *Dogma*, 80–3, 207–12.

to break down in the face of modernity, defenders of tradition used the tools ready to hand in their attempts to stem the tide of change. One of these tools was dogma.

There is a second point which must be raised here. Maimonides achieved a level of personal authority in Judaism that has never been equalled since (and, the first Moses aside, is maybe even unequalled before).[22] His fellow medievals were, it is true, less awed by him than were later generations;[23] but by the close of the Jewish middle ages in 1789 Maimonides had become all but unassailable. This is apparent from the way in which almost every Jew today, from the Rabbi of Leibowitz to the Rabbi of Lubavitch, claims to represent the true teachings of Maimonides.[24] Further evidence is provided by David Bleich's introduction to his anthology, *With Perfect Faith*, discussed in Chapter 2 above. Finding a dogmatic, theological reading of Judaism in Maimonides, Bleich, apparently unwilling or unable to accept that Maimonides would have introduced such a dramatic innovation into Judaism, is forced to read Maimonides back into earlier Jewish texts. One could hardly find a stronger indication of Maimonides' stature: in order to defend his *kashrut*, so to speak, it is necessary to read his ideas into Bible and Talmud, in effect rewriting these texts in a Maimonidean vein.

I suspect that there is another issue at work here as well, which further helps us to understand Bleich in particular and the inability

[22] Isadore Twersky has written widely on the reception of Maimonides by his contemporaries and near-contemporaries. See e.g. his *Introduction to the Code of Maimonides*, 515–37, and, for references to other literature, Kellner, 'Reading Rambam'. Bernard Septimus refers to the 'heroic' conception of Maimonides regnant in the years following his death. See his *Hispano-Jewish Culture in Transition*, 48, 63, 99–100. With respect to a later period, Robert Bonfil, *Rabbis and Jewish Communities in Renaissance Italy* (Oxford: Oxford University Press, 1990), speaks of 'the aura of sanctity which surrounded the Maimonidean corpus' (p. 294). For dramatic expressions of Maimonides veneration, see Ya'akov Spiegel, 'Elliptical Language among the Tannaim and *Pshat* and *Drash* in the Mishnah' (Heb.), *Asufot*, 4 (1990), 9–26 at 25.

[23] Maimonides' writings stimulated considerable debate in the generations immediately after his own. For a recent discussion, with extensive references to the scholarly literature, see Ram Ben-Shalom, 'Communication and Propaganda between Provence and Spain: The Controversy over Extreme Allegorization', in Sophia Menache (ed.), *Communication in the Jewish Diaspora: The Pre-modern World* (Leiden: Brill, 1966), 171–226.

[24] The 'Rabbi of Leibowitz' is a facetious reference to Yeshayahu Leibowitz, some of whose idiosyncratic views on Maimonides may be found in his *Judaism, Human Values, and the Jewish State* (Cambridge, Mass.: Harvard University Press, 1992). The 'Rabbi of Lubavitch' refers to Rabbi Menachem Mendel Schneersohn (1902–94), charismatic leader of the Habad/Lubavitch hasidim.

of today's Orthodox Jews in general to do what almost all medieval authorities did, and politely ignore Maimonides' innovation. This is the way in which the doctrine of 'the decline of the generations' has taken such hold in contemporary Orthodoxy.[25]

It is generally accepted in the contemporary Orthodox world that the generations are in decline: i.e. that each successive generation is intellectually, spiritually, and morally inferior to preceding generations. We dwarves have no right to criticize or disagree with the giants who preceded us, and we don't even see further than they did when perched on their shoulders. It would be hard enough even to appear to disagree with Maimonides, given his heroic stature, even without the doctrine of the decline of the generations; against the background of that doctrine (almost universally accepted in contemporary Orthodoxy as normative, authoritative, and binding), it is almost impossible. Thus, if Maimonides says that Judaism has dogmas and those who reject them are heretics, then Judaism has dogmas and those who reject them are heretics. Thus extra force is lent to what I have called the theologification of contemporary Orthodoxy.

Another factor which may have contributed to the current situation is the influence of the German Orthodox leader Rabbi Samson Raphael Hirsch (1808–88). Hirsch insisted on a policy of *Austritt* or 'separation' from non-Orthodox Jewish institutions in the Frankfurt of his day. Hirsch was, moreover, for all his lack of enthusiasm for Maimonides, a staunch defender of orthodoxy, who went so far as to claim that Orthodox and Reform Jews did not share the same religion. Hirsch's policies on separation and on the nature of religious orthodoxy (but not other policies he espoused—see below) were taken as normative for subsequent generations; they thus helped frame contemporary Orthodox responses to Conservative and Reform Judaism. It is interesting that while in his own day Hirsch's policy of separation from the non-Orthodox was vehemently debated within German Orthodoxy, it none the less became 'official' Orthodox policy in our day. His call for some sort of melding between Jewish and general culture ('Torah and *derekh erets*') and the creation of a new Jewish personality reflecting that meld, '*mensch-Jisroel*', policies which generated much less controversy in his own day, survive today in the circles associated with Yeshiva University, but have been interpreted as time-bound and no longer normative by

[25] On the 'decline of the generations', see Kellner, *Maimonides on the 'Decline of the Generations'*.

other sectors of Orthodoxy.[26] Thus, since Orthodoxy picks and chooses among Hirsch's teachings, his teachings alone are not a sufficient explanation for the contemporary situation.[27]

The Maimonidean Bind

Maimonides' intellectualist perception of the nature of religious faith forced him to espouse a stance based on strict dichotomies, opposing in and out, saved and damned, believer and heretic. Such a stance leaves no room for inadvertence, for *shegagah*. The combination of his position with the separate and independent claim that matters of dogma were matters of halakhah, that theology is normative and actionable, yields a Judaism which must condemn theological deviations as heresy (an absolute innovation in Judaism, as was argued above in Chapter 2) or come up with excuses for not so doing (which will be discussed in the next chapter).

It is the Maimonidean framework which forces Orthodox Jews to relate to non-Orthodox streams of Judaism not as innocently mistaken, but as heretical, deviant, illegitimate, lacking in (Jewish) spiritual dignity. This framework forces Jews like Parnes to seek to find ways to limit what other Jews may study; it further forces Jews like Bleich and Sacks to turn intellectual cartwheels so as to make possible dignified and respectful intercourse with non-Orthodox colleagues. (Of course, many Orthodox rabbis today would insist that the term 'colleague' here is a misnomer—how can a heretic be a colleague?)

Judaism did not have to take this turn. But when modernity burst upon the Jewish world, the leaders of what came to be called Orthodoxy sought tools with which to strengthen the bulwarks of tradition, and found Maimonides' principles of faith ready to hand.

[26] For a recent refutation of this misrepresentation of Hirsch's views, see Shnayer Z. Leiman, 'Rabbinic Openness to General Culture in the Early Modern Period in Western and Central Europe', in Jacob J. Schacter (ed.), *Judaism's Encounter with Other Cultures: Rejection or Integration?* (Northvale, NJ: Jason Aronson, 1997), 143–216 at 194–7.

[27] With respect to the Hirschian policy of *Austritt*, see Mordechai Breuer, *Modernity within Tradition: The Social History of Orthodox Jewry in Imperial Germany* (New York: Columbia University Press, 1992); Robert Liberles, *Religious Conflict in Social Context: The Resurgence of Orthodox Judaism in Frankfurt am Main, 1838–1877* (Westport, Conn.: Greenwood, 1985). For Hirsch's battles with other Orthodox rabbis (pre-eminently Rabbi Seligman Baer Bamberger, the celebrated 'Wurzburger Rav'), see Breuer, *Modernity within Tradition*, 58, and Liberles, *Religious Conflict*, 211–25. On Orthodox and Reform Jews not sharing the same religion, see Breuer, *Modernity within Tradition*, 296, and Liberles, *Religious Conflict*, 208.

In its response to the challenges of the modern world contemporary Orthodoxy has, I fear, missed the boat. It seems clear to me that the strategies adopted by its leadership have met with only questionable success. Non-Orthodox Judaisms have not disappeared, nor is there any apparent likelihood of their doing so. Standard Orthodox apologetics has it that Conservative and Reform Judaism facilitate assimilation, giving excuses for people too lazy or too weak to fulfil all the commandments. So far as I can see, this claim is downright wrong-headed. Non-Orthodox versions of Judaism surely stand in the breach against assimilation, rather than facilitating it. Moreover, what I take to be Orthodoxy's 'hard line' has made it easier for non-Orthodox versions of Judaism to move further away from the tradition, rather than closer to it. My opinion is no more provable than the opposite view: but nor is it any more easily dismissed. As I will urge in the next chapter, labelling others as heretics or even as *tinokot shenishbu*, accomplishes nothing positive; it just makes it harder to attract those others to our understanding of the Torah. And it is no criticism of Maimonides to urge, as I do, that the tools he fashioned for Jewry in twelfth-century Egypt have not proved themselves adequate for the needs of our own age.

SEVEN

How to Live with Other Jews

In this chapter I want to sketch a way in which Orthodox Jews can relate to non-Orthodox Jews and their understandings of Judaism which avoids the language of 'legitimate vs. heretical' without at the same time adopting a pluralist position which sees all (or almost all) expressions of Judaism as equally acceptable. Labelling non-Orthodox Jews and interpretations of Judaism as heretical is too exclusive, while true pluralism is too inclusive. Is there some middle ground which will allow me, as an Orthodox Jew, to eat my cake of Jewish unity while still having the cake of adherence to the doctrine according to which the Torah was given in its entirety to Moses by God on Sinai? In other words, can I arrive at a position of tolerant respect for non-Orthodox Jews and Judaisms without being forced to adopt a position of relativistic approval of them? I think that I can.

Asking the Right Question

In brief, I want to show that one can defend the essential elements of what is now called Orthodox Judaism (the expression of *emunah* in God through obedience to the commandments) without being forced to read out of the community as heretics Jews who question, reject, or are simply unaware of certain elements of Jewish theology. My approach is actually traditional, even though it will probably be seen as radical by those whose thinking has been conditioned by what might be called the 'pseudo-Maimonideanism' of post-Haskalah Orthodoxy.

I should like to make it very clear here that I am urging neither tolerance nor pluralism. By 'pluralism' I mean a view which considers the relevant alternatives equally correct, equally acceptable. In the present context that would mean a position which holds Orthodoxy, Conservatism, and Reform to be equally valid, equally legitimate expressions of Judaism, each with its own unique and important value. By 'tolerance' I mean a view which basically does not recognize the value, legitimacy, and validity of the opposed opinions, but is willing to tolerate or 'suffer' them for a variety of possible reasons. As I often tell students who disagree with me, 'Israel is a democracy; you have the right to be wrong.' That is an expression of tolerance, not of pluralism.[1]

Now, my position in this book is certainly not pluralist: I do not see Orthodoxy, Conservatism, and Reform as equally valid, equally correct expressions of Judaism in our age.[2] But my position is more than simple tolerance, since I am not at all interested in seeking out the 'tolerable' mistakes of non-Orthodox Jews, in order to show how liberal and long-suffering I am in being willing to put up with these mistakes. My whole point in this venture is to urge that pluralism and tolerance are answers to the wrong question—the Maimonidean question. If we frame our questions differently, we will not be forced to choose between tolerance and pluralism (not to mention what appears to be the most popular choice these days, in all camps—intolerance). The question we should be asking is: 'Now that we are all Jews, what can we do together to enhance further the future of the Jewish people?'

I will begin from the assumption that Jews are one community, one family, divided by disputes. A healthy family can survive disputes: the areas of disagreement are not glossed over, they are acknowledged, but areas of agreement, of shared concern, shared past, shared future, are emphasized, and arenas are sought in which all can work together. God made a covenant with the Jewish people. That people has been traditionally defined as *kelal yisrael*. I want to urge that we start with that notion of Israel as basic. Let us move the discussion of Jewish authenticity from the realm of dogma, where Maimonides pushed it,

[1] The term 'pluralism' is often used to mean simply an acknowledgement of diversity. But 'pluralism' is a value term, 'diversity' a description of a state of affairs. A truly pluralist approach insists that each stream of Judaism is equally legitimate, equally normative, equally authoritative, equally the correct manifestation of God's Torah in today's world.

[2] Spokespersons for Conservative, Reform, and Reconstructionist Judaism often maintain that their movements are pluralist while Orthodoxy is not. I do not think that is true: most Conservative and Reform rabbis reject as illegitimate the same-sex marriages celebrated by some Reconstructionist rabbis; most Conservative, Reform, and Reconstructionist rabbis reject as illegitimate the intermarriages solemnized by some of their colleagues. Few Conservative rabbis recognize the authenticity and legitimacy of the Reform decision in favour of patrilinear descent; and few, if any, non-Orthodox rabbis accept as legitimate the Orthodox 'oppression' of women (through the laws of *agunah*) or of bastards (through the laws of *mamzer*). Adherence to these laws is usually rejected as immoral, not as 'acceptable for you but not for me'. For a leader of Conservative Judaism who adopts a clearly 'non-pluralist' approach to Reform and Reconstructionist Judaism, see the statement by the provost of the (Conservative) Jewish Theological Seminary of America, Professor Jack Wertheimer: 'Judaism without Limits', *Commentary*, July 1997, pp. 24–7.

back to the realm of public behaviour, where it traditionally belongs. In effect, I am calling for an inversion of the later Haskalah dictum, urging one to be a Jew in the street and, if unavoidable, an *epikoros* at home.[3]

More precisely, the position I am urging calls for us to worry less about determining whether or not our fellow Jews are heretical, and more about working with them on matters of mutual concern and encouraging them to behave more in accordance with traditional norms. In other words, I think we should let God worry about who the 'kosher' Jews are, and who gets into heaven, while we worry about trying to get Jews to become more Jewish here in this world.

So Who or What is a Jew Anyway?

Maimonides defines Jews, ultimately, as persons who hold certain clearly defined doctrines. In theological terms, he turns Judaism into what may be called a 'church of true believers'.[4] If we reject that view, what alternatives remain? The question is of considerable importance to me, for reasons I explained in the introduction to this book. As noted there, I do not want to go from the frying pan of a theological definition of Judaism into the fire of an essentialist definition of Judaism; nor am I willing to turn allegiance to the Torah into a sentimentalized religious nationalism.

[3] The expression *heyeh adam betsetekha viyehudi be'ohalekha* (which may be paraphrased as 'behave like a human being when on the street, like a Jew when in your tent') was a standard phrase of the later Haskalah, and comes from the poem *Hakitsah ami* by Judah Leib Gordon (1830–92). The 'father of the Haskalah', Moses Mendelssohn (1729–86) sought to move Judaism from the public to the private domain. That is certainly not what I am trying to do here. I am, however, trying to move the issue of theological orthodoxy from the public to the private realm. I hope that none of my readers will confuse my position more broadly with that of Mendelssohn. He sought to turn Judaism into a 'religion of reason' (basically, the affirmation of the existence of one God who guarantees human immortality and demands moral behaviour from human beings) with a revealed law. In his hands, Judaism becomes 'orthopraxy'. I certainly do not deny that the Torah teaches truths about God, the universe, and our place in that universe; my argument concerns the Jewish status of those truths. It is expected that Jews will accept them; traditionally, no great store is set by defining them in a carefully worked out and systematic fashion.

[4] In emphasizing the dogmatic character of Judaism, Maimonides divided Jews into two classes, the saved and the damned. The very fact that his approach can be so neatly summarized in terms borrowed directly from Christian theology shows how unusual it is in the context of classical Judaism. In his book *One People?* Rabbi Jonathan Sacks points out that this 'fundamental dualism between the saved and the condemned' (p. 206) is typical of apocalyptic writings, gnosticism, and the writings of the Qumran community and of Paul the Apostle, but not typical of classical Judaism.

Nor, in rejecting Maimonides' dogmatic version of Judaism, do I wish at the same time to reject the (in Maimonides' eyes) allied claims that Judaism teaches truth and that there is one absolute truth—for these are claims that I am in no way willing to give up.

The solution to my problem is in fact ridiculously simple. Maimonides argued that the Jews became the Jews by accepting the Torah; but he defined the Torah in terms of its core metaphysical teachings. Halevi argued that the Jews were given the Torah because they were already the Jews, the only people capable of receiving the Torah and worthy of it. I propose instead to define Jews as the halakhah does: as persons born Jewish (i.e. born to a Jewish mother) or converted to Judaism. In a very real sense, Halevi accepts only the first half of that formula, Maimonides only the second half.

For Halevi, persons converted to Judaism are not fully Jewish, for they could not possibly have inherited the *inyan ha'elohi*, that special characteristic which sets Jews apart from non-Jews in an essential fashion. For Maimonides, persons born to a Jewish mother are not thereby truly Jewish until they consciously accept the essential doctrines taught by Judaism. This acceptance, it should be remembered, constitutes the core of conversion to Judaism for Maimonides.[5]

Accepting the halakhic definition of what it is that makes a person a Jew has a number of immediate advantages. The first advantage is that it is the halakhic definition. In principle, that, of course (at least in my eyes), gives it immediate legitimacy. In polemical terms, it puts Maimonides and Halevi (and their present-day followers) on the defensive: it is they who have to defend their apparent divergence from the halakhic standard; I, on the other hand, do not have to defend my allegiance to it. Second, the halakhic definition disallows Halevi's essentialist reading of what it is that constitutes a Jew, since it allows for true and complete conversion to Judaism. Third, the halakhic definition disallows Maimonides' theological reading of what it is that constitutes a Jew, since it counts as Jews those persons born to Jewish mothers who are unaware of the theological teachings of the Torah, mistaken about them, or even unwilling to accept them.

[5] For an important discussion of Judah Halevi's attitude towards proselytes, see Daniel J. Lasker, 'Proselyte Judaism, Christianity, and Islam in the Thought of Judah Halevi', *Jewish Quarterly Review*, 81 (1990), 75–91. Halevi's views on proselytes ought to be contrasted with those of Maimonides, on which see Kellner, *Maimonides on Judaism*, 49–57. See there, 85 ff., for proof of my claim that according to Maimonides even individuals born as Jews have, in effect, to 'convert' in order actually to be Jews in the full sense of the term.

Non-Orthodox Jews and Judaisms

Defining Jews as persons considered Jewish by halakhah does not mean that all Jews are good Jews. It certainly does not commit me to accepting every interpretation of Judaism put forward by sincere and concerned Jews. On the contrary, it puts halakhah at the centre of Jewishness, where it belongs, and commits me to encourage myself and other Jews to strive for greater obedience to the dictates of halakhah. It does, however, allow me to reject the Maimonidean language of legitimacy vs. heresy, of in vs. out, of the saved vs. the damned. Changes of language both reflect and bring about changes in attitude. Adopting the halakhic approach allows me to tear down the barriers built between Jew and Jew. It allows me to stop asking 'does so and so believe the right thing?' and encourages me, instead, to ask 'is so and so doing the right thing?' It moves mitzvot (commandments) to the centre of the stage, forcing us to ask 'how many mitzvot does so and so observe?', not 'which of Maimonides' Thirteen Principles does so and so correctly accept?'

This distinction is of cardinal importance. No one, not even Moses, has properly observed all 613 commandments. All Jews, therefore, are on the same continuum, from those who obey more to those who obey fewer. There is no absolute 'in' or 'out' here, saved or damned, orthodox or heretical. Rather, the question becomes: where on the continuum does one stand, and in which direction is one going?[6]

Furthermore, by emphasizing behaviour, and de-emphasizing theology, we can allow ourselves to examine the contributions that individuals make, and ignore the reasons behind those contributions. In doing so, we are on firm traditional footing. The Jerusalem Talmud has God say, 'Would that they abandon Me and observe My Torah—the light within it would return them to the good.'[7] Similarly, in the Babylonian Talmud we find the statement, 'Let a man always concern himself with Torah and commandments even not for their own sake, since performance not for

[6] With respect to the issue of the observance of all the commandments it is worth recalling a text from BT *Makot* 23*b*–24*a* cited in Chapter 2 above:

Amos came and reduced them to one, as it is said: 'For thus saith the Lord unto the house of Israel, Seek ye Me and live.' At this R. Naḥman ben Isaac demurred, saying [Might it not be taken as meaning,] Seek Me by observing the whole Torah and live? But it is Habakkuk who came and based them all on one, as it is said, 'But the righteous shall live by his faith.' Rabbi Nahman ben Isaac was concerned lest it be thought that Jews were required to observe all 613 commandments perfectly to be considered properly Jewish. This mistake is based upon the misconception of Judaism as an 'in vs. out', 'all or nothing', 'saved vs. damned' religion.

[7] JT *Ḥagigah* i. 7.

its own sake will lead to performance for its own sake.'[8] We can thus ask, does a particular individual, institution, or movement behave in such a fashion as to move Jews away from assimilation and in the direction of greater fidelity to the Torah or not? If the answer is yes, we can applaud that individual, institution, or movement, without agreeing with her/his/its theological stance.

There is a further advantage to the approach urged here. As we have seen above, once one accepts the basic Maimonidean orientation, which defines Judaism first and foremost in terms of dogmas, one is locked into seeing those who deny (or, for Maimonides, even question or simply make honest mistakes about) dogma as heretics. Very few rabbinic authorities want to count the vast majority of Jews alive today as heretics. They therefore adopt the fiction of calling these people *anusim* or *tinokot shenishbu*. One is an *anus* (literally, 'coerced' or 'compelled') when one is compelled to violate the law. One is a *tinok shenishbah* when one violates the law because one knows no better. In order to apply the category of *anus* we must say something to the effect that contemporary Jews would, other things being equal, choose to obey the Torah. What keeps them from doing it? The claim is made that the modern world is so dominant and so attractive that one is literally compelled to abandon the life of Torah. In the words of Rabbi Abraham Isaac Hakohen Kook, Jews today who do not live according to the Torah are like 'children who have been turned from Torah ways and the faith by the raging currents of the time . . . They are coerced in every sense of the word.'[9]

Those raised in a cultural environment alien to the values and norms of (Orthodox) Judaism are additionally seen as being almost literally like children taken captive by heathens.[10] They can hardly be expected to believe in the dogmas of Judaism, and obey the commandments, when they barely know of their existence. Even in circumstances where they are taught about Judaism, their exposure to the dogmas and command-

[8] BT *Pesaḥim* 50*b*. The Hebrew there reads: *Le'olam ya'asok adam betorah umitsvot, af al pi shelo lishmah, shemitokh lo lishmah, ba lishmah.*

[9] The quotation from Rabbi Kook is taken from *Responsa* (Heb.) (Jerusalem: Mosad Harav Kook, 1962), 1, 170–1. For an English translation see Tzvi Feldman, *Rav A. Y. Kook: Selected Letters* (Ma'aleh Adumim: Ma'aliyot, 1986), 51–4. My citation is taken from Judith Bleich, 'Rabbinic Responses to Nonobservance', 114–15.

[10] For sources on calling contemporary non-Orthodox Jews 'babes captured by heathens', see Sacks, *One People?*, 125–8; Chinitz, 'Reb Moshe and the Conservatives'; Yehudah Levi, *Facing Contemporary Challenges* (Heb.) (Jerusalem: Olam Hasefer Hatorani, 1993), 71–81. My thanks to my son, Avinoam Kellner, for drawing this last passage to my attention.

ments is such as almost to guarantee that they will not relate to them in a proper (Orthodox) manner. The application of this category in the modern world derives from the writings of Rabbi Abraham Isaiah Karelitz, the Hazon Ish—although he was not the first to use it in this fashion in the modern era.[11]

Without any significant exceptions that I have been able to find, every single Orthodox spokesperson (from all elements in Orthodoxy, with the obvious exception of Satmar hasidim, who draw the circle of who is truly Jewish very narrowly) who has addressed the issue has adopted the Hazon Ish's solution to the problem of living with heretics. (For reasons which need not detain us here, the Hazon Ish is cited much more frequently than Rabbi Kook.) This proposed solution distinguishes between the sinner (who can be exculpated on the grounds of compulsion and having been captured by heathens) and his or her sin (which cannot be forgiven under any circumstances).[12]

What is wrong with this approach? From my perspective, four things: it is unnecessary; it is a fiction; it is unbearably patronizing; and it is counter-productive.[13]

[11] On this point see Samuel Morell, 'The Halachic Status of Non-Halachic Jews', *Judaism*, 18 (1969), 448–57. In his glosses on *Shulḥan arukh, Yoreh de'ah* ii. 16 and ii. 28, the Hazon Ish argues that in our day and age, since we cannot properly rebuke our fellow Jews, and since divine providence is no longer clearly operative in the world, non-observant Jews may be considered as *tinokot she nishbu*, their heresy a matter of compulsion (*ones*) and not choice. The Maimonidean context of his discussion is clearly evident throughout and is reflected in his choice of terms and phrases, much of it drawn directly from Maimonides. This is further indicated by the Hazon Ish's parallel discussion in his commentary on Maimonides' 'Laws of Character Traits', ii. 3. See A. L. Karelitz, *The Hazon Ish on the Yoreh De'ah* (Heb.) (Benei Berak: Greenman, 1973); idem, *The Hazon Ish on Maimonides* (Heb.) (Benei Berak: n.p., 1980).

[12] In the words of R. Meir's wife Beruriah, as used by J. Immanuel Schochet, 'Let Sins be Consumed and Not Sinners', *Tradition*, 16 (1977), 41–61). Other articles which rely upon the Hazon Ish include Shlomo Riskin, 'Orthodoxy and Her Alleged Heretics', *Tradition*, 15 (1976), 34–44; Grunblatt, 'Confronting Disbelievers'; Alan J. Yuter, 'Is Reform Judaism a Movement, a Sect, or a Heresy?', *Tradition*, 24 (1989), 87–98; and a major statement by Norman Lamm, 'Loving and Hating Jews as Halakhic Categories'. On Lamm in particular, see Elliot N. Dorff, 'Pluralism: Models for the Conservative Movement', *Conservative Judaism*, 48 (1995), 21–35. Dorff cites and discusses Lamm's untitled presentation in *Materials from the Critical Issues Conference: Will There be One Jewish People by the Year 2000?* (New York: CLAL, 1986).

[13] I should like to point out that the Hazon Ish's position is problematic *in its own terms*. It is Maimonides who decided that we 'lower and do not raise' (i.e. kill) heretics (after proper rebuke but without benefit of trial—for sources see Kellner, *Maimonides on Judaism*, 136 n. 13). But 'proper rebuke' (a technical term) was no more possible in his day

This approach is unnecessary because it is adopted only to avoid excluding masses of Jews from the community as heretics, with all the extreme penalties and disabilities attached to that status. If we give up the whole approach of heresy, however, this corrective is no longer necessary.

Calling a well-educated non-Orthodox rabbi, or a lay graduate of some of the finer educational programmes in the non-Orthodox world, a *tinok shenishbah* is clearly a fiction. These people know very well what they are rejecting. All legal systems know of legal fictions; in Judaism commercial life would be impossible without the legal fictions called *prozbul* and *heter iska*.[14] These are fairly arcane examples; but most Jews are aware of the custom of 'selling' one's *ḥamets* (leavened food products) before Passover. So why not adopt one more fiction, that of calling the non-Orthodox *tinokot shenishbu*, if that allows us to have a certain level of dealings with them, and allows us to pursue certain crucial projects (such as support for Israel) together?

There are a number of points to be made here. In the first place, legal fictions are, and should be, used only when absolutely necessary. To a certain extent they engender a sense of bluff and hence discomfort. Building one's communal life on a fiction, even a legal fiction, is to build that life on very shaky foundations. They should therefore be used only when essential, and then only sparingly.

Secondly, a legal fiction is one thing, a theological fiction is another. Legal systems, whether divine or human, are constructs of one sort or another and therefore can allow for inconsistencies, loopholes, fictions. Theology, on the other hand, is meant to be a matter of truth and falsehood. A 'theological fiction' is, in effect, a theological falsehood, which should be a contradiction in terms.

Further, theology, especially Maimonidean theology, is very much an 'in vs. out' affair and clear lines are meant to be drawn between those who are in and those who are out. If we say that Conservative Jews are babes stolen by heathens, why not extend the same loophole to include Jews for

than in ours, and divine providence was certainly no more evident then than now. So why are today's heretics compelled and babes captured by heathens while those in Maimoides' time were not? On the notion of 'rebuke' (*tokheḥah*) referred to here, and on the impossibility of actual 'rebuke' in the post-talmudic era, see Yehudah Amital, 'Rebuking a Fellow Jew: Theory and Practice', in Jacob J. Schacter (ed.), *Jewish Tradition and the Nontraditional Jew* (Northvale, NJ: Jason Aronson, 1992), 119–38. For bibliography on the subject see ibid. 208–9.

[14] For explanations of these terms, see the Glossary.

Jesus? Abrabanel raised this point explicitly in the fifteenth century in a critique of earlier attempts to allow for a measure of inadvertence with respect to heresy: if some mistakes are allowed, why not others? Responding to R. Abraham ben David's defence of the Jew who mistakenly attributes corporeality to God, Abrabanel wrote:

> But upon examination this position may be seen to be clearly false, for according to it, [even] one who unintentionally denies every principle will acquire [a portion in] the world to come. Thus, the belief of the Christians—who took the words of Torah and prophecy literally, and believed their meaning to be as they understood it—would not deprive them of the true felicity and we may not say that they are heretics and sectarians. It would be possible, according to this, to find a man who does not believe in any of the principles or beliefs of Torah and yet who would not be called a sectarian or heretic if he were brought to this blind foolishness by his failure to understand the meaning of the Torah.[15]

Abrabanel is demanding consistent application of Maimonides' doctrine of theological orthodoxy. The same demand for consistency, it seems to me, ought to be made of those contemporary authorities who are willing to apply the *tinok shenishbah* label to some forms of heterodoxy but not others.

Most if not all of us have had the experience of being approached by a proselytizer (Mormon, Seventh-Day Adventist, Witness, or Habad hasid) with the request that we do this, that, or the other with or for him. Invariably, these requests are accompanied by a smile and, whatever our response, we are met with consideration and understanding. Many of my readers will, I suspect, recognize as well my feeling that this very positive approach is made possible by the attitude that our views and ideas are deemed, to the extent that they differ from the proselytizer's, to be worthless; if only we recognized reality as it truly is, we too would be Mormons or Habad hasidim. This patronizing attitude is very off-putting. I hate to be patronized; following the first-century *tanna* Hillel the Elder (who urged us not to do to others what we hate), I try not to patronize others. Telling a committed, educated, sincere Reform Jew that her views of Judaism are, at best, childish mistakes born of her unfortunate upbringing is simply obnoxious. I do not think that the Torah demands that I be obnoxious to people who, according to the standard Orthodox view, are not really responsible for holding the views they hold and for behaving as they behave.

Given that the whole *tinok shenishbah* approach is a patronizing fiction,

[15] This passage from Abrabanel's *Principles of Faith* is from ch. 12, p. 112.

is it surprising that it is counter-productive? This view, as Rabbi Sacks puts it so well, attaches 'no significance to liberal Jews' description of their own actions and intentions [thus allowing] Orthodoxy to include individuals within the halakhic community while excluding their ideologies'. How can the non-Orthodox Jew respond to this? Sacks continues: 'It is a strategy of which non-Orthodox Jews might understandably not wish to avail themselves. Explicitly or implicitly, they will feel that it assaults their authenticity.'[16] Sacks writes with admirable British understatement; non-Orthodox Jews indeed find the *tinok shenishbah* approach infuriatingly patronizing.

As anything more than a sop to Orthodox consciences, then, the strategy of calling the non-Orthodox *tinokot shenishbu* is a failure. It cannot be otherwise. Since non-Orthodox Jews know very well that they are not 'babes carried away by heathens' their reactions to the claim that they are range from bemusement through irritation and resentment to anger. I once heard a prominent academic figure in Israel denounce with great passion a rosh yeshiva who had invited the scholar's son to his yeshiva during the young man's army service, thereupon explaining to the officer that he was not at fault for his non-Orthodoxy since he was a 'babe captured by heathens'. In a voice trembling with indignation, the father, who had held high office in the government and had founded one of Israel's universities, proclaimed: 'I did not raise my son among heathens!'

Adopting the Maimonidean approach to the nature of Judaism forces us to choose between two unappetizing alternatives: calling all non-Orthodox Jews heretics, and relating to them as such; or adopting a patronizing, counter-productive fiction as the guiding principle of our shared Jewish life. Were the Maimonidean approach the only option open to us then we would have no choice but to pay the price. But since it is not the only option available to us, as I have shown in the earlier chapters of this book, why not simply abandon it? Such a move would allow us to place our relations with non-Orthodox Jews on a more honest, respectful, and, above all, traditional footing.

Maimonides and the Objectivity of Truth

My position, I fear, is easily misunderstood. My arguments against the claim that Judaism has commandments addressed to the intellect does not mean that the Torah addresses nothing to the intellect. That is clearly

[16] The passage quoted from Sacks, *One People?* is on p. 152.

false. Reducing Judaism to a complex of behavioural norms rubs against the grain of the tradition as much as does reducing Judaism to a series of dogmatic statements. Both are exaggerations and both misrepresent the nature of classical Judaism.

The Torah has important things to say to us on an intellectual plane. These include, for example, the affirmation of God's existence and unity, the rejection of idolatry in all its forms, and ideas concerning the purpose of human and natural existence. That the Torah teaches truth (which it does) does not mean that these truths are expressed in an explicit, detailed, systematic fashion. Nor does it mean that correct and self-conscious affirmation of these truths in all their specificity is the *sine qua non* of being Jewish.[17]

One of the reasons why it is important to take note of this is that we cannot otherwise appreciate the contribution of Maimonides to Judaism. While I have been concerned in this book to argue against a particular aspect of Maimonides' thought, it should not be inferred that I belittle his greatness or underestimate his importance. Maimonides' position that truth is objective and must be accepted whatever its source, and his willingness to understand the Torah in such a way that it cannot conflict with the teachings of reason, are two aspects of his thought that make it possible for many people today to remain faithful to the Torah and Judaism without feeling that they must turn off their brains.[18] These teachings concerning Judaism make sense only if we insist that the Torah addresses the intellect and not just the limbs. My 'argument' with Maimonides in this book is over the nature of that address, not over whether or not it exists.

Let me put this in another way: Maimonides' attempt to place Judaism on a firm dogmatic footing may have reflected, as I have argued elsewhere, particular historical stimuli; but it also reflects an intellectual orientation to the nature of religious faith which many find attractive, even indispensable.

17 With respect to the ever-present need to relearn and re-internalize the truths actually taught by the Torah, I refer the reader to Kenneth Seeskin's marvellous *No Other Gods: The Modern Struggle against Idolatry* (West Orange, NJ: Behrman House, 1995). As Seeskin elegantly shows, idolatry is alive and well, thriving in some really unexpected places, and few are immune to its allure. The teachings of the Torah need not be systematized, dogmatized, and made into a rigid orthodoxy for them to be normative, important, and applicable to our lives.

18 Concerning the possibility of remaining true to the Torah without turning off one's brain, I refer the reader to a splendid book, *Torah and Science*, by Judah Landa (Hoboken, NJ: Ktav, 1992).

This point is important enough to deserve further elaboration. Bahya ibn Pakuda may have been the first Jewish thinker to take explicit notice of the fact that Judaism is not and cannot be a species of 'orthopraxy'. Not only does what we think have a great influence on what we do; how could God command the limbs and ignore the mind? Bahya expresses himself as follows:

Then I examined the duties of the heart as they are commanded by the mind, the Scriptures, and tradition, so that I might see whether they were obligatory or not. And I found them to be the basis of all duties. Were they not, all the duties of the members would be of no avail. As I have said, the duties of the heart are commanded by the mind, for we have already shown that man is composed of a soul and a body—both are God's graces given to us, one exterior, one interior. Accordingly, we are obliged to obey God both outwardly and inwardly . . . Inward obedience, however, is expressed in the duties of the heart, in the heart's assertion of the unity of God and in the belief in Him and His book, in constant obedience to Him and fear of Him, in humility before Him, love for Him and complete reliance upon Him, submission to Him and abstinence from the things hateful to Him. Inward obedience is expressed in the consecration of all our work for His sake, in meditation upon His graces, in all the duties performed by faith and conscience without the activity of the external body members. Thus I have come to know for certain that the duties of the members are of no avail to us unless our hearts choose to do them and our souls desire their performance. Since, then, our members cannot perform an act unless our souls have chosen it first, our members could free themselves from all duties and obligations if it should occur to us that our hearts are not obliged to choose obedience to God. Since it is clear that our Creator commanded the members to perform their duties, it is improbable that He overlooked our hearts and souls, our noblest parts, and did not command them to share in His worship, for they constitute the crown of obedience and the very perfection of worship. For this reason, we are commanded both outward and inward duties, so that our obedience to our glorious Creator might be complete, perfect, and all-embracing, comprising both our outer and inner parts, both mind and body.[19]

Bahya's point cannot be ignored: must Judaism indeed include 'commandments of the heart [i.e. of the intellect]' for the 'commandments of the limbs' to make any sense? Not necessarily. As I have tried to make clear earlier in this book, the Torah can teach truth without necessarily commanding its acceptance.

But if the Torah contains the truth, why not command its acceptance —or, at the very least, teach it in a very clear and unambiguous fashion?

[19] I cite from Bahya ben Joseph ibn Pakuda, *The Book of Direction to the Duties of the Heart*, trans. Menahem Mansoor (London: Routledge & Kegan Paul, 1973), 89.

The reason is that for Bible and Talmud the translation of ultimate truth into clearly defined and manageable statements was a less pressing need than it was for Maimonides. Let me put this as follows: Maimonides and the Talmud agree that God's truth is embodied in the Torah; the Talmud finds pressing the need to determine the practical, this-worldly consequences of that truth, while Maimonides, in addition, finds it necessary to determine the specific, cognitive content of that truth. On one level, Maimonides is clearly right: Judaism does teach truth; but, on the other hand, his insistence on expressing that truth in specific teachings is an innovation in Judaism.

The point I am trying to make here comes out in the well-known talmudic story concerning the oven of Akhnai. The Sages debated whether a particular kind of oven could become ritually impure. The text says:

On that day R. Eliezer brought all the answers in the world [to support his position] but they were not accepted. He said to them: 'If the halakhah accords with my opinion, let this carob tree prove it!' The carob tree uprooted itself and moved 100 *amot* [*c.*50 yards]—some say, it was 400 *amot*. The [other] rabbis said to him: 'One does not bring a proof from a carob tree.' He continued, saying, 'If the halakhah accords with my opinion, let this aqueduct prove it!' The water thereupon flowed backwards. They said to him: 'One does not bring a proof from an aqueduct.' He continued, saying, 'If the halakhah accords with my opinion, let the walls of this house of study prove it!' The walls of the house of study thereupon began to fall inward. Rabbi Joshua reproved them [the walls]: 'By what right do you interfere when Sages battle each other over halakhah?' The walls did not fall [all the way] out of respect for R. Joshua and did not stand upright [again] out of respect for R. Eliezer. To this day, they stand at an angle. He then said to them, 'If the halakhah accords with my opinion, let it be proved by Heaven!' A voice from Heaven [immediately] spoke forth: 'How do you disagree with R. Eliezer, when the halakhah accords with his opinion in every place?' R. Joshua then stood upon his legs and said, 'It is not in Heaven!' [Deut. 30: 12]. [The Talmud then asks,] 'What is the significance of *It is not in Heaven*?' R. Jeremiah answered, 'Since the Torah was given at Mt Sinai we pay no attention to voices from Heaven [in determining halakhah] since You [i.e. God, the source of heavenly voices] have already written in the Torah at Mt Sinai, "turn aside after a multitude" [i.e. follow the majority: Exod. 23: 2].' R. Nathan met Elijah and said to him, 'What did the Holy One, blessed be He, do when this happened?' Elijah replied: 'He smiled and said, "My children have defeated me! My children have defeated me!"'[20]

[20] BT *Bava metsia* 59*b*. For a useful survey of the many ways in which this passage has been interpreted, see Avi Sagi, *Elu ve'elu* (Tel Aviv: Hakibuts Hame'uḥad, 1996), 12–16.

Much can be (and has been) said about this fascinating passage. Here it will suffice to quote an insightful comment of David Kraemer's: 'Of course, we must assume that if the heavenly voice supported R. Eliezer's view, his view must have been closer to the "truth." Nevertheless, his truth is rejected, and the view of the sages, though objectively in error, is affirmed.'[21] Judaism teaches truth, and that fact must never be forgotten. But the ultimate truth taught by the Torah need not necessarily be understood in its detailed specificity for us to live in the world in a decent fashion; while there is one objective 'truth', the Talmud is interested in arriving at a halakhic determination, rather than at a determinate understanding of the final truth. We can safely put off determining the exact truth until 'the earth . . . be full of the knowledge of the Lord, as the waters cover the sea' (Isa. 11: 9); but in the meantime we must know how to live.[22]

The talmudic position, I think, makes it possible for Jews to reach ever greater understandings of the truth taught by the Torah and allows them to express that truth in language appropriate to each age. Had Judaism adopted a Maimonidean, as opposed to talmudic understanding of the nature of our relation to the truth taught by the Torah, we would be forced to express our vision of the universe in terms of the Neoplatonized Aristotelianism adopted by Maimonides. Our situation would be similar to that of Habad hasidim, who feel constrained to accept Maimonides' description of the physical universe as 'Torah from heaven', or to that of those Catholics who accept the medieval theology of Thomas Aquinas and the scholastics as normative and authoritative. But the Torah 'is not in heaven'—it must be lived in this world, while the absolute truth which it embodies remains 'from heaven', a constant challenge to our understanding, a constant critique of our tendency to intellectual complacency. The talmudic position, as hinted at in the story of the oven of Akhnai, allows Judaism to live and breathe in today's world as much as in yesterday's; Maimonides' position (as held especially by today's Maimonideans, if not necessarily by Maimonides himself) would have kept us chained to medieval conceptions of the cosmos.

[21] David Kraemer, *The Mind of the Talmud: An Intellectual History of the Bavli* (New York: Oxford University Press, 1990), 122. I found Kraemer's discussion of the Bavli's understanding of truth very helpful.

[22] Maimonides uses the verse from Isaiah to close his messianic discussion at the very end of the *Mishneh torah*; my use of it, therefore, is not coincidental. In the pre-messianic era we can only approximate to the truth.

I should not like to be misunderstood here (or anywhere, for that matter). I am not claiming, with Peter Ochs, that

In Hebrew Scripture, in rabbinic literature, and for most Jewish thinkers, truth is a characteristic of personal relationships. Truth is fidelity to one's word, keeping promises, saying with the lips what one says with one's heart, bearing witness to what one has seen. Truth is the bond of trust between persons and between God and humanity. In the Western philosophical tradition, truth is a characteristic of the claims people make about the world they experience: the correspondence between a statement and the object it describes, or the coherence of a statement with what we already know about the world.[23]

I am enough of a Maimonidean (i.e. a follower of the 'Western philosophical tradition') to think that the Torah is concerned with truth in both senses of the term isolated by Ochs (senses, by the way, which parallel the distinction used above between 'belief in' and 'belief that'). My claim throughout has been that the Torah teaches truth in both senses, but that Judaism had, until Maimonides, emphasized truth as 'a characteristic of personal relationships' over truth as 'a characteristic of the claims people make about the world they experience', and that we would all be better off were we to revert to that approach, at least until we have reached the days of the Messiah.

Maimonides' position, and my discomfort with it, may be better understood in an Aristotelian context. Aristotle was well aware of the fact that absolute truth is not always determinable. As he wrote in the *Nicomachean Ethics* (i. 3),

Our discussion will be adequate if it has as much clearness as the subject matter admits of; for precision is not to be sought for alike in all discussions . . . for it is the mark of an educated man to look for precision in each class of things just so far as the nature of the subject admits.

In matters of science, however, truth is attainable (as Aristotle argued in *Posterior Analytics*, ii. 19), even if it may take a long time to arrive at. Aristotle makes this last point in *Metaphysics* (ii. 1):

The investigation of the truth is in one way hard, in another easy. An indication of this is found in the fact that no one is able to attain the truth adequately, while, on the other hand, no one fails entirely, but everyone says something true about the nature of things, and while individually they contribute little or nothing to the truth, by the union of all a considerable amount is amassed.[24]

23 Peter Ochs, 'Truth', in A. A. Cohen and Paul Mendes-Flohr (eds.), *Contemporary Jewish Religious Thought* (New York: Scribners, 1987), 1018–23 at 1018.

24 I quote from Aristotle's *Complete Works*, ed. Jonathan Barnes (Princeton: Princeton University Press, 1984), i. 1730; i. 1569.

Maimonides, as I have argued elsewhere,[25] conceived of the Torah on the model of an Aristotelian deductive science and thus thought it necessary that the same canons of exactitude in expressing cognitive truth pertaining to the latter should also be applied in the former. I shall quote just one of his many statements which express this idea:

> The fourth species [of perfection] is the true human perfection; it consists in the acquisition of the rational virtues—I refer to the conception of intelligibles, which teach true opinions concerning the divine things. This is in true reality the ultimate end; this is what gives the individual true perfection, a perfection belonging to him alone; and it gives him permanent perdurance; through it, man is man.

It is on this understanding of truth that Maimonides says, 'For only truth pleases Him, may He be exalted, and only that which is false angers him.'[26] This is clearly not the position of the Talmud in the story of the oven of Akhnai! Surely, God is pleased by (intellectual) truth, but is even more pleased, as it were, by right behaviour. This is the entire burden of my argument in this book.

But, it may be asked, if I agree that Judaism teaches truth, why am I unwilling to admit that untruth is heresy? The reason is simply stated. Heresy is the opposite of truth only in a narrowly theological context. Usually, when we think that someone has become persuaded of untruth, we say that such a person is mistaken, not a heretic. The position advanced in this chapter is that Judaism teaches truth, and that Orthodoxy understands that truth more completely than competing versions of Judaism. Those competing versions are wrong and mistaken; calling them heretical is simply not helpful and is, furthermore, foreign to the historical tradition of Judaism as it developed until Maimonides.

It is further important to realize that even though classical Judaism does not understand the nature of *emunah* as Maimonides does, and therefore places little value and emphasis on precise theological formulations, there are limits to what one can affirm or deny and still remain within the Jewish community. Note my terminology here: there are limits to what one can affirm or deny and still remain within the Jewish *community*. Denying the unity of God, for example, or that the Torah is of divine origin in some significant sense, or affirming that the Messiah has already come, are claims which place one outside the historical community of Israel. This is not to say that such persons are technically

[25] Kellner, 'The Conception of the Torah as a Deductive Science'.

[26] *Guide*, iii. 54, p. 635; ii. 48, p. 409.

heretics—nor is it to say that they are not: that is not the issue here—but it is to say that they have placed themselves beyond the broadest limits of historical Jewish communal consensus.

How to respond to such people is a question which, I think, is best decided on an *ad hoc* basis; indeed, it is a question which cannot be answered in one fashion for all of us. The Israeli Supreme Court faced with a Brother Daniel gives one sort of answer,[27] a parent faced with a rebellious child another sort. Similarly, when faced with such problems, rabbis should match their responses to the problems, without being forced to decide in advance that all persons of a certain type are either heretics or babes captured by heathens.

[27] Daniel Rufeisen (b. 1932), a Polish Jew turned Catholic monk, in 1962 sought recognition as an Israeli citizen on the basis of his birth as a Jew.

Afterword

AUTHORS must usually resign themselves to the slings and arrows of outrageous reviewers, who typically get the last word. Although the reviewers of this book were generally perceptive and generous, I am very grateful to the Littman Library of Jewish Civilization for this opportunity to respond to some of those colleagues who paid me the compliment of writing serious responses to this book.[1]

A central thesis of the book is that the fundamental meaning of 'belief' in Judaism is trust. The reviewer who best understood the implications of that insight was Norbert Samuelson. By way of summarizing my answer to the question, 'What constitutes Jewish belief understood as trust?', Samuelson writes: 'Trust that God is God and should be worshiped, that the Torah and the rabbinic interpretation of it should be observed in service to God, and that the Jewish people were chosen by God to preserve, obey, and teach the Torah.' He continues:

> Hence, despite the title and the initial answer, it is not really the case that Kellner's Judaism does not require belief. It clearly does, namely belief in God, Torah, and Israel. Trust can either be reasonable or unreasonable, and to make this judgment requires critical thinking about the trust. What Kellner rejects is what he calls systematic theology and dogmatism. He argues that Judaism has always emphasized deeds as an expression of the love of God. Although this emphasis entails beliefs, they were never systematized or clearly defined until the time of Sa'adia, and then only as a strategy of defense against threats posed to Jewish identity by Islam and the Karaites. Systematic theology and dogmatism are polemical strategies that the rabbis adopted in defense of rabbinic Judaism against intellectual attacks, but they were never intended to define Judaism as Judaism in any other kind of context. Similarly, once the threat was removed, the activity of systematic, dogmatic theology was abandoned until another external threat emerged—[medieval] Christianity.

I should like to thank David Berger, Raphael Jospe, Jolene S. Kellner, Tyra Lieberman, and Daniel Statman for discussing the issues raised in this afterword with me.

[1] Mention should be made here of Marc Shapiro, *The Limits of Orthodox Theology: Maimonides' Thirteen Principles Reappraised* (Oxford: Littman Library of Jewish Civilization, 2004). Shapiro's seminal work adds important support to many of the points made in this book. See also Howard Wettstein, 'Doctrine', *Faith and Philosophy*, 14 (1997), 423–43, who convincingly argues that 'theological doctrine is not a natural tool for thinking about biblical/rabbinic Judaism' (p. 423).

Up until this point Samuelson succinctly captures what I try to say in this book. The continuation of this paragraph, however, does not reflect my intentions:

> In fact, systematic theology and dogmatism arise in Judaism today only because of Christianity and not because of the inner logic of rabbinic Judaism itself. As such, Bleich and others (notably Yehudah Parnes and Jonathan Sacks), despite their intentions to the contrary, distort Judaism, and they do so because of Christian influence.[2]

Systematic theology and dogmatism arise in Judaism today, I suggest, because of the threats of emancipation and enlightenment, not because of Christianity. To my mind, using tools crafted by Maimonides eight hundred years ago to confront the challenges of his day indicates a failure to realize that the challenges confronting Judaism since the emancipation are dramatically unlike any of those faced by the Jewish religion at any point since the destruction of the Second Temple.

Because my principal focus in this book was on theological issues, I may not have developed this historical point sufficiently. In order to understand what Samuelson describes as the distortions foisted upon Judaism by contemporary rabbis, we must take a brief look at the history of the Jews and of Judaism over the last two hundred years.

Pre-emancipation Judaism was an unselfconscious amalgam of religion and what came, in the nineteenth century, to be called nationality. With very few exceptions (the forced converts of Iberia being the most prominent example), Jewish authorities never had to define who a Jew was, since the matter was clear, both to Jews and to non-Jews. After the French Revolution, when Jews were invited to participate in the world around them, they found a world in which religion had been largely 'privatized', in which it had been severed from nationality, and in which there developed a confusing multiplicity of new ways of being Jewish. It was suddenly no longer so clear who was a Jew, and it was certainly no longer clear who was a 'good' Jew. In a world in which membership in good standing in the Jewish community was no longer determined by descent (since so many Jews by descent had ceased being Jewish in terms of belief and practice, or were adopting new beliefs and practices while still calling themselves 'good' Jews); in a world in which membership in the Jewish community was no longer determined by identity with a shared Jewish past and hopes for a shared Jewish future (since so many

[2] Norbert M. Samuelson, review, *Central Conference of American Rabbis Journal* (Winter 2001), 95–9, esp. p. 98.

Jews who identified with the shared Jewish past hoped for a shared Jewish future defined primarily in national or cultural terms); in a world in which Jews might be willing to violate every single one of the 613 commandments of the Torah while still being prepared to lay down their lives in defence of the Jewish collective, Maimonides' Thirteen Principles, wholly ignored by halakhic authorities since their publication, and largely ignored by theologians (with the exception of those of Iberia between 1391 and 1492), suddenly came into their own and were used, with increasing vigour, to demarcate the line between 'good' Jews and those who must be excluded, those with whom no religious co-operation may be permitted, those who, for the most lenient, are *tinokot shenishbu*, and who, for the most stringent, are out-and-out heretics.

The challenges facing Judaism since the emancipation are thus unlike any faced before; that being the case, the theological toolbox of Judaism must be expanded to include tools for which there was no need in our past. I argued in this book that the tools fashioned by Maimonides are inappropriate and counter-productive when used today. But, before exploring that point, let us return to Samuelson's presentation of my argument: '[Kellner] argues that Judaism has always emphasized deeds as an expression of the love of God.' Samuelson perfectly captures my approach here, while several other reviewers apparently missed the significance of the second part of this sentence and asserted that in this book I argue for a form of orthopraxy. In their view, if Judaism lacks an ortho*doxy*, a substratum of obligatory (but, before Maimonides, not clearly expressed) beliefs, then it resolves itself to an ortho*praxy*, a body of (mindless) rules which could be obeyed by an automaton.

But—and this my critics failed to grasp—to say that Judaism does not demand that we express beliefs about God and God's relationship to the world in the form of dogmas is not to say that all that Judaism demands of its adherents is a kind of mindless practice. They ignore two issues: (*a*) one can love someone and act on that love while knowing very little about the object of that love; (*b*) Judaism prizes *kavanah* (intention) over rote behaviour.

Let me illustrate the first point with a dramatic allegory. Let us imagine a member of a cell in the French resistance during the Second World War. This person might know that she is a member of a cell with perhaps a dozen members, even if she does not know them all. Let us further imagine that our *résistante* does not know the identity of her cell leader. She might not know whether the leader is a man or a woman; she might not even know whether the leader is French, or perhaps someone parachuted in from abroad. At first she might be wary of following instructions from this leader. But time after time, the leader's instructions prove to be wise, leading to many successful strikes against the Nazis, and in many instances they protect our cell member from possibly fatal mistakes. Our *résistante* comes to trust her cell leader and finds that this trust is never betrayed. Would we be surprised to discover that our heroine comes to feel admiration, even awe, for her cell leader, that she is willing to lay down her life for the leader, and, as time goes by, that she devotes herself to her resistance activities as much out of dedication to the leader as for the freedom of France?

Our *résistante* would certainly fail any 'theological' test about her cell leader. Beyond the fact of the leader's existence and, one supposes, the leader's *nom de guerre*, she knows almost nothing at all about him or her. She might imagine all kinds of things about the leader, and could even be wrong about all of them, without that making much difference at all. 'Orthodox' she certainly isn't. But does it make sense to call her 'orthoprax' in her resistance activities? Her motivations are undoubtedly complex (as are all human motivations), but they can include devotion to the cause and its ideals, loyalty to her fellow cell members, trust in her cell leader, and a desire to earn the trust, respect, and approbation of that leader.

It is possible for a Jew to have very few detailed ideas about God, and about the way in which God relates to the cosmos, while still loving God, trusting in God, and yearning to earn God's approval. On this issue (if not on many others, and it pains me even to admit this) Judah Halevi better reflects the traditions of Judaism than does Moses Maimonides. Halevi's spokesman in the *Kuzari* speaks of the experienced God of Jewish history, the God who spoke with Abraham, Isaac, and Jacob, the God who took the Jews out of Egyptian bondage and nurtured them for forty years in the wilderness. Maimonides prefers to speak of the God whose wisdom is manifest in nature. Halevi's Jew knows what God has done for her people, Maimonides' Jew understands the workings of science.

With respect to my second claim, that Judaism prizes *kavanah* over rote behaviour, must a person have a 'firm dogmatic foundation' in order to pray with *kavanah* and in order to fulfil commandments with *kavanah*?[3] Can one pray if one does not have dogmas defining the recipient of

[3] Yitzchak Blau, 'Flexibility with a Firm Foundation: On Maintaining Jewish Dogma', *The Torah Umadda Journal*, 12 (2004), 179–91. Daniel H. Frank, review, *Jewish Quarterly Review*, 92 (2002), 272–5 also interprets me as advocating a kind of orthopraxy.

one's prayers? If the answer to this question is negative, then no Jew before Maimonides prayed with *kavanah* or fulfilled the commandments with *kavanah*, since even my critics admit that before Maimonides there were no clear and explicit statements of theology or dogma in Judaism. As David Berger states, 'Since they [the talmudic Sages] were indeed not interested in systematic theology, they did not articulate these principles until they were challenged, but once challenged, they fleshed out a position they had always taken for granted.'[4] The point that scholars like Berger are trying to make is that, while a religion may lack a clearly expressed statement of dogma, there may still be a wide (if unexpressed) consensus concerning theological matters. My critics claim that Judaism always had a theology, but that no one before Maimonides took the trouble of systematizing it and expressing it in terms of dogma. But my argument is different: if one needs to know to whom one is praying or to whom one is dedicating one's fulfilment of the commandments, then how can one be said to know God if this knowledge has never been systematized or even articulated?

If the answer to my question is positive, and *kavanah* is possible without a firm dogmatic foundation, then the stark dogma versus orthoprax dichotomy is nullified.[5]

The question that needs to be addressed, then, is whether or not *kavanah* must presuppose some sort of systematic theology, even if unexpressed.[6] I want to give my critics the benefit of the doubt, as it were, by examining what Maimonides has to say about the subject.[7] After all, if any Jewish thinker and halakhic authority can be expected to make *kavanah* depend upon theology, it should be Maimonides.

Maimonides opens chapter 4 of 'Laws Concerning Prayer and the Priestly Blessing' in the *Mishneh torah* with the following general statement: 'The set time for prayer having come, it should still be delayed for five reasons: purity of hands, nakedness, purity of the place of prayer, the pressure to rush, and correct intention [*kavanat halev*].' After discussing the first four impediments to prayer, Maimonides devotes four paragraphs to the issue of *kavanah*:

4 David Berger, review, *Tradition*, 33 (1999), 81–9.

5 So, for that matter, is Norman Solomon's criticism that I advocate a vague and hazy theology. See his review in *Journal of Jewish Studies*, 52 (Spring 2001), 152–4.

6 For a discussion of the nature of *kavanah* in general, see Seth Kadish, *Kavvanah: Directing the Heart in Jewish Prayer* (Northvale, NJ: Jason Aronson, 1997).

7 On *kavanah* in Maimonides, see Gerald J. (Ya'akov) Blidstein, *Prayer in Maimonidean Halakha* (*Hatefilah bimishnato hahilkhatit shel harambam*) (Jerusalem: Mosad Bialik, 1994), 77–150.

15. What does correct intention involve? Any prayer recited without correct intention is not prayer. One who prays without correct intention must pray again with correct intention. One who is confused or preoccupied may not pray until he become tranquil. Thus, one who returns from a journey fatigued or distressed is forbidden to pray until he becomes tranquil. The Sages said that such a person must wait three days until he rest and his mind settle before praying.

16. How does one achieve correct intention? One must free his mind of all thoughts and see himself as standing before the Divine Presence [*shekhinah*]. Therefore, one should sit a while before prayer in order to direct his mind, and then pray gently and beseechingly. One must not pray as if it were a burden to be cast aside before one continues on his way. Thus, one should sit a while after prayer and only then leave. The early pietists would wait an hour before prayer, an hour after prayer, and spend an hour praying.

17. One who is drunk may not pray, since he has no correct intention; if he prayed, his prayer is an abomination. Therefore, he must pray again when he becomes sober. One who is slightly drunk should not pray, but if he prayed, his prayer is considered prayer. Who is drunk? One who cannot speak before a king. The person who is slightly drunk is one who can speak before a king after drinking without confusion. Even so, one who has drunk a quarter-*hin* of wine should not pray until its influence pass.

18. So too, one ought not to stand up to pray directly after laughter, frivolity, conversation, argument, or anger, but after words of Torah. Even though a halakhic debate consists of words of Torah, one ought not stand up to pray directly after such a debate, lest one's mind be preoccupied with determining the halakhah. Rather, one should stand up to pray after studying words of Torah that do not demand concentration, such as already determined laws.[8]

From this passage, Maimonides' most extensive treatment of the nature of *kavanah*,[9] we learn that *kavanah* consists in seeing oneself as standing before the Divine Presence. Now it is obvious that certain beliefs are presupposed by this formulation. But is it obvious what they are? Upon examination, the issue turns out to be not so simple.

Minimally, one can only picture oneself as standing in prayer before the Divine Presence if one accepts that God exists and is a fit object of worship. But what further specific beliefs are entailed by the obligation to picture oneself as standing in prayer before the Divine Presence? It turns out, almost none.

First, does God command us to pray? As is well known, that is a matter

[8] I quote from my translation of Maimonides, *The Book of Love* (New Haven, Conn.: Yale University Press, 2004), 28–9.

[9] *Guide*, iii. 51 also contains a discussion of the nature of *kavanah*, but even there Maimonides focuses on the psychological aspects of *kavanah* and not on its object.

of debate in the tradition. Maimonides holds that there is a biblically derived commandment to pray, while Nahmanides disagrees.[10] Since there is a debate among the early authorities over whether or not there can be a biblically ordained commandment to pray, it is obvious that accepting that prayer is commanded by God cannot be a prerequisite for *kavanah*.

Assuming that there is a commandment to pray, how is it to be fulfilled? Maimonides strongly hints that, ideally, prayer should consist of silent (presumably intellectually oriented) meditation; prayers consisting of words (and associated actions, such as fasting and genuflecting) are an accommodation to human weakness.[11] However, be that as it may, all would have to agree that in the biblical and mishnaic periods (before the establishment of standardized prayer), there was a time when Jews prayed without the words we use today. Kabbalists also hold that the prayer of Jews who pray without the requisite intentions (*kavanot*) is, at the very least, defective. Beyond certain halakhic minima, the tradition does not even teach us how to pray.

Must we know something concrete, as it were, about the Divine Presence in order to see ourselves as standing before it? If so, we are in trouble, since the Jewish tradition presents us with a wide variety of opinions concerning the nature of *shekhinah* without finally coming down in favour of any of them.

The term *shekhinah* does not occur in the Torah, but the term *kavod* does.[12] Its first use is illustrative of its other occurrences. Exodus 16 describes one of the episodes of Israelite grumbling in the wilderness. Moses tells the people: 'and in the morning you shall see the *kavod* of the Lord, because He has heard your grumblings against the Lord. For who are we that you should grumble against us?' (Exod. 16: 7). Moses keeps his word: 'Then Moses said to Aaron, "Say to the whole Israelite community: Advance toward the Lord, for He has heard your grumbling." And as Aaron spoke to the whole Israelite community, they turned toward the wilderness, and there, in a cloud, appeared the *kavod* of the Lord' (Exod. 16: 9–10). The ancient Israelites certainly seemed to have beheld something visible. In a later chapter (Exod. 24: 17), the Israelites see the *kavod* as a burning fire on top of Mount Sinai.[13]

[10] See Maimonides, *Book of Commandments*, positive commandment 5, and Nahmanides' gloss. [11] See *Guide*, iii. 32.

[12] Sa'adiah Gaon teaches that the rabbinic term *shekhinah* refers to the entity called *kavod* in the Torah. See *Beliefs and Opinions*, ii.10.

[13] Compare also Lev. 9: 5–7, 22–4; Num. 14: 10, 20–3; Num. 16: 6–7; Isa. 40: 3–5; Isa. 60: 1–3; Ezek. 1: 26–8, 3: 22–7, and 8: 1–4.

As used in rabbinic literature, *shekhinah* may or may not be a hypostasis in the Neoplatonic sense of the term,[14] but there is no reason to doubt that many rabbinic sources attest to an understanding of *shekhinah* as a phenomenon which can be located in specific places at specific times.[15]

Consistent with traditional usage, both Sa'adiah Gaon and Judah Halevi, following Targum Onkelos,[16] understand *kavod* as denoting something corporeal and accessible to the senses.[17] Maimonides, on the other hand, takes great pains to deny this. His ultimate position may be summarized in the following gloss on Isa. 6: 3, 'The whole earth is full of his *kavod*'. The meaning of this verse, Maimonides teaches, is 'that the whole earth bears witness to His perfection, that is, indicates it'.[18]

In sum, the biblical *kavod*, as some sort of sensible manifestation of God's presence, and the post-biblical *shekhinah* readily lend themselves to interpretations according to which God's presence can be located in space and time. Onkelos (followed by Sa'adiah and Halevi) had sought to soften the dangerous idea of a sensible manifestation of God's presence. It fell to Maimonides to analyse many of the places where the terms *kavod* and *shekhinah* are used, in an attempt to show that the key meaning of the term *kavod* is the wisdom of God as expressed in the natural world, and that the way in which we best show *kavod* (= honour) to God and express *kavod* (= praise) of God is by seeking to understand divine wisdom as expressed in nature.[19]

[14] Urbach, *The Sages*, i. 43, denies the hypostatic nature of *shekhinah*, while Gershom Scholem sees it as 'verging on hypostatization'. See Scholem, *On the Mystical Shape of the Godhead* (New York: Schocken, 1991), 147–8.

[15] See e.g. *Gen. Rabbah* 19: 7. Indeed, Alan Unterman opens his *Encylopaedia Judaica* article '*Shekhinah*' with the following definition of the term as used in rabbinic literature: 'God viewed in spatio-temporal terms as a presence'.

[16] As Maimonides presents his position in the *Guide*, i. 21.

[17] For a history of discussions of *kavod*, see Joseph Dan, *The Esoteric Theology of Ashkenazi Hasidism* (*Torat hasod shel ḥasidut ashkenaz*) (Jerusalem: Mosad Bialik, 1968), 104–68.

[18] *Guide*, i. 9. My late teacher Steven S. Schwarzschild presented a Maimonidean understanding of the concept, asserting that *shekhinah* should 'be understood as a somewhat poetic, metaphoric name that classical Judaism has given to the idea of the functioning relationship between the transcendent God, on the one hand, and, on the other hand, humanity in general and the people of Israel in particular'. See Steven S. Schwarzschild, '*Shekhinah* and Eschatology', in Menachem Kellner (ed.), *The Pursuit of the Ideal: Jewish Writings of Steven Schwarzschild* (Albany, NY: SUNY Press, 1990), 235–50, esp. p. 235.

[19] I cite and analyse the relevant texts in my forthcoming *Maimonides' Confrontation with Mysticism* (Oxford: Littman Library of Jewish Civilization, 2006), ch. 6.

I do not want to go too far afield here, but if we admit into our discussion kabbalistic conceptions of the term *shekhinah* as naming one of the *sefirot*, we certainly see how tolerant the tradition has been of dramatically different conceptions of what it means to stand before the Divine Presence.

Let us grant all that I have said up to this point. Have I refuted my critics? My colleague Daniel Statman is not sure. His perceptive critique is worth citing at length:

> According to Kellner, *emunah* in classical Judaism is not propositional belief, but trust in God expressed through the observance of His commandments. But if that is so, then in most cases the conclusion would be less tolerance of non-orthodox Jews, not more tolerance. The reason for this is simple: if *emunah* referred to propositional beliefs, such as the belief that God exists, that He created the world, that He revealed Himself in Sinai etc., then we could ascribe significant *emunah* to many non-orthodox Jews, in the US as well as in Israel. But if *emunah* means faith in God manifested through fulfilling the *mitsvot*, then non-orthodox Jews, namely Jews without commitment to halakha, would clearly count as 'illegitimate'. The suggestion to focus on praxis as the essence of Judaism seems to achieve the exact opposite of what Kellner wanted. In other words, from an orthodox point of view the problem with the non-orthodox is that, by definition, they lack *emunah* in the sense of trust in God expressed in fulfilling the *mitsvot*, and most of them also lack *emunah* in the sense of admitting the truth of the theological principles set by Maimonides, especially those concerning the divine origin and the eternal nature of the Torah.
>
> To this Kellner will probably respond by saying that while the focus on dogma leads to an absolute 'in' or 'out' (either you believe that *x* is true, and you are in, or you don't, in which case you're out), the focus on praxis leads to a continuum . . . Yet this response ignores the fact that *emunah*—even on Kellner's view—is more than merely doing certain things. It is doing them *as an expression of one's trust in God*. Thus, a huge difference exists between Jews who do not accept the yoke of the *mitsvot* (and who often do not believe that God exists or revealed Himself in the Torah) and Jews who do, and only the latter seem to qualify as having *emunah*. Here I think that the late Yeshayahu Leibowitz was right: some minimal religious intention (*kavanah*) is required in order for behaviour to bear a religious meaning. A lucky coincidence between what one does and what halakha requires is insufficient to bestow religious significance on the deed and to place the agent on the same continuum with those who accept the yoke of halakha.[20]

Statman is correct in refusing to adopt the stark 'orthodox–orthoprax' dichotomy. He correctly anticipates my response that traditionally

[20] Review, *Journal of Jewish Studies*, 52 (2001), 202–6.

approved Jewish behaviour is not action on the basis of dogma, but action *leshem shamayim*, done for the sake of heaven. The problem with this approach, Statman sagely notes, is that most contemporary Jews, towards whom I want to be inclusive, do not in fact behave in this way.[21] Their Jewish behaviour does not appear to express trust in God or indeed often expresses no relationship with God at all, and thus fails Leibowitz's test for an act bearing religious meaning.

I cheerfully admit all this, but am still convinced that much is gained by focusing Jewish attention on behaviour and not on dogma, for two reasons. First, Leibowitz is wide of the mark. Jewish tradition recognizes the religious significance of actions done *shelo lishmah*, not for the sake of heaven. The talmudic rabbis, unlike Professor Leibowitz, prized good behaviour done for the wrong reasons. They prized good behaviour done for the right reasons even more, but in no way can they be construed as holding that incorrect intention empties an act of all religious meaning, even if the religious meaning is not intended by the actor. Second, while theological tests are relatively easy to administer (and there is a long history of administering them in Christianity and Islam, a history which contemporary Orthodoxy seems all too eager to ape), tests of intention are much harder to administer. Human motivation, after all, is marvellously complex. On the basis of the approach I champion, the decision of who is in, who is out, who is a good Jew and who is a bad Jew, is removed from the hands of rabbis and returned to the hands, so to speak, of God, where it belongs.

Statman continues:

> Kellner's conclusions regarding contemporary Judaism are undermined from another direction too. The mishnah in Sanhedrin chapter 10, regarding the *epikorsim* who do not have a share in the world to come, seems to assume the existence of dogma, to which Kellner responds by saying that the mishnah did not intend to formulate a list of creeds but 'a list of "public enemies", so to speak' (p. 38). The main enemies the tannaites had in mind here were the Sadducees, hence the reference in the mishnah to him who denies resurrection and him who denies that Torah was from heaven—two well-known heresies of the Sadducees. Generally speaking, the Rabbis could tolerate major doctrinal differences so long as they did not lead to substantial behavioural divergences (p. 42). When they did, as with the Sadducees, they were rather intolerant.
>
> Here again I find Kellner's intriguing suggestion leading to an opposite conclusion from the one he derives regarding contemporary Judaism. First, and most important, if the Sages saw the Sadducees as 'public enemies', it is hard to

[21] Norman Solomon (above, n. 5) makes a similar criticism.

see why they would not react in the same way towards the reformers, the reconstructionists or the seculars. Second, if Kellner is right, then we might learn from this mishnah that one way to fight the 'public enemies' is to define what they believe in as heresy. Why, then, can the orthodox not follow the same tactic in their struggle against the non-orthodox, thereby turning them into *epikorsim* and presenting them as residing beyond the borders of Jewish legitimacy?

As a matter of fact, I think this is precisely what orthodox speakers do today when they use Maimonidean dogma to de-legitimize their perceived enemies. Kellner is right in pointing out the absurdity in the fact that those who do so almost certainly do not subscribe to Maimonides' principles as he stated them . . . and have not even started the philosophical voyage necessary for religious perfection. But this only indicates that their real motivation for using Maimonides is political rather than theological. What really concerns them about the non-orthodox movements is not their erroneous theological views, but rather their lack of commitment to halakha (often coupled with a denial of its divine origin).

Statman's points here force me to make clear some unarticulated assumptions which underlie a lot of what I tried to do in this book. Paraphrasing David Berger's statement quoted above, even though I am indeed opposed to systematic theology, I did not articulate these principles until challenged by Daniel Statman, but once challenged, I shall flesh out a position I had always taken for granted.

There are some crucial assumptions which inform my approach and which need to be made explicit here:

1. commitment to *kelal yisra'el*, the generality of Israel, overrides doctrinal orthodoxy;
2. modernity presents challenges never before faced by the Jewish people;
3. the response to modernity on the part of the founders of what is today called *ḥaredi* Orthodoxy was wrong.

It would take a whole new book to defend these claims, but I think that I may be allowed a few paragraphs here to sketch out the basis for each of them.

My first assumption is that, in many important ways, identification today with the Jewish past and a desire to be identified with the Jewish future is at least as important a criterion of Jewish legitimacy as theological 'orthodoxy' and adherence to halakhah. My espousal of this view probably reflects the fact that I am not only an observant Jew, but also a Jewish nationalist, specifically a Zionist. But it also reflects, I believe, a crucial intuition of traditional Judaism that a Jew is, first, a human being, second, a member of the Jewish people, and only third a believer in the Torah of Israel.

This is the order in which we become aware of our identity; it is also the order in which these stages are presented in the Torah: all human beings were created equally in the image of God. The patriarchs, through covenants with God, established a special relationship with the Creator of all. The descendants of the patriarchs stood at Sinai and in effect converted to Judaism.[22]

Indirect expression of this tripartite approach may be found in Mishnah *Avot* iii. 14:

> [Rabbi Akiva] used to say: Beloved is man in that he was created in the image [of God]. [It is a mark of] superabundant love [that] it was made known to him that he had been created in the image [of God], as it is said: 'for in the image of God made He man'. Beloved are Israel in that they were called children of the All-Present. [It was a mark of] superabundant love [that] it was made known to them that they were called children of the All-Present, as it is said: 'ye are children of the Lord your God'. Beloved are Israel in that a desirable instrument [the Torah] was given to them. [It was a mark of] superabundant love [that] it was made known to them that the desirable instrument, wherewith the world had been created, was given to them, as it is said: 'for I give you good doctrine; forsake not My teaching'.

This text speaks, first, of the creation of all humanity, second, of the establishment of a special relationship between God and the Jewish people, and, third, of the giving of the Torah. We are thus faced with three concentric circles—the first and largest, humanity, encompassing the second, the Jewish people, which in turns encompasses the third and smallest, those people whose lives are governed by the Jewish religion in its various guises. While some Jewish particularists may have problems with the status of the first circle, all Orthodox Jews must admit that the second circle is religiously significant.

But beyond all this, and we now shade into my second claim, modernity presents Orthodoxy with challenges it never had to face before, specifically, a large number of Jews who strongly identify as Jews, and yet who would never knowingly fulfil a single commandment of the Torah if they could help it. This is particularly evident in Israel. Over the last half-century many Jews there, even though wholly disconnected from tradition, have sacrificed their lives for the good of the Jewish people. Modernity has made it possible for individuals to identify as Jews in ways

[22] Above, pp. 58–60, and the sources cited there.

never dreamed of by our classical and medieval forebears. This is a reflection of the fact that what was once an undifferentiated and unselfconscious Jewish identity, consisting of many facets, has been shattered by modernity so that each of the facets (religious, mystical, cultural, national, etc.) has adherents who are convinced that theirs is the truest form of Judaism. Modernity has also presented Judaism with a challenge never dreamed of by any pre-modern Jew (other, perhaps, than Spinoza): the re-establishment of Jewish sovereignty in the Land of Israel without the coming of the messiah. In effect, my argument is that new challenges must be recognized as such, confronted honestly, and not ignored.

This leads to my third assertion, that rabbinic leadership has failed to rise to these challenges. The famous pun made by the Hatam Sofer (Rabbi Moses Sofer, 1762–1839), 'All that is new [*ḥadash*] is forbidden by the Torah', may have been a reaction to the early proponents of religious reform (*meḥadshim*), but it both reflects and was taken to mean not confrontation with modernity, but flight from it. We will never know if Rabbi Sofer and his followers were right in rejecting the model of Orthodox engagement with modernity offered by Rabbi Samson Raphael Hirsch, or the model of Orthodox engagement with Zionism offered by Rabbi Isaac Jacob Reines (1839–1915), or the model of Orthodox engagement with democracy offered by Rabbi Hayim Hirschensohn (1857–1935); but, from where I sit, it seems clear that they missed the boat, and it is possible that they should be held responsible for the assimilation of millions of Jews. Of course, we can never know who is right, but the only reason to assume that they were correct is if one believes that they *must* have been correct. This is certainly the view of *ḥaredi* Orthodoxy, but not likely to be the view of anyone who has read this far in this book.

We may now return to Daniel Statman's critique. He writes: 'First, and most important, if the Sages saw the Sadducees as "public enemies", it is hard to see why they would not react in the same way towards the reformers, the reconstructionists or the seculars.' Indeed, that is precisely what has happened. But to equate Reform Jews with Sadducees, for example, is to pretend that Judaism and the Jewish people exist in a kind of stasis and that nothing of note has happened in the last two thousand years. It is, crucially, simply to ignore the challenges of modernity as outlined above.[23]

[23] Statman's point here raises another issue. A number of readers (including Statman himself, in private communication) understand me to have claimed that the talmudic rabbis would adopt my position. That is not the claim I defend in the book or in this afterword. Rather, I maintain that if we go back to the early Sages instead of to

Statman continues:

> Second, if Kellner is right, then we might learn from this mishnah [*Sanhedrin* x. 1] that one way to fight the 'public enemies' is to define what they believe in as heresy. Why, then, can the orthodox not follow the same tactic in their struggle against the non-orthodox, thereby turning them into *epikorsim* and presenting them as residing beyond the borders of Jewish legitimacy?

Again, Statman is correct. Contemporary Orthodoxy uses the weapons forged against the Sadducees in the first century and against Karaites and others in the twelfth century against a very different sort of opponent in a very different sort of world. It is not that I am unaware of this sort of reaction (were I unaware of it, I would not have written this book); rather, my book is a plea to see this reaction as unwise and self-destructive, in addition to being untrue to the teachings of rabbinic Judaism as outlined in Chapter 2.

Apropos those teachings, David Berger made some important criticisms of my presentation of them. Let us turn then from my response to what might be called Statman's theological critique of the book to Berger's historical critique. Here is the core of his argument:

> Let us begin at the beginning. It is perfectly evident that Hazal [the talmudic rabbis] did not present us with a Maimonidean-style creed. At the same time, it is also evident that they did regard the denial of specific theological propositions as grounds for exclusion from the world to come. When Kellner has completed his discussion of the 'one possible exception' to his rule, he has shown that Mishnah Sanhedrin 10: 1 is not a work of systematic theology but has done nothing to undermine the obvious and unavoidable reality, to wit, that it excludes from the world to come people who deny resurrection and the belief that the Torah is from Heaven. Even if we were to endorse the debatable assertion that only people who advertise their denial forfeit eternal felicity, the fateful action would remain nothing more than a statement of disbelief in a dogmatic proposition.
>
> Now, it may well be that the Rabbis were impelled to single out these doctrines in the wake of attacks by Sadducees and other sectarians (p. 36), but this position does little to salvage Kellner's overall argument. It means that the Rabbis did believe that membership in good standing in the community of Israel rested on certain articles of faith. Since they were indeed not interested in

Maimonides, we can construct a way of dealing with non-Orthodox Jews which does not necessitate invoking the language of heresy, with its absolute 'in' or 'out' implications. Nowhere in the book do I make the claim that the rabbis of the Talmud would adopt the views I defend, were they to walk among us today. (Nor do I say they would not.) The claim I seek to defend is that demanding dogmatic orthodoxy is a (Maimonidean) divergence from rabbinic approaches, and that one can use those approaches to fashion tools better suited to contemporary needs and realities than those based upon Maimonides.

systematic theology, they did not articulate these principles until they were challenged, but once challenged, they fleshed out a position that they had always taken for granted.

In contrast to David Berger, I shall begin at the end. Given all the evidence adduced in this book concerning the nature of religious faith in the Torah and rabbinic writings, it appears to me that there is only one reason why one should assume that the talmudic rabbis believed that 'membership in good standing in the community of Israel rested on certain [unarticulated] articles of faith'. That reason is that Maimonides could not have introduced so massive an innovation into the heart of Judaism. But that assumption lacks all scholarly basis, and, so far as I can judge, is not necessitated by any commitment central to Orthodox Judaism (it is certainly not taught in Maimonides' Thirteen Principles). Orthodox Jews who make this assumption (and Berger is certainly not alone in making it), are, in effect, adopting Solomon Schechter's understanding of Judaism as the religion of catholic Israel, where catholic Israel is defined as that portion of the Jewish people with whose views and practices one identifies. To make this assumption is to read Judaism backwards (surely an odd approach for so excellent a historian as David Berger), but, in more popular terms, it is to say that what my rabbi teaches *must* be what all previous rabbis have taught.

Once this assumption is rejected, as it ought to be, there is no reason in the world to assume that, despite the lack of interest on the part of the talmudic rabbis in systematic theology, they held Judaism to be based on (unarticulated) principles of faith, adherence to which was the single essential criterion for membership in good standing of the community of Israel.[24]

[24] Berger's assumption also underlies another of his criticisms of the position I defend in the book. He attributes to the rabbis the position that 'false belief is a criterion for *minut* ['heresy' for Berger, 'sectarianism' for me] and exclusion from the world to come. To take Kellner's own example of idolatry, his assertion that Hazal saw only action as sinful is incorrect. They explicitly tell us that thoughts of heresy or idolatry are biblically forbidden (*Sifrei* on Numbers 15: 39; BT *Berakhot* 12*b*)' (p. 84). What I find fascinating here is how Berger understands the expressions found in the original—*da'at minim*, *hirhur averah*, and *hirhur avodah zarah*. Depending upon how we understand the term *min* (above, pp. 40–2), the first expression can either mean 'heretical positions' (Berger) or 'sectarian positions' (Kellner). The second expression literally means 'thought of sin' but may also mean 'licentious thought', while the third means 'thoughts of idolatry'. Only a person who reads these rabbinic texts through a theological prism would feel the necessity to render the Hebrew as does Berger. The text here (I found the source in *Berakhot*, not in *Sifrei*) certainly does not prove his point.

What I tried to do in this book was to look at rabbinic texts against the background of the Torah and without the assumption that Maimonides understood them correctly (certainly most of his contemporaries were convinced that he got most non-halakhic aspects of Judaism wrong). Once that assumption is rejected, the reading I gave to those texts makes excellent sense—as is apparent from a careful reading of Berger's own critique. As we just saw, he writes: 'When Kellner has completed his discussion of the "one possible exception" to his rule, he has shown that Mishnah Sanhedrin 10: 1 is not a work of systematic theology but has done nothing to undermine the obvious and unavoidable reality, to wit, that it excludes from the world to come people who deny resurrection and the belief that the Torah is from Heaven.' But, as Berger must readily admit, and as I note in the book itself (p. 37), the expression 'X loses his or her share in the world to come' does not actually mean that the person about whom it was said has no share in the world to come. It is not an expression bearing any serious halakhic or theological weight. It is simply an expression of strong disapproval.[25] Only one who assumes that the Mishnah in *Sanhedrin* is making a theological statement, and only one who assumes that the Mishnah in *Sanhedrin* knows of a category of punishment (eternal damnation) for mistakes concerning certain theological matters, i.e. only one who reads the Mishnah as if it were written by Moses Maimonides, could possibly make the claims that Berger makes here.[26] But the Mishnah was not written by Maimonides!

Let us continue. Does the Mishnah condemn those who deny resurrection, as Maimonides' text has it, or those who deny that the Torah teaches resurrection, as the standard printed editions have it? The issue is of course crucial if there are indeed dogmas in Judaism, even if the first articulation of this alleged dogma is in our mishnah. But, if Berger is

25 BT *BM* 58*b*–59*a* may be added to the sources cited there (n. 16). Compare also Rabeinu Nisim of Marseilles in his *Ma'aseh nisim*, ed. H. Kreisel (Jerusalem: Mekize Nirdamim, 2000), 132. The text cited from *Avot derabi natan* may be found in *The Fathers According to Rabbi Nathan*, trans. Judah Goldin (New York: Schocken, 1974), 151; the chapter contains a long list of individuals and groups excluded from the world to come.

26 Further support for my reading may be found in the following statement by W. D. Davies: 'The anathemas in *Mishnah Sanhedrin* 10 strike one as being haphazard: they are not the considered "dogmatic" pronouncement of an authorized body of leaders nor are they presented with the full-blasted force of a "dogma": they do not stand out in any way from other materials in *Sanhedrin*; they are given no prominence, not to speak of pre-eminence.' See Davies, 'Torah and Dogma: A Comment', *Harvard Theological Review*, 61 (1968), 87–105, esp. p. 89.

right, why is there no discussion outside the world of scholarship of this matter? Maimonides' recension is clearly theological, the standard text, clearly sociological.

Continuing with our gloss of David Berger, he holds that the Mishnah excludes all who deny that the Torah is from heaven from the world to come. Let us grant him his claim for the moment. What does it mean to assert that the Torah is from heaven? Berger is certainly aware of the ways in which twentieth-century theologians tied themselves into knots trying to define this term. Had the authors of the Mishnah really held it to be a dogma of Judaism, does it not seem odd that not one of them, or their amoraic successors, or the *ge'onim* who followed them took the trouble to define the term with any specificity?[27] Assuming that we know what it means for the Torah to be from heaven, do we know which part of Torah is from heaven? Maimonides and Nahmanides famously disagreed about this as well, and Rabbi Isaac Abrabanel, among others, was willing to consider the possibility that the book of Deuteronomy was written by Moses himself, not God.[28]

Speaking more generally, David Berger proposes a category of unarticulated dogmas, rejection of which (whether purposeful or inadvertent, apparently) costs people their share in the world to come. The category seems bizarre on the face of it. But leaving that aside, let us examine some of its consequences. Does a Jew living before the pub-

[27] It is apposite here to contrast David Berger's views with those of another historian:

> Classic Judaism places very little emphasis on dogma. While its adherents and critics might differ sharply in their attitude towards this orientation, they would have been able to agree that this was much more a religion of 'works' than of 'faith', and that one's membership in good standing in the religious community depended on practical observance rather than on formal assertions of belief. We hear of few internal debates on questions of dogma, and even someone who denied one of the few tenets which were deemed essential, such as the belief in resurrection, was only said to be denied a place in the World to Come and his transgression was not punishable by human agency . . . Although a few basic beliefs, such as the existence of God and the revelation of the Torah, may safely be considered part of a universal consensus for the Tanna'im and Amora'im, they were able to entertain an extraordinarily wide range of views on almost any other theological question. Furthermore, to judge by the available evidence, many of the talmudic rabbis devoted little or none of their intellectual energies to theological speculation, and those who did concentrate on this field did not generally present their ideas in explicit, let alone systematic, form.

See Robert Brody, *The Geonim of Babylonia and the Shaping of Medieval Jewish Culture* (New Haven, Conn.: Yale University Press, 1998), 283.

[28] For the first issue, see Maimonides' *Book of Commandments*, principle 2, and Nahmanides' gloss there; for the second, see Abravanel's introduction to Deuteronomy. Abravanel's conclusion (one likely to surprise many contemporary Orthodox Jews) is that Moses wrote the book on his own and that only after it had been written did God, as it were, extend a divine imprimatur to the book.

lication of the Mishnah who denies that the Torah teaches resurrection have a share in the world to come? If the answer is yes, then we seem to have a case of punishment without prior warning (*hatra'ah*). If the answer is no, then theological orthodoxy becomes time-dependent; a person who denied resurrection before the publication of the Mishnah could achieve a share in the world to come while one who denied it afterwards has no share.

Berger continues: 'Even if we were to endorse the debatable assertion that only people who advertise their denial forfeit eternal felicity, the fateful action would remain nothing more than a statement of disbelief in a dogmatic proposition.' Actually, no. The fateful action would be an overt act by which one puts oneself outside the community. In tannaitic Palestine, to state publicly (the Mishnah's criterion, not mine[29]) that one denied the heavenly source of Torah, or to deny that the dead will be resurrected, was not to engage anyone in theological debate; it was to make a statement about the community from which one excluded oneself. I argued this at length in the book itself. Berger is on shaky ground when he refutes the claim; he can only reject it because of his own unarticulated assumption that rabbinic Judaism must have had dogmas, because otherwise Maimonides was a religious revolutionary.

But let us assume for the moment that Berger is right in his reading of Mishnah *Sanhedrin* x. 1 and that (despite the arguments adduced above on pages 33–8 and in the preceding paragraphs) the text means exactly what he takes it to mean, namely, that Jews who deny that the Torah is from heaven and who deny that the resurrection will take place (or that the Torah teaches that the resurrection will take place) lose their share in the world to come. We are still very far away from the kind of dogmatic theology he needs to make his critique stick. He must also argue that an issue of crucial importance is raised in a fairly offhand manner by the Mishnah, discussed briefly and in a desultory manner by the relevant Gemara, and ignored by generations of halakhic decisors.

Let us look at the issue in strictly historical terms. Systematic theology (and its outgrowth, dogma) is entirely absent from the Written Torah. There are a very small number of rabbinic texts which may (but, as I have argued here and in the book proper, do not have to) be read as implying that the Sages understood Judaism to be a religion based upon dogma.

[29] As noted above (p. 36) the Mishnah uses the expression *ha'omer*, 'he who says'. Had the authors of this text meant 'he who thinks' they could have used the biblical expression *amar belibo* (Obad. 1: 3; Pss. 10: 6, 11, 13; 14: 1, and 53: 2) or some variant of the mishnaic *meharher* (Mishnah *Ber.* iii. 4, etc.; see above, n. 24)

Apart from Maimonides, would anyone read those texts in this way? David Berger thinks that the answer is yes, while I remained convinced that I have shown the better answer to be no.

My disagreement with Berger can be made clearer by reference to the case of the rebellious elder. In 'Laws of Rebellious Elders [*mamrim*]', iii. 4 Maimonides defines 'the rebellious elder [*zaken mamreh*] of whom the Bible speaks' as a member of the high court who disagrees with his colleagues in the court 'with regard to a question of law, refuses to change his view, persists in differing with them, [and] gives a practical ruling which runs counter to that given by them'. However, Maimonides clarifies in paragraph 6 that, if the elder 'persists in communicating his opinion to others, but does not give it in the form of a practical ruling, he is not liable'.[30] The rabbis were not seeking uniformity of halakhic thought and teaching; they were interested in communal solidarity. I suggest that, to the extent that they considered theological matters at all, they applied the same approach: one could think pretty much what one pleased, so long as one did not diverge too publicly from the communal consensus.

The clearest proof that Berger's critique of my book misses its target is provided by Berger himself. He has proved conclusively that contemporary Habad hasidism is heretical,[31] yet no Orthodox rabbi that I have ever heard of is willing to follow him in adopting the operative conclusions that follow from this finding. This is so, despite the fact that most Orthodox rabbis persist in saying, with Berger, that 'membership in good standing in the community of Israel rest[s] on certain articles of faith'. Berger is consistent: Habad fails a crucial theological test (divine unity and incorporeality, i.e. the absolute transcendence of God)[32] and followers of Habad cannot therefore be considered members in good standing in the community of Israel. Berger's rabbinic colleagues insist that the test is applicable, and some (in private) are willing to admit that Habad fails the test, but none is willing (in public) to join Berger in his

[30] I cite the translation of Abraham M. Hershman, *The Book of Judges*, 144–5.

[31] See Berger, *The Rebbe, the Messiah, and the Scandal of Orthodox Indifference* (Oxford: Littman Library of Jewish Civilization, 2001). That many followers of Habad see the late Rabbi Menachem Mendel Schneersohn as the Messiah is certainly foolish, but not necessarily heretical. That many of them also attach expressions of divinity to him clearly violates Maimonides' principles of faith.

[32] A test, I might add, probably more important in Maimonides' eyes than the question of how precisely to define the term 'Torah from Heaven' (about which he himself held views at variance with what is considered normative by most Orthodox rabbis today; on this see my forthcoming *Maimonides' Confrontation with Mysticism*).

condemnation of Habad. Why is that? Leaving aside questions of communal policy and the nature of rabbinic leadership, it seems obvious to me that in their heart of hearts the rabbis who agree that Habad is heresy but who refuse to condemn it as such are adherents (without knowing it) of the approach I advocate—other considerations (for them, halakhic obedience; for me, identification with the past and future of the people of Israel) trump theological orthodoxy.

A number of reviewers[33] were disappointed that I did not adopt a thoroughgoing theological pluralism. I regret that I must disappoint them, but to ask a person writing from a standpoint of Orthodoxy (even as I attempted to define it) to applaud versions of Judaism which countenance or advocate large-scale abandonment of halakhah is itself not only unreasonable, but also intolerant.

To my mind there are two other problems with the call for pluralism. The first is the implied trivialization of the decision to be Jewish. In public lectures the late Emil Fackenheim used to confront his listeners with a chilling point: Jews in nineteenth-century Europe who remained Jewish condemned millions of their descendants to death. One's decision to remain Jewish could be fraught with horrifying consequences for people yet unborn; it is not a decision to be taken lightly. The claim that all forms of Judaism are equally true and valid (however one defines these words) trivializes the decision to remain Jewish. It ultimately turns remaining Jewish into a matter of taste or sentiment. I have much greater respect for a Reform Jew convinced that her interpretation of Torah is superior to mine and fervently committed to it than I have for someone whose understanding of Judaism has no truth component. With the first person, I can agree to disagree (the position staked out in this book); with the second, I have very little to discuss concerning matters of Jewish religious importance.

The second problem is inherent in the concept of religious pluralism itself: why not extend the bounds of pluralism beyond the bounds of Judaism? If one relativizes religious truth within Judaism, on what grounds can one refuse to relativize it outside Judaism?

Let me rephrase these two points in extreme terms. For thousands of years Jews have martyred themselves for their faith; to adopt a pluralist view of religious truth is to make a mockery of those sacrifices. It further implies that any Jew who makes such a sacrifice in the future is misguided.

I must hasten to add that, historically, Judaism has been convinced of

[33] Notably Peter Haas, review, *Shofar*, 19 (2001), 178–80.

its own truth without seeking to impose that truth on non-Jews. Indeed, one way of expressing what I am trying to do in this book is to urge Orthodoxy to extend the same attitude of respectful disagreement it maintains towards righteous non-Jews towards righteous non-Orthodox Jews.

Daniel H. Frank seeks to exculpate Maimonides from responsibility for the use to which he has been put by Orthodoxy over the last couple of centuries. He concludes his interesting review by saying:

> I think Maimonides' demands are not unreasonable. He is not hunting heretics, as Kellner believes, nor is he demanding mindless uniformity of belief. Rather, he calls Jews to greater reflection on the foundations of their characteristic way of life. In this regard, I side entirely with Kellner in his own battle against the forces of mindless uniformity—the thought police.[34]

I would rate this a nice try, and I certainly sympathize with its intent. Unfortunately, it founders on the shoals of some fairly hair-raising Maimonidean texts.[35] Maimonides certainly did not demand mindless uniformity of belief, but he definitely preached thoughtful uniformity and seemed to have no qualms about deploying thought police. Gotthold Ephraim Lessing (1729–81) is famous for having maintained that, if God were to offer him all truth in the right hand and the eternal search for truth in the left, he would choose the left. Maimonides, in common with all other medievals, would choose the right hand, and expected others to do so as well. Those who failed to choose the truth were to be condemned.

Rabbi Isaac Abrabanel is reputed to have ended lectures on Maimonides' philosophy with the words: 'This is the opinion of Rabeinu Mosheh [Rabbi Moses Maimonides], not of Mosheh Rabeinu [Moses our teacher].' Abravanel thought that Maimonides held views at variance with those taught in the Torah, but he still taught those views in public. Would that Jews today could put up with each other with as much forbearance!

[34] *Jewish Quarterly Review*, 92 (2002), 275.

[35] Examples include *Mishneh torah*, 'Laws of Repentance', iii. 7; 'Laws of Idolatry', ii. 5–6, v. 5, and x. 1. For discussion, see my *Dogma*, 18–21, and the additional sources cited there.

APPENDIX ONE

Maimonides on Reward and Punishment

THE idea that individuals are rewarded for their good deeds and punished for their transgressions is, according to Maimonides, literally a dogma of Judaism. The eleventh of his Thirteen Principles is

that He, may He be exalted, rewards him who obeys the commands of the Torah and punishes him who violates its prohibitions; and the greatest of His rewards is the world to come while the severest of His punishments is 'being cut off'. We have already expounded sufficiently on this in this chapter.[1] The verse which attests to this foundation is: '. . . if You forgive their sin, and if not, erase me, then from Your book which You have written' (Exod. 32: 32), taken together with His answer, may He be exalted, 'Him who has sinned against Me, shall I erase from My book' (Exod. 32: 33). These verses are attestations to [the fact that] the obedient person and the rebellious person will reach [a point] with Him, may He be exalted, where He will reward the one and punish the other.[2]

On the face of it, this is an unambiguous statement of the doctrine that people are rewarded for good behaviour and punished for evil behaviour. It is certainly no surprise to find a figure like Maimonides, one of the foremost exponents of the rabbinic tradition, presenting the doctrine of divine retribution as a dogma of Judaism.[3] If any teaching finds near-unanimous support in rabbinic literature, it is surely this one.[4]

[1] Maimonides' principles appear at the end of his introduction to his commentary on the tenth chapter of Mishnah *Sanhedrin*, 'Perek ḥelek'. The original Arabic text with modern Hebrew translation may be found in Maimonides, *Mishnah im perush rabenu moshe ben maimon*, 6 vols., ed. and trans. Joseph Kafih (Jerusalem: Mosad Harav Kook, 1963), iv. 195–217. For an English translation, see Isadore Twersky, *A Maimonides Reader* (New York: Behrman House, 1972), 401–23. Maimonides' reference here appears to be to the text at *Mishnah im perush rabenu moshe ben maimon*, ed. Kafih, 210 and Twersky, *A Maimonides Reader*, 412.

[2] I use the translation of David R. Blumenthal, as cited in Kellner, *Dogma*, 15–16, and in Appendix 2 below (p. 150).

[3] Strictly speaking, as I have argued throughout this book, it is surprising to find any exponent of the rabbinic tradition maintaining that any belief is a *dogma* of Judaism, but that is not relevant to our theme here.

[4] On the doctrine of reward and punishment in rabbinic thought see e.g. the discussion in Urbach, *The Sages*, vol. ii, ch. 15, sect. 2.

It is also no surprise, therefore, that readers whose understanding of Maimonides is coloured by the received tradition of Judaism are thunderstruck, often outraged, when confronted by the claim that Maimonides actually maintains that the righteous are not directly rewarded for their good behaviour, nor the wicked directly punished for their evil behaviour. Yet this understanding of Maimonides is the near-unanimous opinion of those of his interpreters whose approach to the 'Great Eagle' is informed by the canons of Western academic scholarship.[5]

Since many of the arguments in this book stand or fall on the question of Maimonides' understanding of reward and punishment, and since some readers of earlier drafts were indeed shocked by my assumption that Maimonides denies that the righteous are clearly and directly rewarded for the fulfilment of the commandments, I thought it necessary to write this appendix. It is my intention here to defend the 'academic' understanding of Maimonides on reward and punishment, show that he could not possibly have accepted the 'traditionalist' approach, and explain exactly in what sense he maintains that the righteous are indeed rewarded and the wicked indeed punished. I will argue further that in his own eyes his position is in no way heterodox (even though he took considerable pains to hide his true views from his less sophisticated readers). Attention will also have to be paid to the nature of Maimonides' esoteric writing in his halakhic works.

I will be demonstrating, in other words, that Maimonides put forward an esoteric teaching on the nature of divine retribution, that that teaching is a consequence of antecedently held philosophical positions, and that he did not himself hold that teaching to be heterodox. In so doing I will be advancing a project to which I have devoted considerable attention, namely showing that Maimonides understood his philosophical and Jewish commitments to coexist harmoniously and that he was in his own eyes an 'orthodox' Jew.[6]

The best place to begin our investigation is with Maimonides' first

[5] Maimonides' view on this matter was well understood by R. Solomon ben Abraham Adret (Rashba; *c.*1235–*c.*1310), the leading halakhist of his generation, who complained about Maimonides' views, 'Are the pious men of Israel without philosophy not worthy of an afterlife?' The text appears in Adret's *Responsa* (Heb.), 2 vols. (Jerusalem: Mosad Harav Kook, 1990), i. 387. I cite it as translated by Moshe Halbertal in *People of the Book* (Cambridge, Mass.: Harvard University Press, 1997), 119.

[6] See the following of my studies: *Dogma*, 10–65; *Maimonides on Human Perfection*; *Maimonides on Judaism*; 'Reading Rambam'; 'The Beautiful Captive'; *Maimonides on the 'Decline of the Generations'*.

statement of his opinions concerning the nature of retribution in this world and the next, his introduction to the tenth chapter of Mishnah *Sanhedrin*, 'Perek ḥelek'. It is at the end of this text that he enunciates his Thirteen Principles and it is in the light of this text, I maintain, that we ought to understand the eleventh principle of faith, cited above. In commenting on the mishnah which begins 'All Israelites have a share in the world to come', Maimonides writes:

I must now speak of the great fundamental principles of our faith. Know that the masters of the Torah hold differing opinions concerning the good which will come to a person as a result of fulfilling the commandments which God commanded us through Moses our Teacher. (p. 402)[7]

After describing five different views about the nature of reward for the fulfilment of the commandments, Maimonides introduces an analogy by way of explaining the correct understanding of divine retribution. A small child will study the Torah only if bribed to do so. Such a child cannot understand that study of the Torah brings us to our perfection and is thus worth doing in and of itself. As the child grows, the nature of the bribes changes (from food, to clothing, to money, to social status). This is deplorable, Maimonides says, but also unavoidable, 'because of man's limited insight, as a result of which he makes the goal of wisdom something other than wisdom itself . . . our Sages called this learning not for its own sake' (p. 405).

Learning the Torah for its own sake, on the other hand, means that 'the end of studying wisdom [should not] be anything but knowing it. The truth has no other purpose than knowing that it is truth. Since the Torah is truth, the purpose of knowing it is to do it' (p. 405).[8] This study and doing should be motivated by nothing extrinsic to itself:

[7] Here and below I cite from the translation found in Twersky, *A Maimonides Reader*, 401 ff. The translation is relatively loose but sufficient for our purposes. Page references in the text are to this edition. I have retranslated passages which require greater precision from the Arabic–Hebrew edition by Kafih, as indicated in the text.

[8] Y. Leibowitz (incorrectly) uses this passage to prove that the fulfilment of the commandments is 'not a means: it is the end in itself'. For Leibowitz's texts and a critique of them see the important article by Hannah Kasher, ' "Torah for its Own Sake", "Torah not for its Own Sake", and the Third Way', *Jewish Quarterly Review*, 79 (1988–9), 153–63 at 157. This fine article provides significant support for the interpretation of Maimonides put forward here. Further on our issue, see the discussion between Hannah Kasher and Michael Zvi Nehorai in *Tarbits*, 64/2 (1995), 301–8. See also Dov Schwartz, 'Avicenna and Maimonides on Immortality: A Comparative Study', in Ronald Nettler (ed.), *Studies in Muslim–Jewish Relations* (Chur, Switzerland: Harwood Academic Publishers, 1993), 185–97. For another very useful and convincing study relevant to my theme here, see

A good man must not wonder, 'If I perform these commandments, which are virtues, and if I refrain from these transgressions, which are vices which God commanded us not to do, what will I get out of it?' This is precisely what the child does when he asks, 'If I read, what will you give me?' (p. 405)

In promising a child some sweet or toy in order to motivate it to learn, we are acting in accordance with Proverbs 26: 5: 'Answer the fool according to his folly.' It is reasonable to extrapolate and see that Maimonides is hinting that when a person is promised some earthly reward for the study of the Torah or the fulfilment of its commandments, that promise is an instance of answering the fool according to his folly.

Maimonides seems to confirm this interpretation immediately: 'Our sages have already warned us about this. They said that one should not make the goal of one's service of God or of doing the commandments anything in the world of things' (p. 406).[9] One who does so does not serve God out of love. The true servant of God, Maimonides continues, quoting the Talmud, desires God's commandments, not the reward of God's commandments.[10]

Maimonides admits that it is hard to motivate the masses to serve God out of love, with no thought of reward or fear of punishment. 'Therefore,' he says, 'in order that the masses stay faithful and do the commandments, it was permitted to tell them that they might hope for a reward and to warn them against transgressions out of fear of punishment . . . just like the child in the analogy which I cited above' (p. 406).

Having made his position tolerably clear, that only fools and children expect rewards for the fulfilment of the commandments or for the study of the Torah, Maimonides suddenly shifts his attention to a new question altogether: how to understand the words of the Sages (in midrashic and aggadic contexts). The suddenness of this shift of attention is actually more apparent than real. Maimonides is interested here in

Jerome Gellman, 'Radical Responsibility in Maimonides' Thought', in Ira Robinson *et al.* (eds.), *The Thought of Moses Maimonides* (Lewiston, NY: Edwin Mellen Press, 1990), 249–65.

[9] i.e. in this earthly world. The passage quoted is from BT *Avodah zarah* 19*a*.

[10] Maimonides' statements on service of God out of love have recently been collected and analysed by Abraham Feintuch, *Upright Commands* (Heb.) (Jerusalem: Ma'aliyot, 1992), 80–2. See further Menachem Kellner, 'Philosophical Misogyny in Medieval Jewish Thought: Gersonides vs. Maimonides', in A. Ravitzky (ed.), *From Rome to Jerusalem: The Joseph Sermonetta Memorial Volume* (Heb.) (Jerusalem: Magnes Press, 1998), 113–28. In addition to the sources cited in these two studies, see also *Guide*, iii. 28–9. For important new insights into the issue, see Howard Haim Kreisel, 'Love and Fear of God in Maimonides' Thought' (Heb.), *Da'at*, 37 (1996), 127–52.

teaching us how to understand rabbinic discussions of reward in the world to come.

There are those who interpret the Sages literally and accept their teachings on that level; there are others who also interpret the Sages literally but therefore reject their teachings as contrary to reason. The very small number of people who interpret the words of the Sages correctly realize that to interpret them literally is to impute nonsense to them. People of this sort understand that 'whenever the sages spoke of things which seem impossible, they were employing the style of riddle and parable which is the method of truly great thinkers' (p. 409).

Having made these introductions, Maimonides can finally 'begin to discuss the matter with which I am really concerned' (p. 410). This is, that true delight is spiritual. Such delight has no physical analogue, being of a different dimension altogether. The angels, heavenly bodies, and spheres 'experience great delight in that they know by experience the true being of God the Creator. With this knowledge they enjoy delight which is both perpetual and uninterrupted' (p. 411). Individuals who purify themselves in this world will achieve this 'spiritual height'.

How does one purify oneself in order to achieve this rarefied existence? Maimonides makes himself fairly clear, commenting on a passage from BT *Berakhot* 17*a* which reads: 'In the world to come there is no eating, drinking, washing, anointing, or sexual intercourse; but the righteous sit with their crowns on their heads enjoying the radiance of the divine presence.' The expression 'crowns on their heads', Maimonides explains,

> signifies the existence of the soul through the existence of that which it knows, in that they are the same thing as the experts in philosophy have maintained . . . The expression, 'enjoying the radiance of the divine presence' means that those souls enjoy what they know of the Creator, as the *ḥayot hakodesh* and other degrees of angels[11] enjoy what they have cognized of His existence. (p. 412; my translation)

Maimonides explains to us here that the reward of the righteous in the world to come is the existence of the soul thanks to what it has learned. This existence is blissful because it involves the cognition of God. This is something taught by the 'experts in philosophy'.

Maimonides sharpens the point in the sequel: the final end of human beings, their ultimate felicity, consists in knowing God, which knowledge 'is the cause [of the soul's] continued existence, as was established in

[11] For Maimonides on the *ḥayot hakodesh* ('holy animals') and other degrees of angels, see 'Laws of the Foundations of the Torah', ii. 7.

first philosophy'. 'First philosophy', of course, is a standard Aristotelian expression referring to metaphysics.

Reward in the world to come, then, is a consequence of achieving a certain kind of knowledge in this life and consists of enjoying that knowledge without change and without end. If that is reward, what is punishment? Maimonides is quick to answer that the ultimate punishment 'consists in the cutting off of the soul so that it perishes and does not exist' (p. 412; my translation).[12] If this is the case, Maimonides continues, what could be 'the meaning of the promises of good and threats of evil punishment which are contained in the Torah?' When the Torah promises a reward, it means that God will remove obstacles to human fulfilment, 'so that men who strive to do the commandments will be healthy and at peace so that their knowledge will be perfected and they will [thereby] merit life in the world to come' (p. 413; my translation).

We may now summarize Maimonides' position as it has been developed to this point. Fulfilment of the commandments enables us to learn about God. Learning about God is the key to the soul's survival after the death of the body. The fulfilment of the commandments itself without learning about God does not bring one to the world to come, while it appears that Maimonides would hold (indeed, has to hold, as I will show below) that learning about God without fulfilment of the commandments does bring one to the world to come.[13]

There is an important point which must be emphasized here. Life in the world to come is not a reward in the sense that if a person does *x* then God responds by granting that person a share in the world to come. For

[12] A consequence of Maimonides' position—a consequence from which he does not shrink—is that there is no actual punishment after death. He makes that point tolerably clear in his discussion of the biblical *karet* ('cutting off') in 'Laws of Repentance', i. 1 and i. 5, and explicitly in viii. 1. His statements on this matter have deeply troubled traditionalist interpreters of the *Mishneh torah*, starting with Nahmanides and continuing through R. Joseph Karo (in his *Kesef mishneh* on 'Laws of Repentance', viii. 1) to our own day in the commentaries of Rabbi Nachum Rabinovitch, and Rabbi Joseph Kafih. The ingenuity of these commentators aside, it will be shown below that Maimonides could not have held any other position. For Nahmanides, see his *Writings and Discourses*, trans. Charles B. Chavel (New York: Shilo, 1978), 390–5, 495–504; for Rabinovitch, see his *Yad peshutah* on the *Mishneh torah*, book 1 (*Sefer hamada*), 2 vols. (Jerusalem: Ma'aliyot, 1990), i. 971; for Kafih, see his commentary on the *Mishneh torah*, book 1 (*Sefer hamada*) (Jerusalem: Makhon Moshe, 1986), 636.

[13] I hasten to add that Maimonides was not optimistic that many could learn about God without fulfilling the commandments, only that the possibility existed. For details, see Kellner, *Maimonides on Judaism*, 29–32.

Maimonides, one achieves a share in the world to come by learning about God. As he puts it,

When one perfects oneself as a human being, and genuinely differentiates oneself from the animals,[14] one becomes a perfected human being; a characteristic of this degree is that nothing external can restrain the soul from existing through that which it cognizes, and this is the world to come, as we have explained. (p. 416; my translation)

In other words, life in the world to come is a consequence of having achieved human perfection, not a reward for a particular sort of behaviour.[15] For Maimonides, correct behaviour (i.e. fulfilment of the commandments) is surely obligatory, and certainly an important condition for achieving human perfection, but in itself it does not constitute that perfection and there is, literally, no direct reward for it.[16]

Maimonides' position here in his commentary on 'Perek ḥelek' is couched in very traditional language, and most readers, expecting to find a traditional account, and not familiar with the Aristotelian background to Maimonides' argumentation (which I will elucidate below), are not even aware that an unusual stance is being taken.

The position on reward and punishment which I have found in

[14] Accepting the Aristotelian definition of a human being as a rational animal (see *Guide*, i. 1–2), Maimonides is committed to the proposition that the specific difference which marks humans off from other animals is their rationality. Thus, one 'genuinely differentiates oneself from the animals' by achieving rationality and thus becoming fully human. Those who do not make the grade remain animals in human form. Such a one 'is not a man, but an animal having the shape and configuration of man' (*Guide*, i. 8, p. 33; cf. iii. 18, p. 475 and commentary on Mishnah *Ḥagigah* ii. 1). This last text is available in an annotated English translation: Menachem Kellner, 'Maimonides' Commentary on *Ḥagigah* ii. 1', in Marc Angel (ed.), *From Strength to Strength* (New York: Sepher Hermon Press, 1988), 101–11

[15] The point is put very well by Kasher in ' "Torah for its Own Sake" '. As Kasher puts it, Maimonides replaces 'the principle of just recompense with a rational doctrine of natural consequence' (p. 157). Further, 'God's rule of the world and his providential actions are not based upon the idea of reward and punishment, but upon a natural process which leads to a desirable outcome' (p. 162).

[16] We are now in a position to understand why there can be no punishment after death for the wicked: nothing remains to be punished! If we are born, live, and die without perfecting ourselves as human beings, then we die as we were born: human beings *in potentia* only. Maimonides' Aristotelian doctrine of the soul makes it impossible for him to posit punishment after death for evildoers. The righteous (= intellectually perfected) create their own immortality and enjoy it when they die; the wicked (= those who have not actualized their intellectual potential even to a small degree) create nothing and therefore are nothing when they die.

Maimonides' commentary on 'Perek ḥelek' is repeated in other of his works, both halakhic and philosophical. I have cited and analysed these texts in another context;[17] here I must be content briefly to summarize them.

In 'Laws of the Foundations of the Torah', iv. 9, Maimonides explicitly connects knowledge of God with the persistence of the soul after death. In 'Laws of Repentance', viii. 3, again quoting from BT *Berakhot* 17*a*, Maimonides repeats that the expression 'their crowns on their heads' 'refers to the knowledge they have acquired, and on account of which they have attained life in the world to come'.

Maimonides' position on fulfilment of the commandments and reward in the world to come finds clear expression in the *Guide of the Perplexed*. A human being's ultimate perfection, Maimonides maintains,

> is to become rational in actu; this would consist in knowing everything concerning all the beings that it is within the capacity of man to know in accordance with his ultimate perfection. It is clear that to this ultimate perfection there do not belong either *actions or moral qualities* and that it consists only of ideas toward which speculation has led and that investigation has rendered compulsory.[18]

Perfection consists only in knowledge.[19] This perfection is purely intellectual; 'actions or moral qualities' do not constitute it all.

What is going on here? Does Maimonides really mean to teach that fulfilment of the commandments is a waste of time, and that in order to reach ultimate perfection one must devote oneself wholly to perfecting one's intellect? Were that his position, he would really have placed

[17] See Kellner, *Maimonides on Human Perfection*, 1–5.

[18] *Guide*, iii. 27, p. 511; emphasis added.

[19] Some students of Maimonides maintain that such perfection is actually impossible and thus hold that he denied that anyone could really achieve a share in the world to come. This view, held by Shlomo Pines, obviously turns Maimonides into a self-consciously heterodox thinker. Pines' position has been criticized by Alexander Altmann and Herbert Davidson. See Shlomo Pines, 'The Limitations of Human Knowledge According to al-Farabi, ibn Bajjah, and Maimonides', in Isadore Twersky (ed.), *Studies in Medieval Jewish History and Literature*, i (Cambridge, Mass.: Harvard University Press, 1979), 82–109; Alexander Altmann, 'Maimonides on the Intellect and the Scope of Metaphysics', in *Von der mittelalterlichen zur modernen Aufklärung* (Tübingen: Mohr, 1987), 60–129; Herbert A. Davidson, 'Maimonides on Metaphysical Knowledge', *Maimonidean Studies*, 3 (1992–3), 49–103. The question of what sort of knowledge constitutes human perfection has also been debated. See Warren Zev Harvey, 'R. Hasdai Crescas and his Critique of Philosophic Happiness' (Heb.), *Proceedings of the Sixth World Congress of Jewish Studies*, 3 (1977), 143–9.

himself so far outside the mainstream of the rabbinic tradition as to justify the claims of those who see him as an *epikoros*, a self-conscious heretic.

Maimonides, however, neither says nor intimates that Jews are not obligated to fulfil the commandments. We are indeed so obligated, and it is good for us to do so. What he does hold is that there is no direct, *quid pro quo* compensation for the fulfilment of the commandments. We ought to fulfil the commandments in a mature fashion, out of love, with no expectation of reward.

What good then are the commandments and their fulfilment? Maimonides essays an answer to this near the very end of the *Guide*:

> all the actions prescribed by the Torah—I refer to the various species of worship and also the moral habits that are useful to all people in their mutual dealings— . . . all this is not to be compared with this ultimate end and does not equal it, *being but preparations for the sake of this end.*[20]

The commandments are preparations which enable human beings to achieve their proper end, intellectual perfection. Through the achievement of such perfection, one constitutes one's own immortality.

How does this work? In order to answer this question we must look at Maimonides' psychology, or theory of the soul. This is a subject to which I have also paid attention elsewhere, and so here, again, I will only summarize the key elements of Maimonides' theory.[21] Maimonides adopted an account of the nature of human psychology called the theory of the acquired intellect. According to this theory, humans are born with a potential to learn, which they may or may not actualize, and it is this

[20] *Guide*, iii. 54, p. 636; emphasis added.

[21] See Kellner, *Maimonides on Judaism, passim* and esp. 9–16. With respect to Maimonides' adoption of the theory of the acquired intellect, Isaac Abrabanel also attributes it to him in his commentary on *Guide of the Perplexed*, i. 1, i. 41 (Abrabanel's commentary is found in the standard Hebrew editions of the *Guide*), in his commentary on Genesis (Jerusalem: Benei Arabel, 1964), 67, and in *Yeshu'ot meshiḥo*, section (*iyun*) 1, ch. 5 (Benei Berak: Me'orei Sefarad, 1993), 92. He sees Alexander of Aphrodisias as Maimonides' source and criticizes the latter heartily for following Alexander in this matter. In his commentary on 1 Samuel 25, third root (Jerusalem: Torah Veda'at, 1955), 286, Abrabanel argues, against Maimonides, that immortality is not restricted to the 'souls of perfected individuals, who survive through their concepts or their desired actions, but the souls of the wicked also survive in the world of souls in order to be punished there'. Abrabanel goes on to connect the view he rejects (that the wicked have no world to come) to the psychology of Alexander of Aphrodisias, according to which the human soul is at birth (only) a disposition. This latter view he also attributes to Maimonides, and he hints rather broadly that Maimonides also accepts the view that the wicked do not survive to be punished in the world to come.

capability and its actualization in which their humanity lies. In slightly more formal terms, we are born with a capacity to know; to the extent that we actualize that capacity by learning truth, we become actual intellects—we have acquired our intellects; if we fail to actualize our intellects, that capacity with which we are born is wasted and nothing survives the death of our bodies.[22] It is important to note here that on the theory of the acquired intellect the only way to achieve immortality, what Jews call earning a portion in the world to come, is through actually acquiring an intellect by perfecting ourselves intellectually. There is simply no other mechanism available to Maimonides on his own understanding of the nature of human beings.

One could reply, of course, that there is nothing to stop God from working a miracle and granting a saintly but simple person a share in the world to come. On Maimonides' theory of miracles this solution is not available. Maimonides' understanding of the stable character of nature, and his consistent attempts to explain miracles in naturalistic terms, make it impossible that he should hold that God works miracle after miracle to guarantee a share in the world to come to every saintly but philosophically unsophisticated person who dies. Maimonides, indeed, explicitly distances himself from the 'masses', who, he says,

> like nothing better, and in their silliness, enjoy nothing more, than to settle the Torah and reason at opposite ends, and to move everything far from the explicable. So they claim it to be a miracle, and they shrink from identifying it as a natural incident . . . But I try to reconcile the Torah and reason, and wherever possible consider all things as of the natural order. Only when something is explicitly identified as a miracle, and reinterpretation of it cannot be accommodated, only then I feel forced to grant that this is a miracle.[23]

Now, Maimonides is quite clear in maintaining that in order to perfect our intellects we must achieve and maintain a high level of moral perfection. In the *Guide of the Perplexed*, he discusses four types of perfection which pertain to human beings (possessions, physical constitution, morals, and intellect). Of the third he says:

> The third kind is a perfection that to a greater extent than the second kind

[22] As we saw above, this is what Maimonides calls *karet*, the biblical punishment of being 'cut off'.

[23] This passage is found in Maimonides' 'Treatise on Resurrection'. I cite it (with slight emendations) as translated by Halkin in *Crisis and Leadership*, 223. Further on this subject see my discussion of Maimonides' understanding of nature and miracles in Kellner, *Maimonides on the 'Decline of the Generations'*, 27–36.

subsists in the self. This is the perfection of the moral virtues. It consists in the individual's moral habits having attained their utmost excellence. Most of the commandments serve no other end than the attainment of this kind of perfection. But this kind of perfection is likewise a preparation for something else and not an end in itself.[24]

Most of the commandments serve to bring us to moral perfection.[25] But this perfection to which we are brought by the fulfilment of the commandments is not an end in itself; rather, it is 'a preparation for something else'. For what is it a preparation? Maimonides answers immediately:

The fourth kind is the true human perfection; it consists in the acquisition of the rational virtues—I refer to the conception of the intelligibles, which teach true opinions concerning the divine things. This is in true reality the ultimate end; this is what gives the individual true perfection, a perfection belonging to him alone; and it gives him permanent perdurance; through it man is man.

Fulfilment of the commandments is thus not valuable in and of itself; it is, rather, a means for achieving the one truly human virtue, the one truly human perfection, the one activity which constitutes us as human beings in this world and guarantees our existence in the next, namely, the 'conception of the intelligibles, which teach true opinions concerning the divine things'.[26]

Maimonides himself stresses this point, stating further

that similarly all the actions prescribed by the Torah—I refer to the various species of worship and also the moral habits that are useful to people in their mutual dealings—that all this is not to be compared with this ultimate end [wisdom] and does not equal it, being but preparations made for the sake of this end.[27]

As we saw above, looking for rewards in this world for the fulfilment of the commandments is a sign of immaturity and foolishness; while the only reward in the next world is an outgrowth and consequence of (not a

[24] *Guide*, iii. 54, p. 635.

[25] Most, but not all, since some commandments bring us to adopt true beliefs, such as observance of the Sabbath, which teaches creation, and the first of the Ten Commandments, which teaches God's existence.

[26] i.e. metaphysics. For an analysis of the many texts in which Maimonides makes the identification, 'secrets of the Torah' = 'Account of the Chariot' = metaphysics, see Kellner, *Maimonides on Judaism*, 65–80. See also the important study by Sara Klein-Braslavy, *King Solomon and Philosophical Esotericism in Maimonides' Teaching* (Heb.) (Jerusalem: Magnes, 1996), 48–75, 203–10.

[27] *Guide*, iii. 54, p. 636.

response to) our intellectual perfection and nothing else. We can now see why for Maimonides there can be no reward or punishment in this world or the next for the fulfilment of the commandments or their violation as such.

Why, then, should we fulfil the commandments? The very question would have given Maimonides a stomach-ache, I think, since in his view it is so wrong-headed. In the first place, Jews are commanded by God to fulfil the commandments. Jews who love God will fulfil the commandments with devotion and joy, with no thought whatsoever of reward. Furthermore, the fulfilment of the commandments is good for you. It makes you into a better person. Even more, a society of individuals fulfilling the commandments of the Torah will be a stable and just society, as Maimonides makes clear in the *Guide* (iii. 27). Finally, in order to realize our potential we must lead ordered, structured, disciplined, and moral lives, otherwise we will never fulfil ourselves as human beings, i.e. as rational animals. Maimonides was convinced that there is no better way to achieve that end than through the fulfilment of God's commandments.

A word of explanation concerning this last point is warranted. Achieving intellectual perfection is extremely hard work, demanding years of disciplined study and devotion in the search of truth, not enjoyment of the pleasures of this world in and of themselves.[28] Very few people can discipline themselves in this fashion. Adopting a mode of life which channels our desires in a healthy fashion, disciplines our behaviour, and leads (those who are able) to intellectual perfection makes the likelihood of perfecting ourselves as human beings much greater.[29] It is not impossible for Gentiles to accomplish this; it is simply much harder for them than for Jews since they do not have the Torah.[30]

Maimonides' position may be summarized thus: fulfilment of the commandments is both an obligation and also certainly good for you, but brings no direct reward, in this world or the next; transgressing the commandments is forbidden and bad for you, but brings no direct punishment, in this world or the next.

All this being said, it is still the case that in not a few places Maimonides

[28] Intellectual perfection must also be constantly renewed. As Lenn Goodman once pointed out to me, it is not like money in the bank, but is, rather, like health or vigour. Without constant exercise, one loses one's vigour. In this sense, intellectual perfection is like treading water: if you stop, you sink.

[29] On this way of life, see Kellner, 'Revelation and Messianism'.

[30] On this point, see Kellner, *Maimonides on Judaism*, 23–32.

clearly speaks as if he accepted a traditionalist account of reward and punishment. Thus, in 'Laws of Repentance', Maimonides writes: 'In that it is known that the reward for the [fulfilment of the] commandments, and the good that we will receive if we observe the way of the Lord as written in the Torah is life in the world to come . . .'. Maimonides here says that life in the world to come is earned through the fulfilment of the commandments.[31] This is, of course, good solid traditional Judaism, but it is a far cry from the doctrine which I hope I have shown here to be espoused by Maimonides and summarized in the previous paragraph.

We have a number of choices here. We can accept the text from the 'Laws of Repentance' as normative and attempt to interpret the texts adduced above in support of the interpretation of Maimonides urged here in its light; or, alternatively, we can take 'my' interpretation of Maimonides as correct and seek to understand why he seems to diverge from it here in the 'Laws of Repentance'. Not surprisingly, I propose to adopt this second alternative, and I would like to explain why.

The interpretation of Maimonides' stance on reward and punishment presented here follows from several other positions which Maimonides clearly holds. If we reject it, we must also reject Maimonides' views on the nature of human beings, their perfection, and his understanding of miracles. That is an unacceptably high price to pay.

Why, though, does Maimonides not present his position clearly and unambiguously? Why does he force us to tease it out of texts like the introduction to 'Perek ḥelek' (as we did above), and why does he seem to contradict it (as in the passage just cited from 'Laws of Repentance')?[32] An answer to this question may be found in *Guide of the Perplexed*, iii. 28. There we are told that in addition to teaching truths in a summary fashion, the Torah 'also makes a call to adopt certain beliefs, belief in which is necessary for the sake of political welfare'. That is, the Torah teaches things which are themselves not strictly and literally true, but are beliefs which the masses must accept so as not to undermine the stability of society. The example cited by Maimonides clearly confirms this inter-

[31] 'Laws of Repentance', ix. 1. For further examples, see 'Laws of Forbidden Intercourse', xiv. 3; Commentary on Mishnah *Makot*, iii. 17.

[32] In actual fact, I think that the contradiction is more apparent than real. If we understand Maimonides here in light of a passage already cited from the commentary on 'Perek ḥelek' ('so that men who strive to do the commandments will be healthy and at peace so that their knowledge will be perfected and they will [thereby] merit life in the world to come'), we can understand him to be saying that obedience to the commandments leads to health and peace, which in turn enables people to devote themselves to the acquisition of knowledge, which brings them to the world to come.

pretation: 'Such, for example, is our belief that He, may He be exalted, is violently angry with those who disobey Him and it is therefore necessary to fear Him and to dread Him and to take care not to disobey.' Now, Maimonides makes it abundantly clear in many contexts that God does not really get angry.[33] But it is certainly useful for religiously immature people to believe that God gets angry so that they 'take care not to disobey'. At the end of the chapter Maimonides sums up his position very clearly:

> In some cases a commandment communicates a correct belief . . . In other cases the belief is [only] necessary for the abolition of reciprocal wrongdoing or for the acquisition of a noble moral quality—as, for instance, the belief that He, may He be exalted, has a violent anger against those who do injustice, according to what is said: 'And My wrath shall wax hot, and I will kill . . .' [Exod. 22: 23] and as the belief that He, may He be exalted, responds instantaneously to the prayer of someone wronged or deceived: 'And it shall come to pass, when he crieth unto Me, that I will hear; for I am gracious' [Exod. 22: 26].

It is hard to state the point more clearly than this: it is important that people believe that God gets violently angry with sinners and it is important for them to believe that God immediately answers the prayers of the wronged. The Torah therefore teaches that these beliefs are true; that does not mean that they are actually true in and of themselves. They are necessary beliefs, not true beliefs.[34]

The notion that the righteous are rewarded for the fulfilment of the commandments in this world and the next, without any reference to their intellectual attainments, and that the wicked are punished in the next world, if not clearly in this world, for their transgressions,[35] is, I submit, a necessary belief without being a true one. As Maimonides himself told us in the introduction to 'Perek ḥelek', very few people are mature enough

[33] See esp. *Guide*, i. 54. Further on Maimonides' extremely negative attitude towards anger, see *Guide*, iii. 8; 'Laws of Character Traits', ii. 3; commentary on *Pirkei avot* ii. 10; and *Book of Commandments*, positive commandment 317.

[34] As we saw above, Maimonides writes in his commentary on 'Perek ḥelek', 'in order that the masses stay faithful and do the commandments, it was permitted to tell them that they might hope for a reward and to warn them against transgressions out of fear of punishment'.

[35] It is crucial to remember that for Maimonides moral perfection is a prerequisite of intellectual perfection. He does not have to 'worry' that an intellectually perfected wicked person will 'sneak' into the world to come. Wicked people do not achieve true intellectual perfection. This position is, I think, objectively false (Martin Heidegger, for example, was a moral pygmy and at the same time an important philosopher); but that does not mean that Maimonides did not hold it. He is allowed to be wrong.

to fulfil the commandments of the Torah for its own sake. They must be motivated by promises of reward and threats of punishment. These promises are in one sense false: there is no *quid pro quo* reward for the fulfilment of the commandments; one does not earn credit points in some heavenly bank account for obeying the commandments of the Torah. But in another sense these promises are true: obeying the commandments of the Torah is surely good for you. In most cases such obedience in and of itself (with no divine intervention) leads to a happier and more fulfilled life, and to a better and more just society. Obedience to the commandments is also a crucially important, if neither necessary nor sufficient, step towards achieving true human perfection and the life in the world to come which is a consequence of that perfection.

APPENDIX TWO

The Thirteen Principles

I use the translation of David R. Blumenthal in his *The Commentary of R. Ḥoter ben Shelomo to the Thirteen Principles of Maimonides* (Leiden: Brill, 1974), pp. 52, 74, 83, 91, 107, 114, 125, 144, 148, 164, 166, 171, and 181.

WHAT is appropriate for me to record now—and this is the most appropriate place to record them—is that the principles of our pure Torah and its foundations are thirteen foundations.[1]

The first foundation is the existence of the Creator,[2] may He be praised; to wit that there exists a being in the most perfect type of existence and that it is the cause of the existence of all other beings. In this being is the source of their existence, and from it derives their [continued] existence. If we were able to eliminate its existence, then the existence of all other beings would be nullified and nothing would remain. However, if we were able to eliminate the existence of all beings other than it, His existence, may He be exalted, would not be nullified nor be lacking, for He is self-sufficient, dependent upon no other for His existence. Everything other than He of the Intelligences,[3] meaning the

[1] As noted above (p. 54), Isaac Abrabanel explains that Maimonides presented the Thirteen Principles in an attempt to define the term 'Israelite' as used in Mishnah *Sanhedrin* x. 1 ('All Israelites have a share in the world to come . . .').

[2] Maimonides' use of this term (*albari* in Arabic) here does not of itself imply a doctrine of creation out of nothing. In the original version of the principles (on which, see n. 18 below) Maimonides does not make acceptance of the doctrine of creation out of nothing a principle of faith. On the term, see Warren Zev Harvey, 'A Third Approach to Maimonides' Cosmogony-Prophetology Puzzle', *Harvard Theological Review*, 74 (1981), 287–301 at 296; also the discussion in Kellner, *Dogma*, 53–61. In this first principle, God is described as cause of the world, not as its creator, even though the term 'creator' is used. This point troubled R. Shimon ben Tsemah Duran (1361–1444), since it appears to be the position of Aristotle and not that of the Torah. See Kellner, *Dogma*, 87–8.

[3] By 'Intelligences' Maimonides means the 'separate intellects' (*sekhalim nivdalim* in Hebrew): those disembodied intellects whose name derives from their being 'separate'—distinct from—matter, as opposed to human intellects, which develop out of a material disposition, and which in Maimonides' Neoplatonized Aristotelianism move the heavenly spheres and constitute the intermediate stages of existence between God and our world. Identifying them with the biblical angels is not to pour new wine into old bottles, as

angels, and the matter of the spheres,[4] is dependent upon Him for its existence. This first foundation is attested to by the verse, 'I am the Lord thy God' (Exod. 20: 2).[5]

The second foundation is God's unity, may He be exalted; to wit, that this One, Who is the cause of [the existence of] everything, is one.[6] His oneness is unlike the oneness of a genus, or of a species.[7] Nor is it like the oneness of a single composed individual, which can be divided into many units.[8] Nor is His oneness like that of the simple body which is one in number but infinitely divisible.[9] Rather, He, may He be exalted, is one with a oneness for which there is no comparison at all. The second foundation is attested to by the verse: 'Hear, O Israel, the Lord our God, the Lord is one' (Deut. 6: 4).

The third foundation is the denial of corporeality to Him; to wit, that this One is neither a body nor a force within a body.[10] None of the characteristics of a body appertains to Him, either by His essence or as an accident thereof, as for example, movement and rest.[11] It is for this reason

Maimonides was convinced that the Torah taught metaphysics and that the actual meaning of the biblical term 'angel' was 'separate intellect'.

[4] This passage is made clearer by 'Laws of the Foundations of the Torah', ii. 3. There Maimonides informs us that all created entities fall into three classes: transitory entities composed of matter and form (all that exists in the sublunar natural world); permanent entities composed of matter and form (the spheres and heavenly bodies); and permanent entities composed of form only (the angels, or separate intellects). Cf. further *Guide*, ii. 10, p. 273. Maimonides' point here would appear to be that everything in the universe, emphatically including unchanging heavenly entities, depends upon God for its existence.

[5] Maimonides' claim that this verse teaches the doctrine of God's existence, commonly accepted today (because of Maimonides' vast influence) was a matter of considerable debate in the Middle Ages. See Kellner, *Dogma*, 127–36.

[6] Once again, God is presented as cause of the universe, not necessarily as its creator. To this Aristotle, who held the universe to be uncreated but not uncaused, would have no objection.

[7] A genus (such as mammals) is one, but not simple, since it is composed of species; a species is one, but not simple, since it is composed of individuals.

[8] Even an individual, which, unlike a genus or a species, is not composed of members, is still composed of components, such as the four elements.

[9] Even simple elements (earth, air, water, fire) can be divided into ever smaller bits (Maimonides could say this since he rejected atomism in favour of the doctrine of matter and form).

[10] i.e. God is neither a body nor a force which exists as the consequence of the existence of a body. An example of the latter in modern terms would be the force of gravity as we experience it.

[11] Movement and rest, that is, are 'accidents' of material bodies, not essential characteristics of them. A material body can be either in motion or at rest; either way it remains a material body.

that they, may they rest in peace, denied to Him division and continuity in saying: 'There is no sitting, nor standing, nor *oref* [lit. "shoulder"], nor *ipui* [lit. "fatigue"] in heaven.'[12] They meant that there is no 'division' which is *oref*, nor is there any continuity (as it is said: *ve'afu bekhatef pelishtim* [Isa. 11: 4], meaning, 'they shall push them with their shoulders [to form a continuous mass] because they are closely packed together,' as the Targum says, 'they shall put their shoulders together').[13] The prophet has said: 'To whom then will you compare Me so that I be similar?' (Isa. 40: 25). Were God a body, He would then resemble bodies.[14] Everything mentioned in the Scriptures which describes Him, may He be exalted, as having the attributes of a body, such as moving from place to place, or standing, or sitting, or speaking, and so on, is all metaphors, allegories, and riddles, as they have said, 'The Torah speaks in human language.'[15] People have philosophized a great deal about this matter.[16] This third foundation is attested to by the verse 'you saw no image' (Deut. 4: 15), meaning, 'you did not perceive Him, may He be exalted, as having an image,' for He is, as we have said, neither a body nor a force within a body.

The fourth foundation is God's precedence;[17] to wit, that this one who just been described is He Who precedes everything absolutely. No other being has precedence with respect to Him. There are many verses attesting to this in Scripture. The verse attesting to it [best] is 'the God of

[12] BT *Ḥagigah* 15*a*.

[13] *Targum* on Isa. 11: 4. The parenthetical expression here is part of Maimonides' text; I have added the parentheses for the sake of clarity. The point of these two sentences is that Maimonides is attributing to the rabbis in BT *Ḥagigah* 15*a* the doctrine of divine incorporeality.

[14] i.e. were God a body, a comparison with other bodies would be possible. Here Maimonides is attributing the doctrine of divine incorporeality to Isaiah.

[15] The statement is drawn from BT *Berakhot* 31*b*. As Abraham Nuriel has shown, Maimonides wholly revised the meaning of this rabbinic statement. Its original use was to claim that not every apparently extra word in Scripture should be understood as teaching something taught nowhere else (on the basis of the rabbinic teaching that there are no unnecessary words in Scripture), since some apparently extra words are necessitated by the way in which Hebrew is actually spoken. Maimonides took it to mean that Scripture couched philosophical teachings in mythological language, suitable for the simple-minded or uneducated. See Abraham Nuriel, '"The Torah Speaks in Human Language" in the *Guide of the Perplexed*', in A. Kasher and M. Hallamish (eds.), *Religion and Language* (Heb.) (Tel Aviv: University Publications, 1981), 97–103.

[16] Maimonides himself devotes the first fifty chapters of the *Guide of the Perplexed* to an analysis of biblical terms which seem to impute corporeality to God.

[17] Arabic: *alkadam*; Hebrew: *kadmon*. This term may denote only ontological, not temporal, precedence. See n. 1 above.

eternity is a dwelling place' (Deut. 33: 27).[18] Know that a foundation of the great Torah of Moses is that the world is created: God created it and formed it after its absolute non-existence. That you see me circling around the idea of the eternity of the world is only so that the proof of His existence will be absolute as I explained and made clear in the *Guide*.[19]

The fifth foundation is that He, may He be exalted, is He Whom it is proper to worship and to praise; and [that it is also proper] to promulgate praise of Him and obedience to Him. This may not be done for any being other than Him in reality, from among the angels, the spheres, the elements, and that which is composed of them, for all these have their activities imprinted upon them.[20] They have no destiny [of their own] and no rootedness [of their own in reality] other than His love, may He be exalted [of them]. Do not, furthermore, seize upon intermediaries in order to reach Him but direct your thoughts towards Him, may He be exalted, and turn away from that which is other than He.[21] This fifth

[18] This principle, as expressed to this point (as it appeared in the earliest 'editions' of the commentary on the Mishnah), seems calculated to upset the philosophically sophisticated but religiously conservative reader, as was indeed the case with R. Shimon ben Tsemah Duran (see n. 2 above). God here is described in terms which Aristotle could easily accept: God is presented as cause of the world, but not as its creator. (For example, I am, I hope, the cause of my students' learning, but am hardly the creator of them or their learning; if I set an example emulated by others, I am the cause of their behaviour, but hardly its creator. In more strictly Aristotelian terms, God can be final cause of the world without being its material, efficient, or formal cause.) It is furthermore stated here that no other being has the same sort of precedence to the world that God has; but, as Duran worries, does that mean that God's precedence is only relative, not absolute? Last, why does Maimonides cite Deuteronomy 33: 27 instead of Genesis 1: 1? What Maimonides may have meant by all this need not concern us here (see the discussion in Kellner, *Dogma*, 53–61), but it should be clear that a proper understanding of his principles requires a fairly lengthy course of study in Aristotelian philosophy.

[19] This sentence was added by Maimonides late in his life; see Kellner, *Dogma*, 54. The reference to the *Guide* is to his explanation there (i. 71, p. 182) of why he appeared to accept the doctrine of the eternity (i.e. uncreatedness) of the world in 'Laws of the Foundations of the Torah', i. 5.

[20] i.e. it is forbidden to worship any entity other than God. Maimonides here makes reference to the three classes of existent beings he later mentions in 'Laws of the Foundations of the Torah': separate intellects (angels), the spheres, and the four elements and all that is composed of those elements (see n. 4 above). None of these may be worshipped; they are all inferior beings determined in their behaviour.

[21] It is on the basis of this passage that several decisors have forbidden the recitation of the passage in the Sabbath eve hymn 'Shalom Aleikhem' beseeching angels (not God) for Sabbath peace. For details, see Shapiro, 'The Last Word in Jewish Theology?'.

foundation is the prohibition against idolatry and there are many verses in the Torah prohibiting it.[22]

The sixth foundation is prophecy; to wit, it should be known that, within the species of humanity, there are individuals who have a greatly superior disposition and a great measure of perfection. And, if their souls are prepared so that they receive the form of the intellect,[23] then that human intellect will unite with the Active Intellect[24] which will cause a great emanation to flow to it.[25] These people are prophets, this [process] is prophecy; and this is its content. The explanation of this principle to its fullest, however, would be very long[26] and it is not our intention to demonstrate each of its basic premises, or to explain the ways by which it is perceived for that is the epitome of all the sciences.[27] Here we shall mention it only in the form of a statement. The verses of the Torah testifying to the prophecy of the prophets are many.

The seventh foundation is the prophecy of Moses, our Teacher; to wit, it should be known that: Moses was the father of all the prophets—of those who came before him and of those who came after him; all were beneath him in rank and that he was the chosen of God from among the entire species of humanity and that he comprehended more of God, may He be exalted, than any man who ever existed or will exist, ever comprehended or will comprehend and that he, peace be upon him, reached a state of exaltedness beyond humanity such that he perceived the level of sovereignty and became included in the level of angels.[28] There remained

[22] Indeed, Maimonides follows the Talmud (BT *Horayot* 8*a*) in making it the central axis of the Torah. See 'Laws of Idolatry', ii. 4; *Guide*, iii. 37, pp. 542, 545.

[23] i.e. actualize the potential intellects with which they were born.

[24] The tenth and last of the 'separate intellects'.

[25] i.e. the unification with the Active Intellect is the cause of the emanation upon the human intellect.

[26] In the *Guide of the Perplexed* it occupies ii. 32–48, pp. 360–412.

[27] i.e. understanding prophecy necessitates understanding all the sciences.

[28] Maimonides here makes a number of unprecedented claims about Moses: (*a*) he is the 'father of all the prophets', including the Patriarchs who preceded him; (*b*) no other prophet ever achieved his rank, nor will any prophet do so (including the Messiah, who, Maimonides teaches in 'Laws of Repentance', ix. 2, will be a prophet 'close' in rank to Moses, but not equal to him); (*c*) unlike other prophets who, in effect, chose themselves, Moses was chosen by God from among all humans; (*d*) Moses' uniqueness was, apparently, a consequence of his having achieved such an exalted level of comprehension of God; (*e*) Moses became an angel, pure intellect only. None of these statements about Moses is commonplace in Jewish tradition. On the contrary, there are several passages in the Talmud in which Hillel is implied to have been as great as Moses (BT *Sukah* 28*b*, BT *Sanhedrin* 11*a*) and one in which the same suggestion is made in respect of Ezra (BT

no veil which he did not pierce, no material hindrance burdened him, and no defect whether small or great mingled itself with him. The imaginative and sensible faculties in his perception were stripped from him, his desiderative faculty was still, and he remained pure intellect only.[29] For this reason, they remarked of him that he discoursed with God without the intermediacy of an angel.[30] I would have been obligated to explain this strange subject, to unlock the secrets firmly enclosed in the verses of the Torah, and to expound the meaning of 'mouth to mouth' (Num. 12: 8) together with the whole of this verse and other verses belonging to the same theme had I not seen that this theme is very subtle and that it would need abundant introductions and illustrations. The existence of angels would first have to be made clear and, then, the distinction between their ranks and that of the Creator. The soul would have to be explained and all its faculties. The circle would then grow wider until we should have to say a word about the images which the prophets attribute to the Creator and the angels. The *Shiur komah* and its meaning would have to enter [into our survey]. And, even if I were to be as brief as possible, this purpose alone could not be attained in even a hundred pages. For this reason, I shall leave it to its place, whether in 'the book of the interpretation of the discourses' which I have promised, or in 'the book of prophecy' which I have begun, or in a book which I shall compose as a commentary to these foundations.[31] I shall now return to the purpose of this seventh foundation and say that the prophecy of Moses is separated from the prophecy of all other prophets by four differences:

The first difference: To every other prophet that ever was, God did not

Sanhedrin 21*b*–22*a*). BT *Menaḥot* 29*b* can be construed as implying that Rabbi Akiva was no less great than Moses. Maimonides deals with the special character of Mosaic prophecy in *Guide*, ii. 39–40, pp. 378–85. On this subject see Menachem Kellner, 'Maimonides and Gersonides on Mosaic Prophecy', *Speculum*, 42 (1977), 62–79.

29 Maimonides is repeating what he has just said. To be an angel is to be 'pure intellect only'.

30 For Maimonides' discussion of this topic, see *Guide*, ii. 39–40, pp. 378–85. Maimonides is here attributing philosophical ideas to the Sages: other prophets received their prophecy through the Active Intellect (= angel). Moses, having become an angel, has no need of an angelic intermediary in order to receive prophecy from God.

31 We see here that Maimonides felt that these principles needed a whole book of commentary. For arguments to the effect that the *Guide of the Perplexed* is that book of commentary, see Menachem Kellner, 'Maimonides' "Thirteen Principles" and the Structure of the *Guide of the Perplexed*', *Journal of the History of Philosophy*, 20 (1982), 76–84.

speak except by an intermediary. But Moses had no intermediary, as it is said, 'mouth to mouth did I speak with him' (Num. 12: 8).

The second difference: Every other prophet received inspiration only when in a state of sleep, as He said in various places: 'in a dream of the night' (Gen. 20: 3), 'he dreamed and he saw a ladder' (Gen. 28: 12), 'in a dream of a vision of the night' (Job 33: 15), and in many other places with similar intent; or during the day, after a deep sleep had fallen upon the prophet and his condition had become one in which his sense-perceptions were rendered inactive and in which his thoughts were empty as in sleep. This condition is called *maḥazeh* ['vision'] and *mareh* ['appearance'] and it is referred to in the phrase 'in visions of God' (Ezek. 8: 3, 40: 2). But to Moses, peace be upon him, discourse came in the day when he was 'standing between the two cherubim', as God had promised him, 'and, there, I will meet with you and I will speak with you' (Exod. 25: 12). And He, may He be exalted, also said, 'If there be a prophet among you, I the Lord, will make Myself known to him in a vision and will speak to him in a dream. Not so my servant Moses. He, in all my house, is faithful' (Num. 12: 6–8).

The third difference: Every other prophet receives inspiration only in a vision and by means of an angel [and] his strength becomes enfeebled, his body becomes deranged, and a very great terror falls upon him so that he is almost broken by it, as illustrated when Gabriel spoke to Daniel in a vision and Daniel said, 'And there remained no strength in me and my dignity became destructive for me' (Dan. 10: 8). He also said, 'I was in deep sleep on my face and my face was towards the ground' (Dan. 10: 16). But not so with Moses. Rather, discourse came to him and no confusion of any kind overtook him as He, may He be exalted, has said, 'And the Lord spoke to Moses face to face as a man speaks to his neighbor' (Exod. 33: 11). This means that just as no man feels disquieted when his neighbor talks with him, so he, peace be upon him, had no fright at the discourse of God, although it was face to face. This was because of the strength of his union with the [Active] Intellect, as we have said.

The fourth difference: Every other prophet did not receive inspiration by his own choice but by the will of God. The prophet could remain a number of years without inspiration, or an inspiration could be communicated to the prophet but he could be required to wait some days or months before prophesying, or not make it known at all. We have seen that there are those among them who prepared themselves by simplifying their soul and by purifying their minds as did Elisha when he declared, 'Bring me, now, a minstrel' (2 Kgs. 3: 15) and then inspiration came to him. It was not, however, necessarily that he received inspiration after he was prepared for it. But Moses, our Teacher, was able to say whenever he wished, 'Stand, and I shall hear what God shall command concerning you' (Num. 9: 8). And He also said, 'Speak to Aaron, your brother, that he not come at any time into the sanctuary' (Lev. 16: 2). [On this], they said, 'Aaron was bound by the prohibition, "that he not come at any time," but Moses was not bound by the prohibition.'[32]

The eighth foundation is that the Torah is from heaven; to wit, it [must] be believed that the whole of this Torah which is in our hands today is the Torah which was brought down to Moses, our Teacher; that all of it is from God [by] the transmission which is called metaphorically 'speech'; that no one knows the quality of that transmission except he to whom it was transmitted, peace be upon him; and that it was dictated to him while he was of the rank of a scribe; and that he wrote down all of its dates, its narratives, its laws—and for this he is called the 'Legislator'[33] (Num. 21: 18). There is no difference between 'the sons of Ham were Cush, Mitsrayim, Fut, and Canaan' (Gen. 10: 6) and 'the name of his wife was Mehetabel, the daughter of Matred' (Gen. 36: 39) on the one hand, and 'I am the Lord your God' (Exod. 20: 2) and 'Hear, O Israel, the Lord, our God, the Lord is One' (Deut. 6: 4) on the other hand. Everything is from the mouth of the Almighty;[34] everything is the Torah of God: whole, pure, holy, true.[35] Indeed, Menasseh became, in the eyes of the Sages, the person strongest in heresy and hypocrisy for he thought that the Torah was composed of kernels and husks and that those dates and these narratives had no value and that they were composed by Moses.[36] This is the issue of 'the Torah is not from Heaven'.[37] And the Sages have said that he who believes that 'the Torah is entirely from the mouth of the Almighty except for this [i.e. any given] verse which was not said by the Holy One, blessed be He, but Moses said it on his own authority' is one to whom the following verse applies, 'He disdains the word of God' (Num. 15: 31).[38]—May God be exalted about that which the heretics say!—Rather, every letter of the Torah contains wisdom and wonders for whom God has given to understand it. Its ultimate wisdom

[32] *Sifra* on Leviticus 16: 2.

[33] Literally, 'copyist'. There is a play on words here.

[34] *Mipi hagevurah*; a reference to BT *Makot* 23*b*–24*a*. For Maimonides' use of this expression see Kellner, *Dogma*, 119–20.

[35] See Psalms 19: 8.

[36] See BT *Sanhedrin* 99*b*.

[37] i.e. one who affirms that only part of the Torah is not from heaven falls under the category (in our mishnah) of one who denies that the Torah is from heaven.

[38] BT *Sanhedrin* 99*a*.

cannot be perceived, as it is said, 'Its measure is greater than the earth and broader than the sea' (Job 11: 9). A man can only follow in the steps of David, the anointed of the God of Jacob, the most pleasant singer of the hymns of Israel who prayed, singing, 'Unmask my eyes that I may see wonders from Your Torah' (Ps. 119: 18). Similarly, its interpretation as it has been handed down is also 'from the mouth of the Almighty'.[39] That which we observe today, such as the form of the *sukkah*, the *lulav*, the *shofar*, the fringes, the phylacteries, and other such forms are the actual forms which God told to Moses and which he told to us. He is the transmitter of the message, faithful in its transmission. The verse on the basis of which this eighth foundation is attested is his [i.e. Moses'] saying, 'By this shall you know that the Lord has sent me to do all these things' (Num. 16: 18).

The ninth foundation is the [denial of the] abrogation [of the Torah]; to wit, that this Torah of Moses, our Teacher, shall not be abrogated or transmuted; nor shall any other law come from God. It may not be added to nor subtracted from—not from its text nor from its explanation—as it is said, 'You shall not add to it, nor subtract from it' (Deut. 13: 1). We have already explained that which it is necessary to explain concerning this foundation in the introduction to this book.[40]

The tenth foundation is that He, may He be exalted, has knowledge of the acts of men and is not neglectful of them. It is not as the opinion of someone who says, 'God has abandoned the earth' (Ezek. 8: 12, 9: 9) but as the opinion of him who says, '[God is] great in counsel, and mighty in work; whose eyes are open upon all the ways of the sons of men' (Jer. 32: 19). It is also said, 'God saw that the evil of man was great' (Gen. 6: 15), and 'the cry of Sodom and Gomorrah was great' (Gen. 18: 20). This attests to this tenth foundation.

The eleventh foundation is that He, may He be exalted, rewards him who obeys the commands of the Torah and punishes him who violates its prohibitions; and the greatest of His rewards is the world to come while the severest of His punishments is 'being cut off'.[41] We have already expounded sufficiently on this in this chapter. The verse which attests to this foundation is '. . . if You forgive their sin, and if not, erase me, then from Your book which You have written' (Exod. 32: 32) taken together

[39] i.e. the Oral Torah is also from heaven. Maimonides here hints at his relatively narrow understanding of the term 'Oral Torah'. For details, see Gerald Blidstein, 'Maimonides on "Oral Law"', *Jewish Law Annual*, 1 (1978), 108–22.

[40] *Mishnah in perush rabenu mosheh ben maimon*, ed. Kafih, i. 4 ff.

[41] On *karet* (being cut off) and the controversy over it see Appendix 1, n. 12.

with His answer, may He be exalted, 'Him who has sinned against Me, shall I erase from My book' (Exod. 32: 33). These verses are attestations to [the fact that] the obedient person and the rebellious person will reach [a point] with Him, may He be exalted, where He will reward the one and punish the other.[42]

The twelfth foundation is the days of the Messiah; to wit, the belief in, and the assertion of, the truth of his coming. He shall not be a long time 'and if he tarries, wait for him' (Hab. 2: 3). No time for his coming may be set nor may the verses of Scripture be interpreted to reveal the time of his coming, as our Sages have said, 'May the wits of those who calculate the date of the end be addled.'[43] One must believe in him by praising him, loving him, and praying for his coming according to that which has been revealed by all the prophets from Moses to Malachi. He who doubts, or treats his command lightly, says that the Torah, which promised his coming specifically in the [weekly readings] of *Balaam* and *Atem nitsavim*,[44] is lying. One of the general ideas of this foundation is that Israel will have no king except from David, and that he will be descended especially from the seed of Solomon.[45] Whoever disobeys the command of this dynasty denies God and the verses of the prophets.

The thirteenth foundation is the resurrection of the dead and we have already explained it.[46]

When all these foundations are perfectly understood and believed in by a person he enters the community of Israel and one is obligated to love and pity him and to act towards him in all the ways in which the Creator has commanded that one should act towards his brother, with love and fraternity. Even were he to commit every possible transgression, because

[42] On Maimonides on reward and punishment, see Appendix 1 above.

[43] BT *Sanhedrin* 99*a*–*b*.

[44] i.e. Numbers 22: 5–25: 9; Deuteronomy 29: 9–30: 2.

[45] As my friend and colleague Daniel J. Lasker once observed to me, Maimonides' emphasis on the Solomonic descent of the Messiah may be aimed at the Christians, who (at Luke 3: 31) traced Jesus' descent through David's 'son' Nathan.

[46] The sum total of Maimonides' explanation was his comment:

> The resurrection of the dead is one of the cardinal principles established by Moses our Teacher. A person who does not believe in this principle has no real religion, certainly not Judaism. However, resurrection is only for the righteous . . . how, after all, could the wicked come back to life, since they are dead even in their lifetimes? Our sages taught: 'The wicked are called dead even while they are alive; the righteous are alive even when they are dead' (Berakhot 18*b*). All men must die and their bodies decompose. (Twersky, *A Maimonides Reader*, 414)

Maimonides' comments here and in his *Treatise on Resurrection* sparked a wide-ranging and long-lived debate on his actual views concerning resurrection of the dead. For details, see Septimus, *Hispano-Jewish Culture in Transition*, 39–60.

of lust and because of being overpowered by the evil inclination, he will be punished according to his rebelliousness, but he has a portion [of the world to come]; he is one of the sinners of Israel. But if a man doubts any of these foundations, he leaves the community [of Israel], denies the fundamental, and is called a sectarian, *epikoros*, and one who 'cuts among the plantings'. One is required to hate him and destroy him. About such a person it was said, 'Do I not hate them, O Lord, who hate thee?' [Ps. 139: 21].

APPENDIX THREE

Yigdal and *Ani ma'amin*

The authorship of these two texts is unknown. *Yigdal* is variously attributed to Daniel ben Judah of Rome and Immanuel ben Solomon of Rome, both writing in the fourteenth century; the translation cited here is that of Philip Birnbaum in the *Daily Prayer Book*, 12–14 and 154–6.[1]

Yigdal

Exalted and Praised be the Living God!
He exists; His existence transcends time.

He is one—there is no oneness like His;
He's unknowable—His Oneness is endless.

He has no semblance—he is bodiless;
Beyond comprehension is His holiness.

He preceded all that was created;
The First He is though He never began.

He is the eternal Lord; every creature
Must declare His greatness and His kingship.

His abundant prophecy He granted
To the men of His choice and His glory.

Never has there arisen in Israel
A prophet like Moses beholding God's image.

The Torah of truth God gave to His people
Through His prophet, His own faithful servant.

God will never amend, nor ever change
His eternal Law for any other law.

He inspects, He knows our secret thoughts;
He foresees the end of things at their birth.

[1] Further on these and other poems derived from Maimonides' Thirteen Principles, see Marx, 'A List of Poems on the Articles of the Creed'.

He rewards the godly man for his deeds;
He repays the evil man for his evil.

At time's end He will send our Messiah
To save all who wait for His final help.

God, in His great mercy, will revive the dead;
Blessed be His glorious name forever.

Ani ma'amin

I firmly believe that the Creator, blessed be His name, is the Creator and Ruler of all created beings, and that He alone has made, does make, and ever will make all things.

I firmly believe that the Creator, blessed be His name, is One; that there is no oneness in any form like His; and that He alone was, is, and ever will be our God.

I firmly believe that the Creator, blessed be His name, is not corporeal; that no bodily accidents apply to Him; and that there exists nothing whatever that resembles Him.

I firmly believe that the Creator, blessed be His name, was the first and will be the last.

I firmly believe that the Creator, blessed be His name, is the only One to Whom it is proper to address our prayers, and that we must not pray to anyone else.

I firmly believe that all the words of the prophets are true.

I firmly believe that the prophecy of Moses our teacher, may he rest in peace, was true; and that he was the chief of the prophets, both of those who preceded him and of those that followed him.

I firmly believe that the whole Torah which we now possess is the same which was given to Moses our teacher, may he rest in peace.

I firmly believe that this Torah will not be changed, and that there will be no other Torah given by the Creator, blessed be His name.

I firmly believe that the Creator, blessed be His name, knows all the actions and thoughts of human beings, as it is said: 'It is He who fashions the hearts of them all, He who notes all their deeds' (Ps. 33: 15).

I firmly believe that the Creator, blessed be His name, rewards those who keep His commands, and punishes those who transgress His commands.

I firmly believe in the coming of the Messiah; and although he may tarry, I daily wait for his coming.

I firmly believe that there will be a revival of the dead at a time which will please the Creator, blessed and exalted be His name for ever and ever.

Note on Transliteration

THE transliteration of Hebrew in this book reflects a consideration of the type of book it is, in terms of its content, purpose, and readership. The system adopted therefore reflects a broad approach to transcription, rather than the narrower approaches found in the *Encyclopaedia Judaica* or other systems developed for text-based or linguistic studies. The aim has been to reflect the pronunciation prescribed for modern Hebrew, rather than the spelling or Hebrew word structure, and to do so using conventions that are generally familiar to the English-speaking Jewish reader.

In accordance with this approach, no attempt is made to indicate the distinctions between *alef* and *ayin*, *tet* and *taf*, *kaf* and *kuf*, *sin* and *samekh*, since these are not relevant to pronunciation; likewise, the *dagesh* is not indicated except where it affects pronunciation. Following the principle of using conventions familiar to the majority of readers, however, transcriptions that are well established (for example *tannaim*) have been retained even when they are not fully consistent with the transliteration system adopted. On similar grounds, the *tsadi* is rendered by 'tz' in such familar words as barmitzvah, mitzvot, and so on. Likewise, the distinction between *ḥet* and *khaf* has been retained, using *ḥ* for the former and *kh* for the latter; the associated forms are generally familiar to readers, even if the distinction is not actually borne out in pronunciation, and for the same reason the final *heh* is indicated too. As in Hebrew, no capital letters are used, except that an initial capital has been retained in transliterating titles of published works (for example, *Shulḥan arukh*).

Since no distinction is made between *alef* and *ayin*, they are indicated by an apostrophe only in intervocalic positions where a failure to do so could lead an English-speaking reader to pronounce the vowel-cluster as a diphthong—as, for example, in *ha'ir*—or otherwise mispronounce the word. Here too, an allowance has been made for convention: *yisrael* has been left as it is, without an apostrophe, since interference in this familar form would constitute an intrusive intervention of no benefit to readers.

The *sheva na* is indicated by an *e*—*perikat ol*, *reshut*—except, again, when established convention dictates otherwise.

The *yod* is represented by an *i* when it occurs as a vowel (*bereshit*), by a *y* when it occurs as a consonant (*yesodot*), and by *yi* when it occurs as both (*yisrael*).

Names have generally been left in their familiar forms, even when this is inconsistent with the overall system.

Thanks are due to Jonathan Webber of the Oxford Centre for Hebrew and Jewish Studies for his help in elucidating the principles to be adopted.

Note on Citation of Classical Sources

The Mishnah and Midrashim

Citations of the Mishnah are given by tractate name (there are over sixty tractates in the Mishnah), chapter number, and paragraph (mishnah) number. Thus, for example, a reference to the first paragraph (mishnah) of the second chapter of tractate *Ḥagigah* would be given as: Mishnah *Ḥagigah* ii. 1.

The Babylonian and Jerusalem (Palestinian) Talmuds are, in effect, commentaries upon the Mishnah and are divided into the same tractates. References to the Babylonian Talmud are prefaced by the letters 'BT' and cite tractate, page, and folio number; references to the Jerusalem Talmud are prefaced by the letters 'JT' and cite chapter and section (halakhah) number.

Sifra is a midrashic commentary on Leviticus; *Sifre* a midrashic commentary on Numbers and Deuteronomy; references to both are keyed to biblical verses. *Genesis rabbah* and *Exodus rabbah* are also midrashim, but are customarily divided into section and subsections, and are referred to accordingly.

Works of Maimonides

Maimonides' *Mishneh torah* is divided into fourteen books and further divided into sections, chapters, and paragraphs. References here follow the customary format of citing section, chapter, and paragraph. Each section within the *Mishneh torah* is called 'Laws of ____'. Thus a reference might read: 'Laws of the Foundations of the Torah', i. 1.

References to Maimonides' *Guide of the Perplexed* are cited by section and chapter number, followed by the page number in the translation of Shlomo Pines (Chicago: University of Chicago Press, 1963).

References to Maimonides' Commentary on the Mishnah are given by citing the relevant passage in the Mishnah itself, by tractate, chapter, and paragraph.

Glossary

aggadah (pl. **aggadot**) Story; non-halakhic (q.v.) material in Talmud (q.v.).

amora (pl. ***amoraim***) An authority cited in the Gemara (q.v.).

anus ('annoos') (pl. ***anusim***) Coerced (and thus not legally liable for one's actions).

avodah zarah Lit. 'alien worship': idolatry.

ba'al teshuvah (pl. ***ba'alei teshuvah***) Repentant individual(s).

da'at torah (Allegedly) authoritative expression of Jewish values by a leading rabbi.

emunah (pl. ***emunot***) Belief(s).

epikoros Rabbinic term of opprobrium; generally taken to mean 'heretic'.

Gehinnom Place of punishment for sinners after death.

Gemara Edited record of discussions on the text of the Mishnah (q.v.) in Palestine, which, with the Mishnah, is called the Jerusalem Talmud; and in Babylonia, which, with the Mishnah, is called the Babylonian Talmud; the Babylonian Talmud was brought to its present form by the year 600 CE.

Habad Philosophy of Lubavitch hasidism; acronym of the three Hebrew words *ḥokhmah* (wisdom), *binah* (discernment), and *da'at* (intellect or knowledge).

halakhah (pl. **halakhot**) Jewish law(s).

ḥamets Food containing fermented dough, forbidden on Passover.

hasid (pl. **hasidim**) Adherent(s) of hasidism (q.v.).

hasidism Spiritual and social movement in Judaism, dating from the eighteenth century, strongly influenced by kabbalah (q.v.), divided into groups led by hereditary leaders called *tzaddikim* (q.v.).

heter iska Legal device enabling Jews to conduct business without violating the prohibitions related to the taking or giving of interest.

hora'at sha'ah Exceptional permission to perform an otherwise forbidden act.

kabbalah Trend in Jewish mysticism from the twelfth century onwards, deriving from the Zohar (q.v.) and having profound impact on hasidism (q.v.) and other forms of contemporary Jewish Orthodoxy.

Karaism Schismatic movement in Judaism (from the ninth century) which rejected rabbinic authority

karet Excision; divine punishment mentioned in the Bible (e.g. Num. 15: 31), ordinarily thought to mean early death.

kelal yisrael The generality or community of the people of Israel, comprehending past, present, and future.

ma'amin (pl. ***ma'aminim***) Believer(s).

malshin (pl. ***malshinim***) Informer(s).

meshumad Lit. 'one who has been destroyed': apostate.

mezid One who sins by prior intention, not inadvertently.

Midrash (adj. **midrashic**) Body of rabbinic literature from the mishnaic and talmudic periods, containing homiletical expositions of biblical texts, sermons, and halakhic analyses of biblical texts; also the (continuing) activity of so treating biblical texts.

mikveh Ritual bath, used primarily by married women in order to purify themselves after menstruation, and in which proselytes immerse themselves on conversion to Judaism.

min (pl. ***minim***) Sectarian(s).

Mishnah First and most authoritative codification of halakhah (q.v.) found in the Oral Torah (q.v.), dating from the early third century.

Mishneh torah Maimonides' comprehensive code of Jewish law, the first of its kind.

mitzvah (pl. **mitzvot**) Commandment(s); colloquially, 'good deed(s)'.

Oral Torah According to Jewish tradition, Moses received the Torah from Sinai in its written form, and in the form of equally authoritative material which was to be transmitted from generation to generation orally; this latter is the Oral Torah.

paskened (Yiddish) Having made a decision in a matter of Jewish law.

pesak Decision in a matter of Jewish law.

Pharisees Immediate antecedents of the *tannaim* (q.v.); forebears of all contemporary versions of Judaism; contrasted with Sadducees (q.v.).

Pirkei avot 'Ethics of the Fathers'; title of a tractate in the Mishnah (q.v.).

prozbul Legal device promulgated by the first-century *tanna* (q.v.) Hillel to make the otherwise forbidden collection of debts in the sabbatical year (Deut. 15: 1–3) permissible.

Rabbanites Opponents of the Karaites (q.v.), faithful to the rabbinic tradition.

reshut Permissible; neither ordained nor forbidden.

responsum (pl. **responsa**) Written answer to a query concerning halakhah (q.v.).

Sadducees First-century movement in Judaism which, among other things, denied retribution after death and rejected the authority of contemporary (Pharisaic) rabbis.

shegagah Inadvertence in committing a sin.

shogeg One who commits a sin inadvertently.

Talmud Mishnah (q.v.) and Gemara (q.v.) taken together.

tanna (pl. ***tannaim***) An authority cited in the Mishnah (q.v.).

teshuvah Repentance.

tinok shenishbah (pl. ***tinokot shenishbu***) Lit. 'captured child'; by extension, one who was raised in such an environment that he or she cannot be held responsible for failure to obey the commandments of Judaism.

Torah Lit. 'teaching': most narrowly, the Pentateuch; more broadly, the Hebrew Bible as a whole; even more broadly, the content of God's revelation to Moses, encompassing the Written and Oral Torah (q.v.).

tzaddik (pl. ***tzaddikim***) Righteous person; leader of a hasidic (q.v.) grouping.

world to come Reward for the righteous after death.

Written Torah Hebrew Bible.

Zohar Key text of that trend in medieval Jewish mysticism known as kabbalah (q.v.); traditionally ascribed to the second-century *tanna* (q.v.) Rabbi Simeon bar Yohai.

Biographical Notes on Jewish Thinkers

Abraham ben David of Posquières (Rabad) Provence, *c.*1125–98; prolific rabbinic writer, most prominently the author of caustic glosses on Maimonides' *Mishneh torah*.

Abrabanel, Isaac ben Judah Iberia, 1437–1508; leader of Spanish Jewry at the time of the expulsion of 1492; author of Bible commentaries, works in theology and philosophy, and especially of Jewish messianism.

Akiva Prominent second-century *tanna*.

Albo, Joseph Iberia, fifteenth century; communal leader and author of *Sefer ha'ikarim*, a popular work of dogmatic theology.

Ba'al Shem Tov or **Besht (Israel ben Eliezer)** Eastern Europe, *c.*1700–60; charismatic founder of hasidism.

Crescas, Hasdai Iberia, d. 1412; leader of Iberian Jewry; author of *Or hashem*, a work of dogmatic theology highly critical of Jewish Aristotelianism.

Duran, Shimon ben Tsemah (Rashbats) Iberia and North Africa, 1361–1444; communal leader, author of theological works and influential responsa.

Emden, Jacob ben Tsvi Germany, 1697–1776; halakhic authority, kabbalist, and fierce opponent of followers of the false messiah Shabbetai Tsvi (1626–76).

Halevi, Judah Iberia, d. 1141; poet and author of *Sefer hakuzari*, a popular and influential work in theology and philosophy.

Hirsch, Samson Raphael Germany, 1808–88; rabbi and leader of German Orthodoxy.

ibn Abi Zimra, David ben Solomon (Radbaz) Egypt, 1479–1573; communal leader and author of influential responsa.

ibn Pakuda, Bahya Iberia, eleventh century; ethical thinker and author of the very popular *Ḥovot halevavot*.

Karelitz, Abraham Isaiah (Hazon Ish) 1878–1953; prominent Israeli talmudic scholar who largely set the tone for what came to be known as *ḥaredi* or 'ultra-Orthodox' Judaism.

Levi ben Gershom (Ralbag; Gersonides) Provence, 1288–1344; radically Aristotelian philosopher, Bible commentator, astronomer, and mathematician.

Moses ben Maimon (Rambam; Maimonides) Iberia and Egypt, 1138–1204; leader of Egyptian and later world Jewry; prolific writer in all fields of Judaism; author of first comprehensive code of Jewish law, *Mishneh torah*, and of the most influential work of Jewish philosophy yet written, *Guide of* *the Perplexed*; probably the single most influential Jewish figure since the first Moses.

Moses ben Nahman (Ramban; Nahmanides) Iberia, 1194–1270; prominent rabbinic leader, prolific author, kabbalist; respectful but determined critic of Maimonides.

Perfet, Isaac ben Sheshet (Rivash) Iberia and North Africa, 1326–1408; communal leader and author of influential responsa.

Sa'adia ben Joseph (Sa'adia Gaon) Born in Egypt, but came to prominence in Babylonia, 882–942; first systematic theologian of Judaism, leading halakhist, communal leader, and anti-Karaite polemicist.

Bibliography

ABRABANEL, ISAAC, *Principles of Faith*, trans. Menachem Kellner (London: Littman Library of Jewish Civilization, 1982); *Rosh amanah*, ed. Menachem Kellner (Ramat Gan: Bar Ilan University Press, 1993).

ABRAMS, DANIEL, 'The Boundaries of Divine Ontology: The Inclusion and Exclusion of Metatron in the Godhead', *Harvard Theological Review*, 87 (1994), 291–321.

ADRET, SOLOMON BEN ABRAHAM, *Responsa* (*Teshuvot harashba*), 2 vols. (Jerusalem: Mosad Harav Kook, 1990).

ALTMANN, ALEXANDER, 'Introduction to Sa'adia's *Emunot ve-De'ot*', in *Three Jewish Philosophers* (New York: Athenaeum, 1972).

——'Maimonides on the Intellect and the Scope of Metaphysics', in *Von der mittelalterlichen zur modernen Aufklärung* (Tübingen: Mohr, 1987), 60–129.

AMITAL, YEHUDAH, 'Rebuking a Fellow Jew: Theory and Practice', in Jacob J. Schacter (ed.), *Jewish Tradition and the Nontraditional Jew* (Northvale, NJ: Jason Aronson, 1992), 119–38.

ARISTOTLE, *Complete Works*, ed. Jonathan Barnes (Princeton: Princeton University Press, 1984).

BAHYA BEN JOSEPH IBN PAKUDA, *The Book of Direction to the Duties of the Heart*, trans. Menahem Mansoor (London: Routledge & Kegan Paul, 1973).

BEN-SHALOM, RAM, 'Communication and Propaganda between Provence and Spain: The Controversy over Extreme Allegorization', in Sophia Menache (ed.), *Communication in the Jewish Diaspora: The Pre-modern World* (Leiden: Brill, 1966), 171–226.

BEN-SHAMMAI, HAGGAI, 'Saadya Gaon's Ten Articles of Faith' (Heb.), *Da'at*, 37 (1996), 11–26.

BERGER, DAVID, 'Judaism and General Culture in Medieval and Early Modern Times', in Jacob J. Schacter (ed.), *Judaism's Encounter with Other Cultures: Rejection or Integration?* (Northvale, NJ: Jason Aronson, 1997), 57–141.

BIALE, DAVID, *Eros and the Jews* (New York: Basic Books, 1992).

BIRNBAUM, PHILIP, *Daily Prayer Book* (New York: Hebrew Publishing Co., 1949).

BLEICH, J. DAVID, *Contemporary Halakhic Problems*, 4 vols. (New York, Ktav, 1989–).

——'Orthodoxy and the Non-Orthodox: Prospects of Unity', in Jonathan Sacks (ed.), *Orthodoxy Confronts Modernity* (Hoboken, NJ: Ktav, 1991).

BLEICH, J. DAVID, 'Reply', *Tradition*, 30 (1996), 100–2.

—— *With Perfect Faith: The Foundations of Jewish Belief* (New York: Ktav, 1983).

BLEICH, JUDITH, 'Rabbinic Responses to Nonobservance in the Modern Era', in Jacob J. Schacter (ed.), *Jewish Tradition and the Nontraditional Jew* (Northvale, NJ: Jason Aronson, 1992), 37–116.

BLIDSTEIN, GERALD J. (YA'AKOV), 'Maimonides' Attitude towards Karaites' (Heb.), *Teḥumin*, 8 (1988), 501–10.

—— 'Maimonides on "Oral Law"', *Jewish Law Annual*, 1 (1978), 108–22.

—— 'Rabbinic Judaism and General Culture: Normative Discussion and Attitudes', in Jacob J. Schacter (ed.), *Judaism's Encounter with Other Cultures: Rejection or Integration?* (Northvale, NJ: Jason Aronson, 1997), 1–56.

—— 'Who is Not a Jew: The Medieval Discussion', *Israel Law Review*, 11 (1976), 369–90.

BONFIL, ROBERT, *Rabbis and Jewish Communities in Renaissance Italy* (Oxford: Oxford University Press, 1990).

BRAUDE, WILLIAM G., *Jewish Proselytizing in the First Five Centuries of the Common Era: The Age of the Tannaim and the Amoraim* (Providence, RI: Brown University Press, 1940).

BREUER, MORDECHAI, *Modernity within Tradition: The Social History of Orthodox Jewry in Imperial Germany* (New York: Columbia University Press, 1992).

BUBER, MARTIN, *Two Types of Faith* (New York: Harper & Row, 1961).

CHINITZ, JACOB, 'Reb Moshe and the Conservatives', *Conservative Judaism*, 41 (1989), 5–15.

COHEN, NORMAN J., 'Analysis of an Exegetic Tradition in *Mekhilta de-Rabbi Ishmael*: The Meaning of *'Amanah* in the Second and Third Centuries', *AJS Review*, 9 (1984), 1–26.

CRESCAS, HASDAI, *The Light of God* (*Or hashem*) (Jerusalem: Sifrei Ramot, 1990).

DAVIDSON, HERBERT A., 'Maimonides on Metaphysical Knowledge', *Maimonidean Studies*, 3 (1992–3), 49–103.

—— 'Maimonides' *Shemonah Peraqim* and Alfarabi's *Fusul al-Madani*', *Proceedings of the American Academy for Jewish Research*, 31 (1963), 33–50.

DAVIS, JOSEPH M., 'Philosophy, Dogma, and Exegesis in Medieval Ashkenazic Judaism: The Evidence of *Sefer Hadrat Qodesh*', *AJS Review*, 18 (1993), 195–222.

DESSLER, ELIYAHU, *Letter from Elijah* (*Mikhtav me'eliyahu*), 5 vols. (Benei Berak: Committee for the Publication of the Writings of Rabbi E. L. Dessler, 1983).

DEXINGER, FERDINAND, 'Limits of Tolerance in Judaism: The Samaritan Example', in E. P. Sanders, A.I. Baumgarten, and Alan Mendelson (eds.),

Aspects of Judaism in the Graeco-Roman Period, vol. ii of *Jewish and Christian Self-definition*, 3 vols. (London: SCM, 1981), 88–114.

DORFF, ELLIOT N., 'Pluralism: Models for the Conservative Movement', *Conservative Judaism*, 48 (1995), 21–35.

ELMAN, YA'AKOV, 'The Book of Deuteronomy as Revelation: Nahmanides and Abrabanel', in Ya'akov Elman and Jeffrey Gurock (eds.), *Hazon Nahum: Studies Presented to Norman Lamm* (New York: Yeshiva University Press, 1997), 229–50

——and GUROCK, JEFFREY (eds.), *Hazon Nahum: Studies Presented to Norman Lamm* (New York: Yeshiva University Press, 1997).

EPSTEIN, J. N., *Introduction to Tannaitic Literature* (*Mevo'ot lesafrut hatanna'im*) (Jerusalem: Magnes, 1957).

FAUR, JOSE, 'Monolingualism and Judaism', *Cardozo Law Review*, 14 (1993), 1712–44.

FEINSTEIN, MOSES, *Responsa* (*Igerot moshe*) (New York: n.p., 1996).

FEINTUCH, ABRAHAM, *Upright Commands* (*Pikudei yesharim*) (Jerusalem: Ma'aliyot, 1992).

FELDMAN, LOUIS, H., *Jew and Gentile in the Ancient World* (Princeton: Princeton University Press, 1993).

——'Proselytism by Jews in the Third, Fourth, and Fifth Centuries', *Journal for the Study of Judaism*, 24 (1993), 1–58.

——'The Contribution of Professor Salo W. Baron to the Study of Ancient Jewish History: His Appraisal of Anti-Judaism and Proselytism', *AJS Review*, 18 (1993), 1–27.

FINKELSTEIN, LOUIS, 'Pre-Maccabean Documents in the Passover Haggadah', *Harvard Theological Review*, 36 (1943), 1–38.

FINOCCHIARO, MAURICE A. (ed. and trans.), *The Galileo Affair: A Documentary History* (Berkeley: University of California Press, 1989).

FOX, MARVIN, *Interpreting Maimonides* (Chicago: University of Chicago Press, 1990).

GELLMAN, JEROME, 'Radical Responsibility in Maimonides' Thought', in Ira Robinson, Lawrence Kaplan, and Julien Bauer (eds.), *The Thought of Moses Maimonides* (Lewiston, NY: Edwin Mellen Press, 1990), 249–65.

GOODMAN, LENN EVAN, *God of Abraham* (New York: Oxford University Press, 1996).

GRUNBLATT, JOSEPH, 'Confronting Disbelievers', *Tradition*, 23 (1987), 33–9.

GUTTMANN, JULIUS, *The Philosophy of Judaism* (Northvale, NJ: Jason Aronson, 1988).

HALBERTAL, MOSHE, *People of the Book* (Cambridge, Mass.: Harvard University Press, 1997).

—— and MARGALIT, AVISHAI, *Idolatry* (Cambridge, Mass., Harvard University Press, 1992).

HALEVI, JUDAH, *The Book of the Kuzari* (*Sefer hakuzari*), trans. Joseph Kafih (Kiryat Ono: Makhon Moshe, 1997).

HALPERIN, DAVID, *The Merkabah in Rabbinic Literature* (New Haven: American Oriental Society, 1980).

HARRIS, JAY, 'The Image of Maimonides in Nineteenth Century Jewish Historiography', *Proceedings of the American Academy for Jewish Research*, 54 (1987), 117–39.

HARVEY, WARREN ZEV, 'A Third Approach to Maimonides' Cosmogony-Prophetology Puzzle', *Harvard Theological Review*, 74 (1981), 287–301.

——'R. Hasdai Crescas and his Critique of Philosophic Happiness' (Heb.), *Proceedings of the Sixth World Congress of Jewish Studies*, 3 (1977), 143–9.

HAZON ISH, *see* KARELITZ, A. L.

HEINEMANN, ISAAC, 'Faith' (Heb.), in *Entsiklopediyah mikra'it*, i. 426–8.

HIRSCH, SAMSON RAPHAEL, *The Nineteen Letters of Ben Uziel*, trans. Bernard Drachman (New York: Funk & Wagnalls, 1899).

IBN ABI ZIMRA, DAVID, *Responsa* (*She'elot uteshuvot haradbaz*), ed. Yitshak Sofer (Benei Berak: Et Vesefer, 1972).

IDEL, MOSHE, 'Kabbalistic Prayer in Provence' (Heb.), *Tarbits*, 62 (1993), 265–86.

JACOBS, LOUIS, *Faith* (New York: Basic Books, 1968).

——'Theological Responsa', *Judaism*, 16 (1967), 345–52.

——*Theology in the Responsa* (London: Routledge & Kegan Paul, 1975).

KADUSHIN, MAX, *The Rabbinic Mind*, 3rd edn. (New York: Bloch, 1972).

KAFIH, JOSEPH, Commentary on the *Mishneh torah* (Heb.), book 1 (*Sefer hamada*) (Jerusalem: Makhon Moshe, 1986).

KARELITZ, A. I., *The Hazon Ish on Maimonides* (*Ḥazon ish al harambam*) (Benei Berak: n.p., 1980).

——*The Hazon Ish on the Yoreh De'ah* (*Ḥazon ish al yoreh de'ah*) (Benei Berak: Greenman, 1973).

KASHER, HANNAH, '"Torah for its Own Sake", "Torah not for its Own Sake", and the Third Way', *Jewish Quarterly Review*, 79 (1988–9), 153–63.

KELLER, CHAIM DOV, 'Modern Orthodoxy: An Analysis and a Response', *Jewish Observer*, June 1979, pp. 3–14, repr. in Reuven Bulka (ed.), *Dimensions of Orthodox Judaism* (New York: Ktav, 1983), 233–71.

KELLNER, MENACHEM, 'A Suggestion Concerning Maimonides' Thirteen Principles and the Status of Non-Jews in the Messianic Era', in M. Ayali (ed.), *Tura: Oranim Studies in Jewish Thought—Simon Greenberg Jubilee Volume* (Heb.) (Tel Aviv: Hakibuts Hame'uḥad, 1989), 249–60.

——*Dogma in Medieval Jewish Thought: From Maimonides to Abravanel* (Oxford: Oxford University Press, 1986).

——'Gersonides and his Cultured Despisers: Arama and Abravanel', *Journal of Medieval and Renaissance Studies*, 6 (1976), 269–96.

——'Gersonides on the Role of the Active Intellect in Human Cognition', *Hebrew Union College Annual*, 65 (1994), 233–59.

——'Gersonides on the Song of Songs and the Nature of Science', *Journal of Jewish Thought and Philosophy*, 4 (1994), 1–21.

——'Heresy and the Nature of Faith in Medieval Jewish Philosophy', *Jewish Quarterly Review*, 76 (1987), 299–318.

——'Maimonides' Allegiances to Torah and Science', *The Torah Umadda Journal*, 7 (1997), 88–104.

——'Maimonides' Commentary on *Ḥagigah* ii. 1', in Marc Angel (ed.), *From Strength to Strength* (New York: Sepher Hermon Press, 1988), 101–11.

——*Maimonides on the 'Decline of the Generations' and the Nature of Rabbinic Authority* (Albany: SUNY Press, 1996).

——'Maimonides and Gersonides on Astronomy and Metaphysics', in Samuel Kottek and Fred Rosner (eds.), *Moses Maimonides: Physician, Scientist, and Philosopher* (Northvale, NJ: Jason Aronson, 1993), 91–6, 249–51.

——'Maimonides and Gersonides on Mosaic Prophecy', *Speculum*, 42 (1977), 62–79.

——*Maimonides on Human Perfection* (Atlanta, Ga.: Scholars Press, 1990).

——*Maimonides on Judaism and the Jewish People* (Albany: SUNY Press, 1991).

——'Maimonides on the Science of the *Mishneh torah*: Provisional or Permanent?', *AJS Review*, 18 (1993), 169–94.

——'Maimonides' "Thirteen Principles" and the Structure of the *Guide of the Perplexed*', *Journal of the History of Philosophy*, 20 (1982), 76–84.

——'Philosophical Misogyny in Medieval Jewish Thought: Gersonides vs. Maimonides', in A. Ravitzky (ed.), *From Rome to Jerusalem: The Joseph Sermonetta Memorial Volume* (Heb.) (Jerusalem: Magnes Press, 1998), 113–28.

——'R. Isaac bar Sheshet's Responsum Concerning the Study of Jewish Philosophy', *Tradition*, 15 (1975), 110–18.

——'Reading Rambam: Approaches to the Interpretation of Maimonides', *Jewish History*, 5 (1991), 73–93.

——'Revelation and Messianism: A Maimonidean Study', in Dan Cohn-Sherbok (ed.), *Torah and Revelation* (Lewiston, NY: Edwin Mellen Press, 1992), 117–33.

——'The Beautiful Captive and Maimonides' Attitude towards Proselytes', in Stephen Benin (ed.), *Jewish–Gentile Relations through the Ages* (Detroit: Wayne State University Press, forthcoming).

——'The Conception of the Torah as a Deductive Science in Medieval Jewish Thought', *Revue des études juives*, 146 (1987), 265–79.

——'The Virtue of Faith', in Lenn Goodman (ed.), *Neoplatonism and Jewish Thought* (Albany: SUNY Press, 1992), 195–205.

KELLNER, MENACHEM, 'What is Heresy?', in N. Samuelson (ed.), *Studies in Jewish Philosophy* (Lanham, Md.: University Press of America, 1987).

KIMELMAN, REUVEN, '*Birkat ha-Minim* and the Lack of Evidence for an Anti-Christian Jewish Prayer in Late Antiquity', in E. P., Sanders, A. I. Baumgarten, and Alan Mendelson (eds.), *Aspects of Judaism in the Graeco-Roman Period*, vol. ii of *Jewish and Christian Self-definition*, 3 vols. (London: SCM, 1981), 226–44.

KITTEL, GERHARD, *Bible Key Words from Gerhard Kittel's Theologisches Wörterbuch zum Neuen Testament*, 4 vols., vol. iii, trans. and ed. Dorothea M. Barton, P. R. Ackroyd, and A. E. Harvey (New York: Harper & Row, 1960).

KLEIN-BRASLAVY, SARA, *King Solomon and Philosophical Esotericism in Maimonides' Teaching* (*Shelomoh hamelekh veha'ezoterizm hafilosofi bimishnat harambam*) (Jerusalem: Magnes, 1996).

KOOK, A. Y., *Correspondence* (*Igerot hare'iyah*) (Jerusalem: Mosad Harav Kook, 1962).

KRAEMER, DAVID, *The Mind of the Talmud: An Intellectual History of the Bavli* (New York: Oxford University Press, 1990).

KREISEL, HOWARD HAIM, 'Love and Fear of God in Maimonides' Thought' (Heb.), *Da'at*, 37 (1996), 127–52.

LAMM, NORMAN, 'An Open Reply to Professor Aaron Twersky', *Jewish Observer*, June 1988, pp. 13–16.

——'Loving and Hating Jews as Halakhic Categories', *Tradition*, 24 (1989), 98–122, based upon idem, 'Love of Israel and Hatred of Evildoers', in *Laws and Customs* (*Halakhot vehalikhot*) (Jerusalem: Mosad Harav Kook, 1990), 149–59.

——'Seventy Faces', *Moment*, June 1986, pp. 23–8.

——untitled presentation in *Materials from the Critical Issues Conference: Will There be One Jewish People by the Year 2000?* (New York: CLAL, 1986).

LANDA, JUDAH, *Torah and Science* (Hoboken, NJ: Ktav, 1992).

LASKER, DANIEL J., 'Proselyte Judaism, Christianity, and Islam in the Thought of Judah Halevi', *Jewish Quarterly Review*, 81 (1990), 75–91.

——'Rabbanism and Karaism: The Contest for Supremacy', in Raphael Jospe and Stanley M. Wagner (eds.), *Great Schisms in Jewish History* (New York: Ktav, 1981), 47–72.

——'The Influence of Karaism on Maimonides' (Heb.), *Sefunot*, 5 (1991), 145–61.

LEIBOWITZ, YESHAYAHU, *Judaism, Human Values, and the Jewish State* (Cambridge, Mass.: Harvard University Press, 1992).

LEIMAN, SID [SHNAYER] Z., 'Inspiration and Canonicity: Reflections on the Formation of the Biblical Canon', in E. P. Sanders, A. I. Baumgarter, and Alan Mendelson (eds.), *Aspects of Judaism in the Graeco-Roman Period*, vol.

ii of *Jewish and Christian Self-definition*, 3 vols. (London: SCM, 1981), 56–63.

——'Rabbinic Openness to General Culture in the Early Modern Period in Western and Central Europe', in Jacob J. Schacter (ed.), *Judaism's Encounter with Other Cultures: Rejection or Integration?* (Northvale, NJ: Jason Aronson, 1997), 143–216.

LEVI, YEHUDAH, *Facing Contemporary Challenges* (*Mul etgarei hatekufah*) (Jerusalem: Olam Hasefer Hatorani, 1993).

LEVIN, Y., 'The Conservative Movement as Reflected in the Responsa of R. Moshe Feinstein', in Y. Raphael (ed.), *Aviad Memorial Volume* (*Sefer aviad*) (Jerusalem: Mosad Harav Kook, 1986), 281–93.

LEWIS, BERNARD, *Islam and the West* (New York: Oxford University Press, 1993).

LIBERLES, ROBERT, *Religious Conflict in Social Context: The Resurgence of Orthodox Judaism in Frankfurt am Main, 1838–1877* (Westport, Conn.: Greenwood, 1985).

LIEBERMAN, SAUL, *Greek in Jewish Palestine* (New York: Jewish Theological Seminary, 1942).

——*Hellenism in Jewish Palestine* (New York: Jewish Theological Seminary, 1950).

LIEBES, YEHUDAH, *Elisha's Sin* (*Ḥeto shel elisha*) (Jerusalem: Academon, 1990).

MAIMONIDES, MOSES, *Crisis and Leadership: Epistles of Maimonides*, trans. A. S. Halkin, discussions by David Hartman (Philadelphia: Jewish Publication Society, 1985).

——*Ethical Writings of Maimonides*, trans. Raymond Weiss and Charles Butterworth (New York: Dover, 1983).

——*Guide of the Perplexed*, trans. Shlomo Pines (Chicago: University of Chicago Press, 1963).

——*The Book of Judges*, trans. A. M. Hershman (New Haven: Yale University Press, 1949).

——*The Mishnah with Maimonides' Commentary* (*Mishnah im perush rabenu mosheh ben maimon*), 6 vols., ed. and trans. Joseph Kafih (Jerusalem: Mosad Harav Kook, 1963).

MANEKIN, CHARLES, 'Hebrew Philosophy in the Fourteenth and Fifteenth Centuries', in D. H. Frank and O. Leaman (eds.), *History of Jewish Philosophy* (London: Routledge, 1997), 350–78.

MARTY, MARTIN, and APPLEBY, R. SCOTT (eds.), *The Fundamentalism Project*, 5 vols. (Chicago: University of Chicago Press, 1991–5).

MARX, ALEXANDER, 'A List of Poems on the Articles of the Creed', *Jewish Quarterly Review*, 9 (1919), 305–36.

MILLER, STUART, 'The *Minnim* of Sepphoris Reconsidered', *Harvard Theological Review*, 86 (1993), 377–402.

MOORE, GEORGE FOOT, *Judaism in the First Centuries of the Christian Era*, 3 vols. (New York: Schocken, 1971).

MORELL, SAMUEL, 'The Halachic Status of Non-Halachic Jews', *Judaism*, 18 (1969), 448–57.

NADLER, ALLAN, 'Piety and Politics: The Case of the Satmar Rebbe', *Judaism*, 31 (1982), 135–52.

NAHMANIDES (R. MOSES BEN NAHMAN), *Writings and Discourses*, trans. Charles Chavel (New York: Shilo, 1978).

NOVAK, DAVID, Review of Menachem Kellner, *Maimonides on Judaism and the Jewish People*, *Shofar*, 11 (1992), 150–2.

—— *The Theology of Nahmanides Systematically Presented* (Atlanta, Ga.: Scholars Press, 1992).

NURIEL, ABRAHAM, '"The Torah Speaks in Human Language" in the *Guide of the Perplexed*' (Heb.), in A. Kasher and M. Hallamish (eds.), *Religion and Language* (*Dat usafah*) (Tel Aviv: University Publications, 1981), 97–103.

OCHS, PETER, 'Truth', in A. A. Cohen and Paul Mendes-Flohr (eds.), *Contemporary Jewish Religious Thought* (New York: Scribners, 1987), 1018–23.

PAGELS, ELAINE, *Adam, Eve, and the Serpent* (New York: Vintage, 1989).

PARK, DAVID, *The How and the Why: An Essay on the Origins and Development of Physical Theory* (Princeton: Princeton University Press, 1988).

PARNES, YEHUDAH, 'Torah u-Madda and Freedom of Inquiry', *The Torah Umadda Journal*, 1 (1989), 68–71.

Passover Haggadah, ed. David Goldschmidt (Jerusalem: Mosad Bialik, 1947).

PELIKAN, JAROSLAV, *The Growth of Medieval Theology (600–1300)* (Chicago: University of Chicago Press, 1978).

PINES, SHLOMO, 'The Limitations of Human Knowledge According to al-Farabi, ibn Bajjah, and Maimonides', in Isadore Twersky (ed.), *Studies in Medieval Jewish History and Literature*, i (Cambridge, Mass.: Harvard University Press, 1979), 82–109.

PRICE, H. H., 'Belief "In" and Belief "That" ', *Religious Studies*, 1 (1965), 5–28.

RABINOVITCH, N., *Yad peshutah* on the *Mishneh torah*, book 1 (*Sefer hamada*), 2 vols. (Jerusalem: Ma'aliyot, 1990).

RAMBAN, *see* NAHMANIDES.

REGEV, SHAUL, 'The Choice of the People of Israel in the Thought of R. Isaac Abrabanel' (Heb.), *Asufot*, 2 (1988), 271–83.

RISKIN, SHLOMO, 'Orthodoxy and Her Alleged Heretics', *Tradition*, 15 (1976), 34–44.

ROBINSON, IRA, 'Because of Our Many Sins: The Contemporary World as Reflected in the Responsa of Moses Feinstein', *Judaism*, 35 (1986), 35–46.

ROKEAH, DAVID, *Jews, Pagans and Christians in Conflict* (Leiden: Brill, 1982).

ROSENBERG, SHALOM, 'The Concept of *Emunah* in Post-Maimonidean Jewish Philosophy', in Isadore Twersky (ed.), *Studies in Medieval Jewish History and Literature*, ii (Cambridge, Mass.: Harvard University Press, 1984), 273–307.

SACKS, JONATHAN, *One People? Tradition, Modernity, and Jewish Unity* (London: Littman Library of Jewish Civilization, 1993).

——(ed.), *Orthodoxy Confronts Modernity* (Hoboken, NJ: Ktav, 1991).

SAGI, AVI, *Elu ve'elu* (Tel Aviv: Hakibuts Hame'uḥad).

SCHACTER, JACOB J., 'Rabbi Jacob Emden's *'Iggeret Purim*', in Isadore Twersky (ed.), *Studies in Medieval Jewish History and Literature*, ii (Cambridge, Mass.: Harvard University Press, 1984), 441–6.

SCHECHTER, SOLOMON, 'The Dogmas of Judaism', in *Studies in Judaism* (Philadelphia: Jewish Publication Society, 1906), 147–81.

SCHIFFMAN, LAWRENCE, *Who Was a Jew? Rabbinic and Halakhic Perspectives on the Jewish–Christian Schism* (Hoboken, NJ: Ktav, 1985).

SCHILLER, MAYER, '*Torah Umadda* and *The Jewish Observer* Critique: Towards a Classification of the Issues', *The Torah Umadda Journal*, 6 (1995–6), 58–90.

SCHLESINGER, GEORGE, *New Perspectives on Old-time Religion* (Oxford: Clarendon Press, 1988).

SCHOCHET, J. Immanuel, 'Let Sins be Consumed and Not Sinners', *Tradition*, 16 (1977), 41–61.

SCHOLEM, GERSHOM, *Origins of the Kabbalah* (Princeton: Princeton University Press, 1987).

SCHWARTZ, DOV, 'Avicenna and Maimonides on Immortality: A Comparative Study', in Ronald Nettler (ed.), *Studies in Muslim–Jewish Relations* (Chur, Switzerland: Harwood Academic Publishers, 1993), 185–97.

SCHWARZSCHILD, STEVEN, 'J.-P. Sartre as Jew', *Modern Judaism*, 3 (1983), 39–73, repr. in M. Kellner (ed.), *The Pursuit of the Ideal: Jewish Writings of Steven Schwarzschild* (Albany: SUNY Press, 1990), 161–84.

SEESKIN, KENNETH, 'Judaism and the Linguistic Interpretation of Jewish Faith', in Norbert Samuelson (ed.), *Studies in Jewish Philosophy: Collected Essays of the Academy for Jewish Philosophy, 1980–1985* (Lanham, Md.: University Press of America, 1987), 215–34.

——*Maimonides: A Guide for Today's Perplexed* (West Orange, NJ: Behrman House, 1991).

——*No Other Gods: The Modern Struggle against Idolatry* (West Orange, NJ: Behrman House, 1995).

SEGAL, ALAN F., *Two Powers in Heaven: Early Rabbinic Reports about Christianity and Gnosticism* (Leiden: Brill, 1977).

SEPTIMUS, BERNARD, *Hispano-Jewish Culture in Transition: The Career and Controversies of Ramah [R. Meir ha-Levi Abulafia]* (Cambridge, Mass.: Harvard University Press, 1982).

SHAPIRO, MARC B., 'The Last Word in Jewish Theology? (Maimonides' Thirteen Principles)', *The Torah Umadda Journal*, 4 (1993), 187–242.

SHEM TOV IBN FALAQUERA, 'Letter on the *Guide of the Perplexed*' (*Mikhtav al devar hamoreh*), in J. Bisliches (ed.), *Minḥat kena'ot* (photo-edition, Israel, 1968).

SHEM TOV IBN SHEM TOV, *Book of Beliefs* (*Sefer ha'emunot*) (Ferrara, 1556; photo-edition, Jerusalem, 1969).

SHERWIN, BYRON L., 'Bar-Mizvah', *Judaism*, 22 (1973), 53–65.

SILVER, DANIEL JEREMY, *Maimonidean Criticism and the Maimonidean Controversy, 1180–1240* (Leiden: Brill, 1965).

SIRAT, COLETTE, *A History of Jewish Philosophy in the Middle Ages* (Cambridge: Cambridge University Press, 1985).

SOLOMON, NORMAN, *The Analytic Movement: Hayyim Soloveitchik and his Circle* (Atlanta: Scholars Press, 1993).

SPIEGEL, YA'AKOV, 'Elliptical Language among the Tannaim and *Pshat* and *Drash* in the Mishnah' (Heb.), *Asufot*, 4 (1990), 9–26.

SUSSMANN, YA'AKOV, 'The History of *Halakha* and the Dead Sea Scrolls: A Preliminary to the Publication of the 4QMMT', *Tarbits*, 55 (1989–90), 11–76.

TWERSKY, AARON, 'A Rejoinder', *Jewish Observer* June 1988, pp. 17–26.

——'Open Letter to Dr. Norman Lamm', *Jewish Observer* April 1988, pp. 6–9.

TWERSKY, ISADORE (ed.), *A Maimonides Reader* (New York: Behrman House, 1972).

——*Introduction to the Code of Maimonides* (New Haven: Yale University Press, 1980).

——*Rabad of Posquières*, rev. edn. (Philadelphia: Jewish Publication Society, 1980).

URBACH, EPHRAIM, 'Self-Isolation and Self-Affirmation in Judaism in the First Three Centuries: Theory and Practice', in E. P. Sanders, A. I. Baumgarten, and Alan Mendelson (eds.), *Aspects of Judaism in the Graeco-Roman Period*, vol. ii of *Jewish and Christian Self-definition*, 3 vols. (London: SCM, 1981), 269–98.

——*The Sages*, 2 vols. (Jerusalem: Magnes, 1975).

WENSINCK, A. J., *The Muslim Creed* (Cambridge: Cambridge University Press, 1932).

WERTHEIMER, JACK, 'Judaism without Limits', *Commentary*, July 1997, pp. 24–7.

WOLFSON, ELLIOT R., 'Negative Theology and Positive Assertion in the Early Kabbalah', *Da'at*, 31–2 (1994), pp. v–xxii.

Wolfson, Harry Austryn, *The Philosophy of the Kalam* (Cambridge, Mass.: Harvard University Press, 1976).

Yuter, Alan J., 'Is Reform Judaism a Movement, a Sect, or a Heresy?', *Tradition*, 24 (1989), 87–98.

Index